Integrating tl

ALSO BY BOB LUKE

Dean of Umpires: A Biography of Bill McGowan,
1896–1954 (McFarland, 2005)

Integrating the Orioles

Baseball and Race in Baltimore

BOB LUKE

McFarland & Company, Inc., Publishers
Jefferson, North Carolina

Library of Congress Cataloguing-in-Publication Data

Names: Luke, Bob, author.
Title: Integrating the Orioles : baseball and race in Baltimore / Bob Luke.
Description: Jefferson, North Carolina : McFarland & Company, Inc.,
  Publishers, 2016. | Includes bibliographical references and index.
Identifiers: LCCN 2015048138 | ISBN 9781476662121 (softcover : acid
  free paper) ∞
Subjects: LCSH: Baltimore Orioles (Baseball team)—History. |
  Discrimination in sports—Maryland—Baltimore. | Baseball—Social
  aspects—Maryland—Baltimore. | Baseball—Maryland—Baltimore—
  History. | Baltimore (Md.)—Race relations.
Classification: LCC GV875.B2 L84 2016 | DDC 796.357/64097526—dc23
LC record available at http://lccn.loc.gov/2015048138

British Library cataloguing data are available

ISBN (print) 978-1-4766-6212-1
ISBN (ebook) 978-1-4766-2302-3

On the cover: Baltimore Orioles players Frank Robinson (left) and
Brooks Robinson (Photograph by Morton Tadder)

Printed in the United States of America

*McFarland & Company, Inc., Publishers
  Box 611, Jefferson, North Carolina 28640
  www.mcfarlandpub.com*

For Judy

Table of Contents

Acknowledgments

Many people made valuable contributions to this book, among them former Orioles executives Bob Brown, Frank Cashen, Hank Peters, and Jerry Sachs, and former Orioles players Paul Blair, Al Bumbry, Don Buford, Gil Coan, Chuck Diering, Joe Durham, David Ford, Joe Gaines, Ron Hansen, Willie Kirkland, Bob Kuzava, Don Larsen, Don Lenhardt, Jim Marshall, Billy O'Dell, Willie Tasby, and Fred Valentine.

Many baseball writers contributed their experience and expertise including Vince Bagli, Bijan Bayne, Howard Bryant, Paul Dickson, John Eisenberg, Michael Gesker, Mark Hyman, Bob Maisel, E. Ethelbert Miller, Bill Nowlin, Larry Moffi, and Bill Tanton.

People who know Baltimore firsthand, having lived in, worked in, and written about the city, told me a lot about the city's history and culture, especially Curtis Anderson, Richard Armstrong, Chris Bready, William Davis, Joseph Haskins, Jr., J. Howard Henderson, Frederick Lonesome, Frank McDougald, William Murphy, Jr., Michael Olesker, Quay Rich, former mayor Kurt Schmoke, and members of the Orioles administrative staff Monica Barlow, Matthew Death, Kristen Schultz, and Bill Stetka.

Others deserving of thanks are Library of Congress reference librarians Thomas Mann and Anthony Mullan, and staff members in the Library's Manuscript and Prints and Photographs Divisions; Michele Casto at Washington, D.C.'s Martin Luther King, Jr. Library; Aiden Faust at the University of Baltimore's Langsdale Library; Carol Brooks, Linda Whittaker, and Matthew Whittaker at the Arizona Historical Society; Ellen Greene and Rob Spindler at the Arizona State University Library; Jacob Pomrenke at the Society for American Baseball Research; Edward Papenfuse, Maryland State Archivist; Phoenix Municipal Court Judge Elizabeth Finn; Amber Kohl and Laura French at the University of Maryland's Hornbake Library; and Jeff Idelson, Jim Gates, Freddy Berowski, Pat Kelly,

John Horne, and Cassidy Lent at the National Baseball Hall of Fame and Museum.

A special word of thanks to Jim Hennenman, Baltimore native, long-time sports writer, scorer for Orioles games, and author of *Baltimore Orioles: 60 Years of Orioles Magic,* for reviewing an earlier draft of the manuscript. Comments by Mark Hyman and Fred Valentine on an early draft are also appreciated. Deborah Patton compiled the index.

Any errors are mine alone.

Preface

This book shows how one major league baseball team, the Baltimore Orioles, traveled the path to integration. This book also examines the push by civil rights organizations, Baltimore residents, and several players to integrate the Orioles' front office, which was, and is today, where the organizational power lies.

The reader will also see the ongoing struggle for civil rights in the city of Baltimore, how the racial tensions in the city affected the team and how the Orioles contributed to integration in the city.

The Orioles' play on the field is discussed only in passing. The team's ups and downs, and there have been many of each, have been well documented elsewhere.

The book draws heavily on primary sources. They include weekly and daily newspapers of the time, especially the *Baltimore Afro-American* and the columns of Sam Lacy, Baltimore's leading African American sportswriter, and the *Baltimore Sun*. Other weeklies included the *Chicago Defender, Pittsburgh Courier, Afro-American Red Star,* and *Philadelphia Tribune.* Daily papers include the *New York Times, Washington Post, Hartford Courant, Wall Street Journal, Boston Globe,* and *Christian Science Monitor.* I consulted the papers of Edward Bennett Williams, the team's owner from 1980 to 1988, and those of the National Association for the Advancement of Colored People at the Library of Congress. Information from the National Baseball Hall of Fame and Museum, University of Baltimore's Langsdale Library, the Arizona Historical Society, Arizona State Library, University of Maryland's Hornbake Library, and the Martin Luther King, Jr. Library in Washington, D.C., proved very helpful. Forty interviews with former players, executives, sportswriters, ushers, and Baltimore residents add human perspectives to the written records.

The number of baseball books, especially biographies, autobiographies, and team histories, is legion. Many such books mention integration but not in great detail. Notable exceptions are the many books written about Jackie Robinson's historic debut in 1947 and several authored by Frank Robinson. It is the rare baseball book that makes integration of a team its single thesis. Two come to mind. Howard Bryant wrote a similar book about the Boston Red Sox, and Stephanie M. Liscio wrote one about the Cleveland Indians.[1] This is the only book about the integration of the Baltimore Orioles.

Introduction

Jackie Robinson courageously broke major league baseball's color barrier with the Brooklyn Dodgers in 1947. Yet the integration of major league baseball to where it became the national pastime, and not just the white national pastime, took much longer. By 1951, only 11 other African Americans had signed a major league contract. That number grew steadily until 1959, when 115 black players had worn a major league uniform.[1] Many had brief careers lasting only a few seasons or less. Some, such as Willie Mays, Frank Robinson, and Roy Campanella, joined the ranks of the game's superstars. Some teams embraced black players early, among them the Brooklyn Dodgers, the Cleveland Indians, and the New York Giants. Others, such as the Boston Red Sox, New York Yankees, and Detroit Tigers, resisted integrating their squads until they could hold out no longer.

The struggle to integrate major league baseball in general and the Orioles in particular mirrored the fight for civil rights throughout the country that intensified following the end of World War II. African American soldiers still served in segregated units during the war. Not until the Korean conflict in the early 1950s would the armed forces become integrated. The Orioles arrived in Baltimore, Maryland, from St. Louis, Missouri, another Civil War border state, when a group of Baltimore businessmen bought the St. Louis Browns in September 1953. The following year, the Orioles' maiden season, the *Brown v. The Board of Education* Supreme Court decision struck down the legal underpinnings of segregated public schools. Protests, demonstrations, sit-ins, bussing, white flight from inner cities to suburbs, freedom riders, attack dogs, fire hoses, church bombings, marches, riots, and assassinations followed.

Organized league baseball did not experience such violence, which is not to say the process was a smooth one. White fans called out all man-

3

ner of racial epithets at black players in both the major and the minor leagues. Many African Americans refused to attend games with all white players, threatened legal action, and criticized owners in letters to newspaper editors. Massive differences of perspective between white and black players went unrecognized and unacknowledged, the most common being white players' accepting segregated facilities simply "as the way it was" and black players resenting them.

Integration of the Orioles, as was the case with many teams, came slowly. A rocky, uphill journey strewn with empty promises, a tin ear toward African Americans' (players' as well as city residents') concerns, and revolving cameo appearances by black players, primarily outfielders, marked the Orioles' early years. The O's breakthrough came in 1966 with the arrival of a more enlightened owner, front office staff, and African American superstar Frank Robinson. As more African American players joined the team, friendships blossoming among players where there had previously been little mixing of white and black players, the Orioles dominated the American League, and city residents' opinions of the team improved. Attempts to integrate the Orioles' executive suite proved to be a more fractious process with a less successful outcome than achieving integration on the field.

CHAPTER 1

"I've Seen the Best Player I've Ever Seen"

Segregated professional baseball in Baltimore goes back to 1874, when the Lord Hannibals and the Orientals—the city's first professional black teams—opened their seasons in Newington Park.[1] Black baseball soon became an entertainment staple for African Americans in Baltimore, with such semi-pro teams as the Baltimore Stars, whose owner and first baseman, Ben Taylor, was inducted into the Hall of Fame. His successor at first base and fellow inductee in Cooperstown, Buck Leonard, played for the Stars before joining the Homestead Grays in Pittsburgh. During the Great Depression the Stars played their home games in Druid Hill Park, without benefit of a stadium, in front of 3–5,000 spectators seated on the grass who tossed coins into a hat that was passed around. A seven-passenger Buick and a 1929 Ford, complete with rumble seat, carried players to games throughout South Carolina, West Virginia, and Pennsylvania.[2]

Two teams from the Negro leagues made their home in Baltimore from the mid-teens to the early 1950s. The Maryland Black Sox, a Baltimore fixture from 1916 to 1934, initially played at Maryland Park, near the intersection of Bush and Russell Streets just a few blocks south of where Oriole Park at Camden Yards stands today. Spectators didn't have to sit on the grass, but the *Baltimore Afro-American* called the park "a sewer ... which featured broken seats, holes in the roof, non-working toilets, and weeds on the field."[3] Fans brought liquor to the games and shared it with the players.[4] Baltimore businessman Joe Cambria bought the Black Sox in 1932 and installed the team in Bugle Field, located at 1500 Edison Boulevard in East Baltimore. He named the stadium after his company: The Bugle Coat, Apron, and Towel Supply Company.[5] The Black Sox featured two future Hall of Famers, Satchel Paige in 1930, about whom we will hear more later, and another pitcher, right-handed fireballer Leon Day in 1934.

Day grew up in the Mount Winan neighborhood in South Baltimore along the Baltimore and Ohio Railroad tracks. Famous for delivering his pitches without a windup, Day made his mark with the Newark Eagles in the National Negro League before returning to Baltimore in 1949 to play for the Baltimore Elite Giants. The Elites had arrived in town in 1938. Their best season came in 1949 when they won the championship of the American Negro Leagues, the Negro leagues equivalent of the major leagues' World Series. Two other Elites, both catchers, James Raleigh "Biz" Mackey and Roy Campanella, also have plaques in Cooperstown.

Major league baseball arrived in Baltimore not long after the Lord Hannibals and the Orientals faced off for the first time. Named after the Maryland state bird, the first Baltimore Orioles joined the American Association when it formed in 1882. After the American Association folded in 1891, the Orioles joined the already existing National League, which the team called home until 1901, when the American League came into existence. The team reached its high water mark during the 1894–1896 seasons under manager Ned Hanlon, when the Orioles won the pennant. In addition to Hanlon, future Hall of Famers Dan Brouthers, Hugh Jennings, John McGraw, Willie Keller, and Wilbert Robinson combined to make the Orioles the best team in the National League, the only major league at the time.

With three exceptions, no African American had appeared on the roster of any American Association, National League, or American League team. Moses Fleetwood Walker and his brother Wendy had short stints with the Toledo Blue Stockings of the American Association in 1884. Moses appeared in 42 games and Wendy in six. William Edward White, the son of a white Georgia plantation owner and a mulatto slave mother, who likely successfully passed as white, thereby escaping classification as black, played one game at first base for the Providence (Rhode Island) Grays of the National League in 1879.[6]

The subsequent ban barring African American players from the majors did not dissuade Orioles player-manager John "Little Napoleon" McGraw from trying to sign a black player in 1901. McGraw, of Irish descent, had established a reputation as a superb player who used every trick in the book to his advantage. He would continue to polish that reputation as a manager. Slick-fielding infielder Charlie Grant, a light-skinned African American with straight hair, of slight build, weighing 115 pounds, caught McGraw's eye in Hot Springs, Arkansas. Umpire E. H. Wood described Grant as "fast as lightning ... and fully as great as Eddie Collins, the Hall of Fame second baseman whose career with the Philadelphia Athletics and Chicago White Sox spanned twenty-five seasons." McGraw had gone to Hot Springs in February to soak in the thermal baths. Grant was a bellboy at Hot Springs' Eastland Hotel and played on the hotel's team.[7] Knowing that major league officials would never tolerate an African American, McGraw passed Grant off as a Cherokee Indian. He dreamed up the name Tokohama for Grant, Toko for short. "Toko is a little uncivilized as yet," McGraw told the press with a straight face, and added that he found him "in Indian Country."[8] "Toko" went along with the ruse. "I used to play second base on our team out in the Indian nation, and I was supposed to be the best player on the team,"[9] Grant told a *Baltimore Sun* reporter. A rumor circulated that Toko might really be Grant. The rumor proved true, of course, and Grant returned to the Chicago Columbia Giants, an all-black team, for whom he had played the two previous seasons.[10]

McGraw's Orioles departed Baltimore in 1903 for New York City, where they eventually become the New York Yankees. With them went any interest in integrating baseball in the city. A minor league team of the same name took their place. Jack Dunn, an early owner of the now International League Baltimore Orioles, barred blacks from the team. He relegated black spectators to the bleachers and the first and third base pavilions in Oriole Park. Whites only sat in the covered grandstand. Following an upgrade of the seats in the third base pavilion in 1933 into more comfortable and pricier grandstand seats, Harry F. Dawson, the O's general manager, informed the *Baltimore Afro-American* (*AFRO*) that blacks must now sit

John McGraw, who tried but failed to integrate the 1901 Baltimore Orioles, is seen here in 1913 as manager of the New York Giants (Library of Congress, Prints and Photographs Division, LC-DIG-ggbain-13535).

only in the bleachers or in the first base pavilion.[11] Nor would Dunn allow his team to play a black team. He refused lucrative offers from promoters for exhibition games between his O's and the Baltimore Black Sox. The *AFRO* suggested "racial purity" as the reason for Dunn's actions.[12]

* * *

Dunn's attitude reflected Baltimore's culture of segregation. Nowhere was segregation more rigidly enforced than in housing. On December 19, 1910, for example, the city council, by a unanimous vote, prohibited "any black" from living in a house on a block where more than half of the residents were white. The ordinance similarly prohibited any white person from living on a predominately black block. Violators faced a maximum fine of $100 and a prison term of 30 days to a year. The *Baltimore Sun* cited "colored people *invading* Northwest Baltimore" (emphasis added) in 1909 as the cause of the ordinance.[13] Democratic Mayor J. Barry Mahool earnestly told a *New York Times* reporter that the measure "was not passed in a spirit of race antagonism but passed to meet a critical condition." The condition included the decline, according to Mahool, by more than half of property values in white neighborhoods after a black family moved in, and a loss of social status.[14]

The ordinance sat well with many whites. "Experience and time," said Edgar Allan Poe, city attorney and grand nephew of the poet, "have conclusively proved that the co-mingling of white and colored races invariably leads to grave public disaster." Poe did not elaborate. A white woman, whose ancestry traced back to the days of the Calverts, the family that founded Maryland in the 1630s, recalled for a *New York Times* reporter her fond feelings for "my old Negro mammy and my little nurse girl playmate." Yet, she added, "It is a most deplorable thing that even the best of the well-to-do colored people should invade our residential districts. The idea of Negroes living next door to me is abhorrent."[15]

Contrary to the popular beliefs of whites at the time, African Americans did not always aspire to live next to them. Anna McMechen, wife of black lawyer George W. McMechen, whose lease of a house at 1834 McCulloh Street Mayor Mahoor was cited as an example of the need for the ordinance, rebuffed Mahool's assertion that the first thing a black does after acquiring money and property "is to leave his less fortunate brethren behind and nose into the neighborhood of white people." "I have," said Mrs. McMechen, "no desire to associate with white women one whit more than they have to associate with me. My husband and I moved into the house because we wanted to be more comfortable."[16]

The Maryland Court of Appeals unanimously invalidated the ordinance on August 5, 1913, for technical reasons but upheld the council's right to pass such an ordinance. The Council passed a suitably modified ordinance a month later. Hours after its passage, a race riot broke out over, as the *Washington Post* put it, "the invasion earlier in the day at the 1300 block of North Mosher street by a negro family." White and blacks threw bricks and stones and fired marbles from slingshots at each other and nearby homes, injuring three people, smashing windows, and splintering plate-glass store windows.[17] The ordinance stood until 1917, when the U.S. Supreme Court declared it and others like it unconstitutional.

Unfazed by the Court's decision, whites filed covenants with the Baltimore Superior Court. Covenants allowed home owners to refuse to sell or rent property to an African American or any other person whose racial, ethnic or religious background they deemed undesirable.[18] Covenants flourished until May 3, 1948, when, in *Shelley v. Kraemer*, the U.S. Supreme Court ruled them unconstitutional.

* * *

The first crack in Dunn's legacy appeared on May 16, 1937, nine years after his death. On that day two Negro leagues teams, the Baltimore Elite Giants, the Black Sox's replacement in the Negro leagues, and the Pittsburgh Crawfords, played a doubleheader in Oriole Park.[19] Crawford's center fielder, Cool Papa Bell, reputedly the fastest man in the Negro leagues, opened the first game with a towering home run off the first pitch of the afternoon. The Elites, nevertheless, won both games.[20] Dawson now allowed the Elites to rent the park on Sundays when the O's were on the road. Two years later, a team of white major leaguers and a team of National Negro League All-Stars set foot in Oriole Park for an exhibition game on October 8, 1939, to inaugurate professional interracial play in Baltimore.[21] Two thousand spectators saw the major leaguers, or "Nordic standouts," as the *AFRO* referred to the white team, prevail, 3–1.[22]

The Elite's pact with Dawson unraveled in 1942 after whites complained about "rowdyism" by blacks in the stands and on the streets surrounding the park. The ban followed the team to Municipal Stadium, where the O's moved after Oriole Park burned to the ground in 1944. White stadium owners in other cities, meanwhile, welcomed Negro leagues teams. The Elites played many a Negro leagues game in white-owned stadiums in New York, Newark, Philadelphia, Boston, Detroit, Brooklyn, Chicago, and Washington, D.C. The stadium owners in those cities, likely no more egalitarian in their racial attitudes than were the

Orioles' officials, put money ahead of Jim Crow. They reaped handsome profits from renting their stadiums to Negro leagues teams.[23] It took until May 1950 for Orioles officials to reach the same conclusion. On Sunday, May 7, the Elite Giants and Philadelphia Stars opened their Negro leagues seasons in Municipal Stadium before 10,511 fans, most of them black. The Elites won a hard-fought game, 4–3. The *AFRO* noted that the game "marked the first time in history—and the culmination of a long fight— that colored teams were permitted to use the city park."[24]

Black teams playing in Oriole Park was one thing. African Americans playing for the Orioles was quite another. In April 1950, Dunn's grandson, Jack Dunn, 3rd, a 1939 graduate of Baltimore's prestigious Boys' Latin School and of Princeton University and now the O's owner, citing a loss of $200,000 over the past two years, asked the city's Department of Recreation and Parks Board to reduce the rent it charged for the Orioles to use Municipal Stadium. If the rent was not reduced, Dunn said, he might be forced to build another stadium. Dr. Bernard Harris, a physician for whom the Dr. Bernard Harris, Sr. Elementary School is named[25] and the only black Board member, suggested the O's could increase attendance and, thereby, revenue by signing black players.

"Have you looked into it for the Baltimore Orioles?" Harris asked Dunn.

"Yes ... seriously," Dunn replied.

"Are you still considering it?" responded Harris.

"Yes," Dunn replied.

Dunn never went beyond considering, but he did acknowledge to Harris that three teams in the International League, the Montreal Royals, Jersey City Giants, and Springfield [Massachusetts] Cubs, used black players. The Board accommodated Dunn's request.[26]

* * *

Orioles officials, with one notable exception, never made public their opposition to black players. In 1944, Alphonse (Tommy) Thomas, a Baltimore native, former major league pitcher, and manager of the minor league Orioles from 1940 to 1949, solemnly told an Afro-American sportswriter, "You of course understand that ever since I have been playing baseball and managing I have been associated with 'Organized Baseball' and do not feel I can have any opinion on the subject except as is expressed by organized baseball."[27]

Organized baseball, as everyone knew, had banned African Americans since before 1900 even though many could play as well as or better than their white counterparts. Proof of black players' abilities was not hard to come by, even in Baltimore. In 1943 an International League All-Star team faced off against the Elite Giants for a seven-game exhibition series at Bugle Field. Baltimore's "tan" players, as the black press of the day referred to black players, won six of the games. A similar series took place two years later, again at Bugle Field, with the same result.

The Elites impressed several white spectators in the stands for the 1945 games. Philip Reinsfelder, who lived on Bailey Street, thought it "a damned shame" none of the Elites could play for the O's. "I think they could have won the pennant this year," Reinsfelder said, "with just one of these [Elites] pitchers." William B. Siems of Elmley Avenue said, "They [Elite players] do everything surprising well, better than a lot of those fellows in the International." William F. Mellendick of Carlisle Avenue, father of Birds outfielder Joe Mellendick, concluded, "These boys are excellent players.... They've outhit, outfielded, outrun our boys, including Joe, all through this series."[28]

Other whites in Baltimore, however, could not abide blacks on the same diamond with white players. Jackie Robinson felt the brunt of white hatred during his first game at Municipal Stadium in April 1946 as a member of the Montreal Royals. "As soon as we took the field," Robinson recalled, "they began screaming all the typical phrases such as 'nigger, son of a bitch.' Soon insults were coming from all over the stands."[29] Other insults such as "Here comes the midnight express" and "Who's that ink-spot?" cascaded onto the field. Robinson said it was hardest on his wife Rachel, who was "forced to sit among the hostile spectators." She kept her temper," he said, "only because her dignity was more important to her than descending to the level of those ignorant bigots."[30] The harassment continued after the game. Large numbers of whites crowded around the Royals' dressing room door. "They weren't after autographs," Baltimore sportswriter Frank Lynch said in an interview.[31] Police dispersed the crowd.

Some O's players shared the same sentiments. Returning to the Royals' dugout after grounding out during a July game in Montreal, Robinson heard the usual catcalls and insults. This time they came from the visiting team's dugout. "I can still see him, stone faced, looking straight ahead as he passed our dugout on the way back to his," recalled Richard Armstrong in 2012. Recently discharged from the Navy, son of the O's business manager Herb Armstrong, Richard worked out with the team, threw batting practice, and sat on the bench during games. "I was absolutely shocked, dismayed, embarrassed and ashamed at the way O's players treated Robinson. It was like a verbal lynch mob. I wanted to be somewhere else," Armstrong said.[32]

* * *

White fans' and Orioles players' antipathy toward Robinson mirrored the continued prejudice many whites displayed towards blacks in Baltimore. Baltimore's other source of cultural friction involved its ethnic groups of European descent who had established neighborhoods by the 1940s. The east side of town served as home to the Poles, Germans, Latvians, Lithuanians, Ukrainians, Greeks, and Slovaks. The Italians had their own Little Italy. Jews clustered in the northwest part of town, while most African Americans lived in West Baltimore.[33]

Each newly arrived group met with some discrimination from established immigrants, but all eventually entered mainstream life as the ethnic frictions mellowed over time. Mayor Thomas D'Alesandro, Jr., for example, recalled overhearing one Italian saying to another in a confectionary shop in the 1940s, "Ain't it awful that Italian married a Pole? You're supposed to marry an Italian girl—it's heresy," the man moaned. Forty years later his son, Thomas D'Alesandro III, who followed his father into the mayor's office from 1967 to 1971, said he did not consider such marriages to be heresy but did admit, "I'm still looking for Italians in the box scores."[34] Baltimore writer Michael Olesker observed that, in Baltimore, as in other cities, "We are a nation of cultural mutts trying to reconcile the normal human desire to fit in while holding on to the things that give us comfort and make us unique."[35]

African Americans also wanted to fit in, but friction between whites and blacks did not diminish over time. African Americans continued to occupy the bottom rung on the city's social, economic, and political ladders. Far more blacks than whites in Baltimore lived in sub-standard housing and worked at menial jobs. A 1955 report noted "By and large Baltimore remains a racially segregated city with the Negroes in poorer jobs and the poorer housing."[36]

One of them, Frank McDougald, lived with his family, which had migrated from Rowland, North Carolina, in 1942, in a third-story, cold water flat at 915 McCullough Street from 1942 to 1957. The building had one bathroom for all third floor residents until the city council passed an ordinance requiring a bathroom in each apartment. A kerosene-powered stove provided heat. An ice box kept food from spoiling. As a young boy, McDougald pulled his wagon ten blocks to the local ice house for a block of ice. "A cold stream of water always ran down my neck each time I carried it up to the third floor," he said. He thought people in the nearby projects, high-rise apartments that replaced many single-family houses and concentrated the poor of all backgrounds into small areas, were well-to-do. They had central heat and hot and cold running water. His family moved to a three-story apartment building on Carrolton Avenue when he turned 15. The new apartment had gas and electric appliances.[37]

Black political muscle could be found only in churches, unions of brick makers, wagoners, grain trimmers, stevedores, and the *AFRO* newspaper which gave voice to African Americans' aspirations, concerns, and achievements.[38]

Several African Americans made their discontent and aspirations clear in a series of interviews with the *AFRO* in 1952, just two years before the major league Orioles would open for business. Robert Watts, an attorney for the National Association for the Advancement of Colored People (NAACP), looked for "an end to police brutality, a colored assistant State's attorney, traffic court magistrate, and above all, clerical and supervisory positions on both the city and state levels." Pastor of the Payne AME Church, W.P. Mitchell, cited "improved relations between the races" and "laws observed by both citizens and law enforcement officials." Magistrate John Berry called for the speedy return of soldiers from the Korean War and "colored players sparking a winning Baltimore Orioles baseball team." The Reverend Wilbur H. Waters, pastor of the Emmanuel Christian Community Church, spoke up for "wider participation in all municipal activities especially colored firemen and more policemen." The Reverend W. Clayton, pastor of Macedonia Baptist Church, put in a bid for "restaurants serving all citizens alike regardless of color of skin, a police department that majors in protection rather than prosecution, more financial services, and less liquor." Walter T. Dixon, president of Cortez Peters Business School, echoed Berry's call for "tan" Orioles. Born in South Carolina and raised in Williamstown, Massachusetts, Dixon held masters degrees from Columbia and Howard University. A visible civil rights leader in the city, Dixon introduced many bills to the City Council, including one that would require the city to fill all positions with those scoring highest on civil service examinations.[39] Dixon added, "If 1952 would provide a big eraser to be used by those in high places in our municipal and state government to forever eradicate the barriers of race, I would be most happy."[40]

The stark nature of segregation in Baltimore prompted Walter White, executive secretary of the NAACP, to telegraph American League President Will Harridge on September 25, 1953, urging him to deny the transfer of the St. Louis Browns to Baltimore. White gave as his reason "the city's rigid pattern of segregation including the exclusion of Negroes from hotels and restaurants." White cited the Lyric Theater's recent refusal to book the internationally famous contralto, Marion Anderson, as an example of the city's "racist spirit." He complimented baseball on having recently "been an important factor in extending the American ideals of civil rights and fair play." Approving the transfer, however, White stressed, "would be a step backward."[41] His telegram went unanswered.

* * *

As the diamonds in Baltimore remained segregated save for the occasional exhibition game, integration in major league baseball could be seen sprouting elsewhere. Following Robinson's historic signing with the Brooklyn Dodgers in 1947, two American League teams, in rapid succession, signed African Americans. Larry Doby, star player for the Newark Eagles in the Negro National League, became the first player of color in the junior circuit when he agreed to terms with Cleveland Indians owner Bill Veeck on July 5, 1947. Doby would go on to a Hall of Fame career. Two weeks later Henry J. "Hank" Peters, 22, World War II veteran and the Browns' assistant farm director, signed outfielders Hank Thompson and Willard Brown, both from the Kansas City Monarchs in the Negro American League. Peters, whose career as a major league baseball executive included 12 as Orioles general manager (1975–1987), hoped the two ballplayers would improve the Browns' dismal record and dwindling attendance. Fewer than 500 paying customers had seen a Browns game in early July, while a game in St. Louis between two Negro leagues teams drew 14,000, most of them black.[42]

Thompson's and Brown's arrival marked the first time two African Americans played for the same major league team. Many black St. Louis residents, however, still resented the segregated seating in Sportsman's Park that had been in effect until two years earlier. They stayed away. Only 1,163 fans attended a Saturday Browns-Philadelphia Athletics game with both Thompson and Brown in the lineup. Whites expressed their displeasure by flooding the Browns' front office with letters threatening a boycott. The St. Louis-based *Sporting News* noted the two men took jobs from whites.[43] Their new teammates directed icy stares their way. One threatened to quit if they remained with the team. "The gloom that pervaded the dressing room and the bench was thick enough to make one gasp for air," noted a St. Louis sportswriter.[44] The Browns released both a month later. "Neither one did that well for us, but why we let Thompson go, I don't know. He developed into a decent major league player," Peters said later.[45] Thompson played eight years with the New York Giants. Brown finished his career with the Monarchs.

The Browns remained an all-white team until 1951, when Bill Veeck, who had sold the Indians in 1949 and bought the Browns in 1951, signed Satchel Paige, who had pitched for him in Cleveland. The best known of any of the Browns, and better known by the general public than most major league players, "Satch" reportedly pitched in over 2,500 games, mostly for Negro leagues and barnstorming teams dating from the 1920s. Standing a slender six foot four inches tall and weighing 180 pounds, he combined a blazing fastball with pinpoint control. Joe DiMaggio, who faced Paige in the California Winter League, called him "the toughest pitcher I ever faced."[46] Considered a relic by many at age 45, Paige confounded the critics by posting a respectable 18–23 won-lost record from 1951 to 1953 for a team that lost 292 games out of 464 while finishing in last place twice and next-to-last once.

Veeck sought out other African American players. "We tried out a lot of blacks through Veeck's connection with Abe Saperstein (Chicago-based sports promoter known for his work with the Negro leagues and the Harlem Globetrotters). I can't tell you how many we must have tried out at Sportsman's Park," Peters said, "but we didn't sign many."[47] Those Peters did sign, other than Thompson and Brown, played in the minor leagues. They included Joseph Vann Durham, who would become the second African American to play for the new major league Orioles.

Veeck's scouts scoured the country for African American talent. One scout, former Yankees and Red Sox backup catcher Freddy Hofmann, reported back to Veeck from a tournament in Alabama that the player Veeck had sent him to scout "was just so-so, but," Hofmann excitedly told Veeck, "I've seen the best player I've ever seen," Peters recalled.[48] That player, Willie Mays, had, unfortunately for the Browns and later the Orioles, already signed with the New York Giants.

Other teams also scouted and signed players of color. By the end of the 1953 season, 40 minorities, including four Cubans and three Puerto Ricans, had signed major league contracts with nine major league teams. The Cleveland Indians led the way with ten, followed by the Brooklyn Dodgers with seven.[49] The Browns still had only one, the ageless wonder, Satchel Paige. How many would don an Orioles uniform soon became known.

CHAPTER 2

"When the Public Is Ready"

September 30, 1953, holds a special place in the hearts of Baltimore baseball fans. On that hot, muggy day the *Baltimore Sun* announced in a two-inch headline: BIG LEAGUE BASEBALL BACK IN CITY AS BROWNS' DEAL IS APPROVED. Two men of dissimilar backgrounds—Baltimore's Democratic mayor, Thomas D'Alesandro, Jr., known as "Tommy" to most, and attorney Clarence W. Miles, a member of the Social Register—had finally sealed the deal. D'Alesandro had tried since 1949 to bring big league baseball to Baltimore.[1] At exactly 6:00 pm on September 29, 1953, the mayor dashed out of the conference room in New York City's Hotel Commodore, where American League owners had been acrimoniously deliberating the Browns' new destination for three days, and "let go with a jubilant shout."[2] D'Alesandro, Miles, and City Solicitor Thomas Biddleson, who had advised the duo on legal matters as the talks ground on, retired to a well-deserved night's sleep after a celebration dinner.

The news, which came to the city over the dinner hour, at first stunned people in Baltimore, few of whom thought D'Alessandro would be successful in his negotiations. Before long, however, a feeling of exhilaration swept through the city like wildfire. Many heard the news over their car radios on the commute home. They honked their horns, flashed their headlights, and stopped in the middle of the street to pass on the good news. A patron of Barber Joe Pecora on East Gay Street, with lather on his face and the cloth around his neck, sprung from his chair to collect on a 15–1 bet he had placed. Two hours later he had not returned. Major league baseball coming to Baltimore was, an East Baltimore bartender exclaimed, "the greatest thing since the Armistice." Bars and restaurants filled up quickly. Late editions of newspapers were hard to come by. Dreams of reconstituting glories past when the National League Orioles had won three straight pennants from 1894 to 1896 danced in many a head. While Baltimoreans celebrated, the mayor's secretary, Thomas O'Donnell, worked through the night to arrange for a band and hundreds of people to be on hand to meet the mayor's train when it would arrive at the Baltimore & Ohio Mount Royal Station at 4:13 the next day.[3]

Thousands of cheering people and a marching band met their train the next day at Mt. Royal Station. The "wildly grinning, enthusiastic" mayor and the "noticeably tired and drawn" Miles made their way in a motorcade through throngs of well-wishers, car horns, posters, balloons, and confetti to City Hall.[4] Former Maryland Governor and United States Senator Herbert R. O'Conor organized a 1,300-person testimonial dinner. Television and radio stations carried part of the festivities live.[5]

* * *

The newly minted Orioles carried one African American on the roster, Satchel Paige. The lanky pitcher's performance with the 1953 Browns, however, did not impress the club's general manager, Art Ehlers. "I don't feel that he put out last year as he should have as a $25,000-a-year-man," Ehlers, 57, a Baltimore native, former minor league player, and Philadelphia Athletics general manager, told members of Baltimore's Frontiers Club, a group of African American civic, business, and religious leaders.[6] Ehlers offered Paige's contract to every other American League club but to no avail. Award-winning sportswriter for the *AFRO*, Sam Lacy, a savvy, articulate, and persistent advocate for civil rights, disagreed. The Orioles "couldn't very well drop an established performer ... and a good gate," Lacy wrote. Such a move, he warned, "would not sit well with the colored citizenry of Baltimore and Washington.[7] The O's, however, could and they did. "Satch, just because of his age, wouldn't fit into our plans,"[8] Ehlers told the Baltimore press when he released Paige on January 26, 1954.

"Brother Art's thinking could stand a small hypodermic," Lacy opined upon hearing of Paige's release.[9] Lacy's colleague, Reid E. Jackson, went further, stating "Baltimore's colored citizens are already sour on the Orioles. They cannot understand why a stellar attraction like Satchel Paige was 'sold down the river.'" Jackson called on blacks everywhere "to flood the Oriole front office with protest letters."[10]

Conventional wisdom held that any pitcher aged 47, black or white, was well past his prime. Such wisdom, however, did not apply to Paige.[11] His earned run average, though a bit on the high side at 3.53, rated third-best among Browns hurlers in 1953 and bested those of three younger pitchers that Ehlers would take to Yuma, Arizona, for spring training.[12]

In addition, Paige had led all Browns pitchers by saving 11 games that season. By releasing him, the O's passed up a chance to bolster the league's worst pitching staff and boost attendance (not only in Baltimore but throughout the American League as well).

Paige packed his bags and continued his career in high style. He barnstormed until 1956, when Bill Veeck, who as owner of the Browns had sold the team to Baltimore and now owned the International League Miami Marlins, signed him. For three years Paige did well enough financially with the Marlins that he spurned three offers from major league clubs.[13]

Controversy over Paige's release cropped up as late as 1978. *Sun* reporters Sandy Banisky and Bill Carter quoted an unnamed but longtime fan of the O's as attributing Paige's release to "40% racism and 60% stupidity." The fan lamented that the team "had kissed away 100,000 tickets." Rising to Ehler's defense, Joseph A. W. Iglehart, one of the club's original owners and board members, denied the existence of any ulterior motive. "I never heard one word about Satchel Paige," Iglehart told the reporters. "There was nothing said about it, not one thing."[14]

Paige himself had harbored mixed feelings about playing for the O's. When he first heard the Browns might go to Baltimore, he told teammate Gene Bearden, "I never got treated too good in that town, you know I played a couple of exhibitions there. But of course if it's Mr. Bill [Veeck] that goes there, I'll go right along with him. I'd play anywhere for him—even in Afghan-

Photographer Robert Lerner took this photograph of Satchel Paige as a St. Louis Brown in Sportsman's Park for a July 1953, story for *Look* magazine. The story's apt headline read "Old Satchel Paige—Still Winning." A portion of Sportsman's Park can be seen in the background (Library of Congress, Prints and Photographs Division, LC-DIG-ppmsca-18778).

istan."[15] Veeck had earned Paige's loyalty when, as owner of the Cleveland Indians, he had signed Paige to his first major league contract in 1948.

* * *

Two months before Paige's release, Miles, now the Orioles president, in acknowledging the city's 45 percent black population, promised a *Sun* reporter that "We are going to exhaust every human effort to find at least a couple of outstanding colored ball players for the team.... The Orioles will be counting on Baltimore's colored population for support and therefore the club will do its part by seeking good colored players."[16] Miles, however, added the caveat that he did not want to interfere with Ehlers' player selection decisions.

Ehlers added his own caveat. "I will not," he told a reporter, "sign a colored player simply to attract Negro fans." Any black player, he made clear, would have to be one capable of helping the club. "To do otherwise would be an affront to the colored fan."[17]

After clearly signaling he would not be pressured into signing a black player, Ehlers, at a December luncheon of the Frontiers Club, promised that neither would a player's race be considered when it came to deciding whom to sign. "My sole objective," he promised the group, "is to build a winning team regardless of the race or religion of the best available players." He went on to lament that certain unnamed factions in Baltimore "that should be working together are constantly at war."[18]

Ehlers could have gone beyond statements of good intentions had he told the Frontiers Club members of his efforts, three weeks earlier, to obtain two African American players. He had offered two Orioles starters, outfielder Vic Wertz and catcher Clint Courtney, to the Cleveland Indians for two African American players of undisputed talent, outfielders Larry Doby and Al Smith. Indians General Manager Hank Greenberg, not surprisingly, nixed the deal. Perhaps Ehlers kept silent because he knew the proposed swap was too one-sided, a future Hall of Famer (Doby) and a future two-time All Star (Smith) for two O's of lesser talent.[19] Ehlers did, however, feel compelled to assure his listeners that any concerns they may have about the attitudes of several Orioles officials who had previously worked for the International League O's "would be found unwarranted."[20]

Ehlers had good reason to offer up such assurance. He had hired Jack Dunn 3rd as a vice-president.[21] Ehlers also knew that Herb Armstrong, public relations director for both the minor and major league Orioles, had expressed "great surprise" at Jackie Robinson's signing by the Montreal Royals, a farm team of the Brooklyn Dodgers, in October 1945. "Naturally, it will pose a number of arresting problems. As it is now, it is strictly a club matter, but no doubt it will now be necessary for some general legislation," Armstrong told the *Baltimore Sun*.[22] Members of the Frontiers Club no doubt also knew that Ehlers and Dunn frequently attended meetings of the International League together.[23] As a Baltimore native, Ehlers knew full-well that segregation had reigned supreme in the city of Baltimore, as well as on the diamond. If he expected his words alone to convince Baltimore's African American community that the new white baseball team in town had its best interests at heart, he had set himself an impossibly high bar.

* * *

Ehlers, hoping he had assuaged the doubts of Baltimore's African Americans, turned his attention to 1954. As to how many black players would go to Yuma, Ehlers had told the Frontiers Club that he could not say for sure. He said he felt reasonably sure, however, that Jehosie Heard would be among them. Heard, a native of Athens, Georgia, stood five feet, seven inches tall, weighed 147 pounds, and seemed a promising southpaw prospect, having compiled a 16–12 record and a 3.19 earned run average with the 1953 Portland Beavers of the Pacific Coast League. Ehlers also mentioned Charles White, a stocky catcher at 190 pounds and five feet 11 inches who hailed from Kingston, North Carolina, as a possibility. Peters had signed White as a free agent for the Browns in 1951 and assigned him to the minor league Toronto Maple Leafs. White came to Ehlers' attention with his stellar play for the San Antonio Missions in the Texas League, a Browns farm club.[24]

* * *

As promised, Ehlers took Heard and White to Yuma, located in the southwest corner of the state. Movie stars came to the town of 20,000 to wed. Dubbing it the "hottest little town in the U.S.A.," city fathers who were eager that Yuma be known for something besides once being the site of the Territorial Prison, initiated a building boom that included the Flamingo Hotel, the second largest "motor court" in the state. A $100,000 renovation had been completed just in time for the team's arrival. The ranch-style motel surrounded a swimming pool and boasted 22 new units, air conditioning, and a TV in every room. The O's worked out at the city's municipal baseball park, home to the Yuma Panthers of the Southwest International League.[25]

The remodeled hotel housed all the Orioles save for Heard, his wife

Mildred, and White. They were forced by Arizona's segregationist culture to stay elsewhere. Heard, whom *The Sporting News* described as "a diminutive Negro lefty," enjoyed spring training. Mildred, however, was lonely. "We don't know many people here," Heard explained to Ehlers, who had asked him how he liked his first big league camp. Ehlers immediately sent his TV set, which he said he was not using because of business pressure, to their room. *The Sporting News* cited Ehlers' act as a "big league move." The article did not say how the TV set affected Mildred's loneliness.[26]

Before spring training ended, Ehlers sent White back down to the San Antonio Missions. The catcher, one of the first blacks to play for the Missions in the Texas League, which had just integrated in 1952,[27] soon graduated to the majors but with the Milwaukee Braves. He appeared in 62 games over the course of the 1954 and 1955 seasons.

With little fanfare, Ehlers brought the Orioles' first Mexican player to Baltimore, second baseman Chico Garcia, 30, a native of Vera Cruz. While still in Philadelphia, Ehlers had arranged for the A's to make Garcia their number one minor league draft choice based on his .305 batting average in the Texas League. Since Baltimore had the first pick while the A's had to wait for the third pick, Ehlers snatched Garcia for the Birds, thereby "engendering the wrath of his former bosses."[28] The A's got the last laugh, however, as Garcia failed to impress during the 1954 season, getting into only 39 games and hitting an anemic .111 to end his major league career.

Ehlers also brought Heard east, thereby giving the southpaw the distinction of being not only the Orioles' first African American player but also the

Jehosie Heard winding up to deliver a pitch in an exhibition game during the Orioles' first spring training camp, 1954, in Yuma, Arizona (National Baseball Hall of Fame Library, Cooperstown, New York).

The Baltimore Orioles in the spring of 1954. Heard is in the middle row, fourth from the right. The curvature of Memorial Stadium which gave the grandstand its nickname—The Bowl—can be seen in the background. Back Row (left to right): Edward Weidner (*trainer*), Sam Mele, Jim Brideweser, Cal Abrams, Lou Kretlow, Don Larsen, Dick Kryhoski, Jim Fridley, Marlin Stuart, Mike Blyzka, Bobby Young, Jack Phillips (*honorary batboy*). Middle Row: Duane Pillette, Bob Turley, Clint Courtney, Harry Brecheen (*coach*), Francis Skaff (*coach*), Jimmy Dykes (*Mgr.*), Thomas Oliver (*coach*), Jehosie Heard, Chico Garcia, Billy Hunter, Gil Coan. Front Row: Eddie Waitkus, Chuck Diering, Joe Coleman, Howie Fox, Ray Murray, Vic Wertz, Bob Kennedy, Vern Stephens, Les Moss, George Diering (*batboy*) (National Baseball Hall of Fame Library, Cooperstown, New York).

team's oldest-ever rookie at age 34. Wishing to appear younger for obvious reasons, Heard claimed 1925 as his birth year. His high school transcript gives the year as 1920.[29]

* * *

Born in High Shoals, Georgia, where his father John worked in the cotton fields before taking a factory job making skillets and pots in Birmingham, Alabama, Heard had pitched six years in the Negro leagues with the Birmingham Black Barons, Houston Eagles, and New Orleans Eagles.[30] His performance in the Negro leagues All-Star Game, the East-West Game, in 1951 in Chicago caught an Orioles scout's attention. Heard went

3⅓ innings, giving up only one run.[31] Bill Gleason, a teammate of Heard with the Barons and later a Baptist minister, said of Heard's delivery, "He didn't have a fast ball to go with those breaking balls, but he threw strikes and he was just one of those guys who got you out."[32] Gil Coan, an outfielder for the Washington Senators from 1946 to 1953 before being traded to the Orioles in 1954, did not share Gleason's assessment of Heard. He was "meek and mild and easy to get along with. But he did not throw hard and was not a major league pitcher," Coan said.[33]

* * *

The Birds opened the 1954 season in Detroit against the Tigers, one of four major league teams yet to sign an African American player. Heard and his mates left the Motor City with a split of the two-game series. An overnight train ride brought the team to Camden Station, the future site of Oriole Park at Camden Yards, on a wet and drizzly Thursday morning, April 15. They changed into their uniforms on the train and disembarked into the station's central waiting room. From there Baltimore's largest-ever parade got under way. Players rode two to three abreast in gleaming new convertibles. Heard rode with right-handed pitcher Mike Blyzka.[34] An estimated 350,000 loudly cheering well-wishers, standing ten deep in some places, lined the route. The school board declared a holiday. Players tossed styrofoam baseballs to the crowds of adults and kids, some of whom ran into the street to shake hands with players. Five-year-old Curt Anderson, a future member of the Maryland House of Delegates' Black Caucus, caught one of the balls. "It was white with the Orioles' logo on it," he said. "I hadn't seen styrofoam before, and I kept it 'til the logo wore off."[35] Twenty bands and 18 floats, made by Earl Hargrove of Cheverly, Maryland, at a cost of $1,000 to $5,000 each, made their way along the three and-a-half-mile parade route.[36] The biggest float showed an animated, 12-foot-tall Baltimore native, Babe Ruth, swinging his bat. Another featured two Miss Marylands and three Mrs. Marylands clad in swimsuits and furs valued at over $100,000. A third paid tribute to the ten Orioles of yore enshrined in the National Baseball Hall of Fame. The parade took an hour and a half to pass a given point. Thousands of pennants and balloons in the O's black and orange colors dotted the parade route. By noon the parade had reached Memorial Stadium at 1000 East 33rd Street, where a sell-out crowd of 46,354 took their seats. "This is a real big thrill for me. The major league is great and the spirit here in Baltimore makes me proud I'm starting here. I only hope I can help the club pay off for these fans," Heard told a reporter.[37]

"This is a great day for baseball and a great day for Baltimore," Vice President Richard M. Nixon announced from his box seat near the O's dugout. Then, after cocking his arm and loudly voicing the hopes of all in the stands, he said, "May the new Orioles be as good and strong as the old Orioles,"[38] and threw out the ceremonial first pitch. Baltimore-born home plate umpire Eddie Rommel cried "Play ball!" Right hander Bob Turley tossed a complete game against the Chicago White Sox for a 3–1 win with home run help from catcher Clint Courtney and third baseman Vern Stephens.[39] Manager Jimmy Dykes, whom Ehlers had brought with him from Philadelphia, had led the team to an impressive .667 start.

* * *

Heard warmed the bench until April 24, when Dykes tapped him to relieve parade-mate Mike Blyzka. The Birds were trailing the White Sox, 10–0, at Comiskey Park in Chicago. As the fourth Orioles pitcher in a debacle of a game being telecast coast to coast as the Saturday "Game of the Week," Heard acquitted himself admirably. He got four outs without giving up a run. Dykes lifted him for a pinch-hitter. The O's lost, 14–4, but Heard's performance earned him a spot on the final 25 man roster. On hearing the news in late May, Heard exclaimed, "It sure feels great to know I'll remain with the Orioles."[40] The southpaw fared less well during his second and last appearance on May 28 at home against the same White Sox. The Sox shellacked the portsider for six hits and five earned runs in two innings before Dykes pulled him.[41]

Ehlers released Heard back to the Portland Beavers on June 6. "It was our feeling that he was not fast enough for the major leagues and we had no alternative than to farm him out," Ehlers explained.[42] *The Sporting News* reported that the O's had sent Heard to Portland to make way for $15,000 bonus pitcher Billy O'Dell.[43]

There may have been more to Ehlers' decision. Suggestions of trouble between Heard and Mildred had surfaced earlier. Heard reported her missing to the police on June 2, saying she left with $80, might be on her way to visit relatives, and had a scar over her right eye. At the same time, the *AFRO* had reported signs of a struggle including broken furniture and blood smears in the house the couple had rented on Bentalou Street. Neighbors reported hearing a "serious disturbance" in mid–May about the time a couple strongly resembling the Heards, but identifying themselves as Joseph and Hazel Thomas and giving their address as being on a non-existent block of Bentalou, arrived at Providence Hospital. The woman received treatment for cuts to her right earlobe, upper right eyelid, and scalp. Heard denied any problems. He failed, however, to show up for the June 6 doubleheader with the Yankees, saying he had "a stomach ailment." Ehlers told the press he accepted the pitcher's explanation and that "club officials knew nothing of Heard's private life that would influence their disposition of him."[44]

* * *

Heard's departure left the O's without an African American player until September, when Ehlers called up 22-year-old Joe Durham from the San Antonio Missions. He had played in the Class B Piedmont League for the York [Pennsylvania] White Roses in 1953 before being promoted to the Missions. A six-foot, one-inch, 190-pound outfielder from Newport News, Virginia, Durham scored the winning run against the Washington Senators in his first game to give the O's a 4–3 win at Memorial Stadium.[45] He appeared in ten games with the Birds that month and managed nine hits in 40 at-bats. With one of those hits, in the nightcap of a doubleheader against the Philadelphia Athletics on September 12, Durham became the first African American to homer for the Birds. His 350-foot shot into the left field bleachers, *Sun* reporter Ned Burks noted, "dropped near a cluster of happy Negro fans."[46] Memorial Stadium did not have segregated seating, but black fans who bought bleacher tickets usually found themselves "surrounded by other blacks."[47] Those who occasionally bought a more expensive seat "in the bowl" (as the grandstand was referred to because of its curved shape) found that the white ushers would do their best to ignore them.[48]

The O's brush with black players ended when Durham started a three-year military commitment with Uncle Sam at the end of the 1954 season.[49] While the Orioles were technically an integrated team in 1954, their two black players, Heard and Durham, had only short, insignificant stints. The couple of outstanding black players promised by Miles had not appeared.

Such players did, however, appear on other major league rosters. Twenty-six African Americans played all or most of the 1954 season, the great majority of them in the National League. They included rookie Hank Aaron as well as veterans Monte Irvin, Roy Campanella, Luke Easter, Junior Gilliam, Ernie Banks, Don Newcombe, Larry Doby, Jackie Robinson, Hank Thompson, and Willie Mays. Mays took the National League's Most Valuable Player honors, and, with teammates Irvin and Thompson, led the New York Giants to a four-game sweep of the 1954 World Series over the Cleveland Indians. The Indians had won the American League pennant with the help of four black players: Luke Easter, Al Smith, Dave Pope, and Larry Doby. Fans across the country elected four African Americans—

Doby, Campanella, Mays, and Frank Robinson to the All-Star Game, two as starters, Robinson and Campanella. Many African Americans in Baltimore wondered why players of that stripe were not wearing the Orioles' orange and black. Had the Orioles really exhausted every human effort, as Ehlers had promised the Frontiers Club they would, to find a star black player or two? It would appear not.

* * *

If Ehlers' promises to the Frontiers Club went unfulfilled—to the disappointment, no doubt, of many African Americans in the city—the scarcity of black players did not rise to a level of concern to players and front office staff. Billy O'Dell, a native of Whitmire, South Carolina, who pitched for O's from 1954 to 1959, recalled in a 2012 interview that "I never thought about it. I didn't see any problems with anybody. We had three or four black guys, they were just like everybody else—that's how we accepted them."[50] Shortstop Ron Hansen, raised in Oxford, Nebraska, and a starter for the O's from 1960 to 1962, agreed. Except for blacks having to live in "a separate hotel in another part of town during spring training, everyone had the same opportunities and the same chances, as far as I remember," Hansen said. "It didn't make any difference, race, nationality, religion, or whatever. The object was to win ball games. Everybody was treated that way," he added.[51]

Orioles front office personnel, all white, had the same outlook. Baltimore native Jerry Sachs, who grew up in a Jewish neighborhood in the northwest section of town and worked in public relations for the O's from 1960 to 1965, echoed O'Dell's and Hansen's comments for the period 1960–1965. "It [skin color] just wasn't anything that I'm aware of that anybody focused on, positively or negatively. My recollection was they [O's management] were just after the best ball players."[52]

Sachs, like many in the O's front office, had had little personal contact with African Americans. "My days in high school," Sachs recalled in 2012, "were totally segregated. There was no mixing. The city was totally segregated, just starting to break out. Until I went to college I was never in a classroom with a black person. The only place that wasn't segregated was on the ball field, both the Colts [the city's professional football team] and the O's."[53]

* * *

Looking back on his debut with the Orioles, Durham said he did not recall any racial slurs or insults from Orioles fans as had Jackie Robinson seven years earlier. "They treated me okay," he said.[54] Such, however, had not been the case for him in the minor leagues. "When I first signed with the Browns in 1951," Durham said, "they wanted to send me to places where I couldn't play, like Arkansas and South Carolina, so they hooked me up with the Chicago American Giants of the American Negro League where I played for one year." The next year the O's assigned him to the York [Pennsylvania] White Roses in the Class B Piedmont League. "Most teams didn't bother me," Durham said, "except Norfolk [Virginia], which could be vile, and Hagerstown [Maryland] which was outrageously poor," Durham said, shaking his head with a small chuckle. "I always figured it this way. If they want to talk about me or my parents, which they didn't know, I'm not from Hagerstown, I let 'em talk as long as they didn't bother me." Teammate Willie Tasby, a five-foot, 11-inch, 170-pound outfielder from Shreveport, Louisiana, took a different stance. "Tasby," Durham said, "had a little problem. He wanted to go up in the stands. I said 'there's 1,800 people up there and we are going up there to meet 1,800 people? You gotta be out of your mind.' I said, 'let 'em talk.'"[55] The talk didn't faze the 22-year-old outfielder. He hit .308 with 14 homers in 129 games with the White Roses and excelled in the field.[56]

In both the Piedmont and the Texas League, Durham lived in separate housing. In Houston, he recalled, "Everyone else is at a downtown hotel, and you're in a tourist home, two stories with one bathtub." Asked if it was hard to play that way, he replied, "It made it harder. Baseball's a team game, a family game, and when the family's split, that's tough."[57]

* * *

Integration, though taken in baby steps by the Orioles, went more smoothly on the ball field than it did in the city. The city's racial structure got a legal jolt of seismic proportion on May 17, 1954, a month after Opening Day. On that day the U.S. Supreme Court, in *Brown v. The Board of Education*, reversed the "separate but equal" doctrine that had controlled the nation's public schools since 1896. Baltimore native and later the first African American U.S. Supreme Court Justice, Thurgood Marshall, played a major role in prosecuting the case. Baltimore's Board of Education quickly voted to support the decision, but it made no effort to integrate the schools. The Board merely authorized parents to enroll their students in any school in the city that had room for them. African American parents soon discovered, however, that custom trumped the new law.[58]

Schools opened in September to hate-filled rhetoric and action. Two hundred white students hurled insults and bottles at 12 African American

Students joined the demonstrations protesting school integration. These teenagers swarmed Baltimore's city hall in 1955 with signs and shouts decrying integration of their schools (Library of Congress, Prints and Photographs Division, LC-USZ62–126454).

students as they entered Southwest Baltimore's Southern High School, the alma mater of future Hall of Fame outfielder Al Kaline, injuring two of them. Unfortunately for the O's, Kaline had started his career with the Tigers a year earlier. A "Stay at Home" movement kept 2,000 white students in six other schools home while pickets surrounded each school with signs and banners protesting integration.[59] A group of mothers surrounded elementary school #54, carrying signs opposing integration, as only 50 of 750 students showed up for class.[60] Charles Luthardt, a 46-year-old carpenter and former cab driver with three sons at Southern, joined the board of the newly formed Maryland chapter of the National Association for the Advancement of White People (NAAWP). The group's purpose, Luthardt explained to the *Sun*, "is to block integration in Maryland public schools by all peaceful and legal means. We don't want any Communists," Luthardt added proudly. "We aren't that kind of an organization."[61]

George Washington Williams, Baltimore attorney and former Federal district judge in the Virgin Islands, added his voice, more inflammatory than many, to those opposing integration during an unsuccessful 1956 campaign for a U.S. Senate. He called the Court's ruling "the most vicious and inexcusable invasion of the rights and powers of the State of Maryland. This is," he added, "no time for pussyfooting." He called on citizens, for their own security, to "fight against the segregation cases being jammed down our throats."[62] At a city council meeting, Williams called the Court's decision "one of the foulest, most unjustified ever handed down. I cannot imagine the court doing a more evil thing," he thundered.[63] The candidate supported U.S. Senator William Langer's (R. ND) proposed bill to send all African Americans to Africa.[64] Neither Williams' rhetoric nor his Democratic primary campaign impressed many voters. He ran so far behind Millard Tawes, who would become Maryland's governor in 1959, and George P. Mahoney, a perennial and unsuccessful office-seeker best known for his anti-open housing slogan, "Your home is your castle, protect it," that the *Sun* did not bother to report Williams' vote total.

* * *

The battle over school desegregation did not affect the Orioles directly, but the Jim Crow custom that banned blacks from registering at white-owned downtown hotels did. Black players from the American League's three teams that had blacks on their rosters in 1954 (Cleveland Indians, Chicago White Sox, Philadelphia Athletics) had to stay at the York Hotel in northwest Baltimore or at a private residence. Their white teammates resided at the Lord Baltimore, Emerson, or Southern Hotel.

On April 7, 1954, just eight days before Opening Day, Republican Governor Theodore Roosevelt McKeldin took on the hotel owners. The governor, who grew up in a white working class neighborhood in south Baltimore, had already established himself as a champion for equal rights. During his first term as mayor from 1943 to 1947, he hired black staff members, including his secretary, appointed the first black assistant city solicitor and school board member, and removed race from the application form for city jobs. "McKeldin was vilified, McKeldin was loved," recalled Democratic city council member Solomon Liss.[65]

Four hotel owners, their attorney, Charles D. Harris, and members of his Governor's Commission on Interracial Problems met in McKeldin's office. Harris told McKeldin that the owners, while they personally would like to accept African Americans as guests, would lose money "if they went ahead of public opinion. When the public is ready to accept mixed patronage," Harris assured everyone, "hotels will be happy to admit Negroes."[66] To admit "Negro" ballplayers would, Harris argued, "discriminate against Negro doctors, lawyers, and other professional men." Besides, Harris continued, the hotels had made progress "because Negroes are permitted to attend meetings, dinners, and other affairs in major downtown hotels."[67] Continuing the registration ban, McKeldin countered, would bring "a lot of unfavorable publicity" down on both Baltimore and Maryland.[68]

Such publicity, McKeldin estimated, had already cost Baltimore at least 20 conventions. Twenty-six national organizations were on record against holding their conventions in Baltimore or any other city where hotels maintain a discriminatory policy. The organizations included the League of Women Voters, the American Mathematical Society, the American Health Association, the Congress of Industrial Organizations (C.I.O.), and the American Veterans Committee.[69] Rabbi Israel M. Goldman, the commission's vice chairman, told the owners the public was ready, as evidenced by successful integration in department stores, at some restaurants, and at Ford's theater. The meeting ended with a round of handshakes but no change in the hotel owners' stance.[70]

Concern about public opinion was not the only factor behind the owners' reluctance to allow African Americans to sign in at their hotels. They were also angry at McKeldin. A mimeographed letter addressed to but not delivered to the governor circulated among owners after the meeting. The letter charged, "the whole matter has been magnified far beyond its own boundary. Why? We are unable to state unless it be due to the desire of some person [read McKeldin] or persons for personal gain." The letter went on to charge that the issue "was not being pushed by the real leaders of the Negro race but by agitators or persons seeking personal glory or reward." The owners further claimed that McKeldin's statement to the Variety Club a week earlier, in which he criticized the owners' stance, put them "in the untenable position of being publically tried without having had an opportunity to present our side of the problem." The governor did not respond to the letter but "marveled" that the missive made its appearance "after such an amiable meeting."[71] He, nevertheless, kept up pressure on them with the statement, issued at a meeting of his commission and representatives of two Baltimore hotels three weeks later, that their position was "morally wrong."[72]

The owners were not entirely wrong in their assessment of public opinion. Several city residents, in letters to the *Sun's* editor, supported them. George H. Wagner warned, "If a price we have to pay for a big league team is the breakdown of our social standards, it is too high a price." Douglas Sompayrac wondered why all the "hullaboo" and pointed out, "Other races (which he did not name) have been denied certain privileges down through the years and still are, but they have been too proud to make a fuss about it." R. D. Spicer challenged those who equated the owners' position with a return to the gaslight era "to show that Americans of the gaslight era were not just as good and intelligent as the Americans of today."[73]

Several black players took the situation in stride. "It's just a matter of time before they change the policy," Luke Easter, the Cleveland Indians' first baseman, told an *AFRO* reporter during a card game at the York Hotel. "I think Luke is right," agreed fellow outfielder Al Smith, "Things are really changing all over the country. I feel the hotels will open up in due time." Dave Pope added, "There is nothing we can do about it, but all of us would like to have the privilege of staying with the rest of the club."[74]

One who did not take the situation in stride was Cuban-born Saturnino Orestes Armas Arrieta "Minnie" Minoso, the White Sox's first black starting player when he joined the team in 1951. Minoso, a flashy dresser and bon vivant, took the ban personally. "I've been to every movie in town. I have no one to visit with, no teammates to play cards with. It is terribly lonely. I wish Baltimore was not in the league, I do," he told Sam Lacy.[75] Elston Howard, the first African American to crack the New York Yankees' line-up a year later, in 1955, avoided the York Hotel altogether. He either stayed with friends in Baltimore when the Yankees were in town or commuted from the Shoreham Hotel, 40 miles south in Washington, D.C. His teammates stayed at the Emerson Hotel in downtown Baltimore.[76]

* * *

Durham and the Birds' maiden season came to a close with reality swamping the city's initial euphoria. Despite the city-wide excitement of major league baseball reappearing in Baltimore, many had kept their expectations in check. A newsboy's response, a week before the season started, to a reporter's question, "Whatta you think about the O's?" spoke for many. He replied, "I've got my ticket for Opening Day, but I'm like most people in this town. We know what we've got is the St. Louis Browns in different uniforms so we're not expecting miracles."[77]

A miracle the city did not get. With a 54–100 won-lost record, the same miserable record the Browns had posted the year before, the O's struggled to a seventh-place finish, barely escaping last place by only two games over the moribund Philadelphia Athletics. Attendance, predicted to top 1,800,000, the figure attained by the Milwaukee Braves in 1953 following their move from Boston, barely topped one million. Miles told a news conference in Boston in late August that "there might be drastic changes in the direction of the Orioles"[78] and that "no one's job is safe."[79] Reports surfaced that the O's Board of Directors would seek Miles', Ehlers', and Dykes' heads at their September meeting. The Board, however, re-elected Miles as president but remained silent on Ehlers' and Dykes' fates.[80]

CHAPTER 3

"We'd Be the Most Stupid People in Baseball"

It did not take long for Ehlers' and Dykes' heads to roll. On September 14, 1954, Miles fired Dykes and signed White Sox manager Paul Richards to a three-year pact. Richards had led the Sox to four first division finishes from 1951 to 1954. Ehlers stayed on as an assistant GM. Dykes finished out the last two weeks of the season but not before letting off some steam. An Orioles executive, who had second-guessed Dykes all season, offered him one more piece of advice in late September. Dykes, knowing the advice would be forthcoming, rubbed the seat of his uniform in grass a few hours before the meeting. He made sure the exec saw the stain. The man exclaimed, "Jim, you've got grass stains on your pants!" Dykes looked him straight in the eye and said, "That's not grass, that's mistletoe."[1]

A native and resident of Waxahachie, Texas, 30 miles south of Dallas, the 45-year-old, tall, slim and slow-talking Richards played a dominant role in the Birds' early years. He began his baseball career in 1926 as an 18-year-old infielder for the Eastern Shore League's Crisfield Crabbers in Crisfield, Maryland, a small fishing community on Maryland's Eastern Chesapeake Bay shore near the Virginia border. Crabbers from both states routinely poached each other's pots. The year the young shortstop arrived, a patrol boat for the Virginia Fisheries Commission, the Marquerita, had been outfitted with a machine gun in response to having taken rifle fire from Maryland crabbers.[2]

Trading an infielder's mitt for a catcher's glove upon making the majors, Richards was a backup catcher for the Brooklyn Dodgers, New York Giants, and Philadelphia Giants from 1932 to 1935. He managed several minor league teams until 1943, when the Detroit Tigers signed him for what would be a four-year career that ended after 1946 when the regular players returned from World War II. Richards returned to managing. There he gained a reputation as a master strategist, often moving players, including pitchers, from one position to another during the same game. He would walk the pitcher so the leadoff batter couldn't steal second base. He introduced both the oversize catcher's mitt for catching knuckleballers and the batting practice pitching machine to the majors. Opposing skippers, with equal part praise and scorn, called him "The Brain."[3]

Players praised his baseball knowledge. "Paul Richards was one of the best baseball people I ever knew," exclaimed Brooks Robinson, the Hall of Fame third baseman for the O's. "He knew every position and he knew what made that position tick."[4]

Personally, Jerry Sachs, Orioles public relations manager from 1960 to 1965, recalled Richards as "a Texan and I dare say not a liberal. He was difficult to get to know; not a great communicator and a taciturn sort of guy."[5] Dunn said of Richards, "if he'd had two beers every morning instead of his orange juice, he would have had the greatest personality.... After two beers at dinner, he could tell the best baseball stories ever."[6] Sachs also said that Richards and Jim McLaughlin, the O's farm system director and the only executive to have transferred with the Browns to Baltimore, constantly disagreed with each other on questions of strategy and players. Richards usually prevailed.[7]

Richards loved being the boss. He demanded total control. Miles gave it to him in the form of general manager and field manager titles.[8] When asked by the press if he had full control, Richards curtly answered that such "was implied" when he signed on. "It would be mighty unpleasant if it should be otherwise," he added.[9]

The new skipper laid out a plan to rebuild the Orioles with young players through trades and scouting. When asked about money for rebuilding, Richards told a reporter, "I'll let you know when the man says 'That's all' and we'll have another meeting."[10]

His first Baltimore trade involved 17 Orioles and Yankees and took from November 18 to December 1, 1954, to complete.[11] Keys to the trade included the Yankees' acquisition of Bob Turley, the O's star pitcher who led the American League in strikeouts in 1954 with 185, and shortstop Billy Hunter, who worked magic with his glove at shortstop. The O's gained quantity—ten players including shortstop Willie Miranda, a Cuban native. Miranda had defected to the United States with the help of an American Airlines flight crew. They hid him in the cockpit of a Miami-bound airplane.[12] Gus Triandos and Gene Woodling also joined the O's. Slapping himself heartily on his back, Richards predicted, "I believe we gained a better club and skipped a full year in our rebuilding."[13] Of the ten players, only catcher Hal Smith, first baseman Gus Triandos, both 25, and Miranda, 28, still wore Orioles colors on Independence Day.[14] Richards traded the others to various clubs, and pitcher Bob Kuzava went to the Philadelphia Phillies on waivers. "We were," Kuzava said in 2012, referring to the new Orioles, "a lot of old guys [Kuzava was 32 and had been in the majors for nine years] and the ball club had to start getting younger guys and a farm system. Paul Richards cleaned house with us older guys. That's the way it worked."[15]

"The Brain" spent freely to rebuild the Birds. Some said too freely. "We wasted a lot of money in the early Richards years. Richards and his people were just throwing the money all over, and they didn't care a whole lot about following rules," Orioles scout Jim Russo said in his autobiography.[16] Richards' disregard for rules cost the Orioles and himself. In 1955, Commissioner Ford Frick fined the team $2,000 and Richards $2,500. Frick promised to suspend Richards for a year or more from baseball for a similar infraction. Richards had attempted to hide the fact that he had signed pitcher Tom Borland to a large bonus and sent him to the minors while, at the same time, releasing pitcher Bruce Swango after also signing him for a hefty sum.[17] At the time, players paid more than $4,000 in bonus money had to remain with the parent club for two years.

He also had a penchant for trickery. In 1961, "The Waxahachie Wizard," as he later became known, staged an injury in an attempt to prevent either of the two American League expansion clubs, the Washington Senators and the Los Angeles Angels, from taking Chuck Hinton, an African American outfielder in the Birds' farm system, in the winter expansion draft. Richards arranged for Hinton to "crash" into the left field fence while going after a fly ball during a game in Arizona's fall league.[18] Hinton was to stay on the ground until a stretcher arrived. The word spread that Hinton needed surgery on his left shoulder, but to no avail. The Senators drafted Hinton anyway. Richards told the press, "They don't know what they're doing."[19] Hinton went on to an 11-year career with the Senators and Indians.

In addition to his manager and general manager role, Richards assigned himself the role of chief scout. "The best way to scout," Richards told reporters, "is to do it yourself."[20] Realizing he could not do it all himself, however, he promised to hire more scouts. By March 1955 17 scouts reported to Richards, including former St. Louis Browns scout Fred Hofman, who spent a month scouting service teams in Europe. Among Hofman's finds was African American shortstop Jesse James, Jr., a member of the 142nd Artillery Team. James signed a contract with the York White Roses after receiving his discharge.[21] Richards received a scouting report from an unexpected source, Harley P. Brinsfield, Sr., well-known to Baltimoreans as host of "The Harley Show." The jazz program aired for 17 years over radio stations WBAL and later WITH.[22] Brinsfield touted first baseman Johnny Washington, a Baltimore resident and consistent .300 hitter during an 18-year career in the Negro leagues, including four with the Elite Giants. Ehlers interviewed Washington but declined to sign the 40-or-so-year-old player.[23]

Richards spent the 1954–1955 winter scouting in Arizona, Texas, and New Orleans before joining the pitchers and catchers for an early spring training session in Miami Beach, Florida. Asked if he had any luck in recruiting a long-ball-hitting outfielder, whom Richards thought imperative for a first division finish, he responded, "Na, but we are trying frantically in the high schools and colleges."[24] Richards had earlier made an unsuccessful overture, to the astonishing, at the time, tune of $250,000, to Casey Stengel, New York Yankees manager, to obtain slugging African American rookie catcher-outfielder Elston Howard.[25] The first black player for the Yankees had won the Most Valuable Player Award while a member of the 1954 International League Toronto Maple Leafs. Stengel was more interested in a pitcher than in money. He declined to forward Richards' offer to Yankees general manager George Weiss. In spite of his exhaustive search, the "Wizard of Waxahachie" found, other than Howard, no players of color deserving of an invitation to either Miami Beach, or to Daytona Beach where the full team gathered in mid–March.[26]

On Opening Day 1955, the O's joined three other major league teams (Tigers, Red Sox, and Phillies) who had no "tan" players on their rosters.[27] By the end of May, after all big league teams had trimmed their rosters to the 25-man limit, 34 black players had won jobs with 12 of the 16 teams. An article in *The New Journal and Guide*, a black weekly, noted the fact but said that the four all-white teams are "in the market for colored talent" and had signed "colored" players to minor league contracts.[28]

During spring training Rex Greaves, one of Richards' scouts and a Baltimore resident, did sign two "colored players," Sonny Glover and Dave Roberts, in late March. Richards assigned the 20-year-old, 195-pound, switch-hitting Glover, a graduate of Baltimore's Armstrong High School, to an Orioles farm team in Quebec, Canada. Glover left for spring training in Thomasville, Georgia, following a banquet friends put on in his honor at the First Baptist Church of Georgetown, Maryland, in nearby Kent County.[29] Roberts, a 21-year-old, left-hand-hitting first sacker, went to

Paul Richards was the driving force of the Orioles from 1955 to 1961. His knowledge of the game was universally respected, but some questioned his attitude towards black players. Always the hands-on manager, here he demonstrates the finer points of pitching to a group of aspiring hurlers during spring training in Miami Beach before the start of the 1955 season (National Baseball Hall of Fame Library, Cooperstown, New York).

spring training with the San Antonio Missions, where scouts gave his performance high marks.[30]

Most black players signed by the O's and dispatched to the minors in the 1950s ended up either playing for another major league team or never made the majors. Such was the case with James, Roberts and Glover. Roberts, a native of Panama, spent the next six years in the minors before catching on with the Houston Astros for two seasons and the Pittsburgh Pirates for one. Glover and James never played in the majors.

Richards' overture to Stengel and his willingness to sign James, Glover and Roberts demonstrate that the Birds' manager was not totally opposed to signing black players, but he was, nevertheless, a controversial figure on racial matters during his tenure in Baltimore. For his part, he proclaimed himself free of prejudice. "You know, we white Southerners, when we get rid of the poison, we're more natural about white and black," he told Lester Rodney, a reporter for the Communist newspaper *The Daily Worker*.[31] Orioles players would deliver a mixed verdict on Richards' racial attitudes.

* * *

Three men who played major roles in the Orioles' early seasons (left to right), Gov. Theodore McKeldin, Paul Richards and Mayor Thomas D'Alesandro, Jr., are shown leaving the Southern Hotel for Memorial Stadium on Opening Day, April 11, 1955 (photographer is Ellis Malashuk, courtesy the *Baltimore Sun*).

Many in Baltimore's African American community continued to wonder why the "Wizard" could not lure a black player of stature to Baltimore. After all, African American players continued to make their presence felt on other teams, most notably the Brooklyn Dodgers. After having won the National League pennant in 1952 and 1953 but falling both times to the Yankees in the World Series, the Dodgers, with five black players, took the 1955 Series from the Yankees. Even the Yankees now carried a full-time African American, Elston Howard. The rookie appeared in 97 games and hit for a .290 average. Five other black players, including Puerto Rican-born Roberto Clemente, made their major league debut in 1955.

The O's would not, however, go the entire 1955 season without an African American player. Dave Pope, the third African American to wear an O's uniform, arrived at Memorial Stadium in June 1955 via a trade that Richards engineered with his former team, the White Sox.

Richards wanted Pope, 29, a native of Talladega, Alabama, and a stocky left-handed hitter, for defensive reasons, calling him "an outstanding fly-chaser."[32]

Pope's name had come up in a speech that Miles, like Ehlers the year before, gave to the Frontiers Club, this time at its May 1955 luncheon. "We'd be the most stupid people in Baltimore if we didn't want a colored ballplayer," Miles assured them. To prove his point, he told the group that he had earlier offered the Indians $25,000 plus two Orioles players in exchange for Pope, but the Indians had rejected his offer.[33] Sam Lacy, by now growing ever more skeptical of such claims by Orioles executives, wondered "whom Miles thought he was kidding." That amount of money, Lacy argued, "wouldn't buy a good batboy on today's market."[34]

Miles proved Lacy's skepticism to be misplaced in this case. A month after the luncheon, the two clubs ended up making the trade but, as it turned out, at no cost to the O's. Miles had offered to trade hard-hitting outfielder Gene Woodling and veteran third baseman Bobby Cox to the Indians in exchange for Pope, fellow outfielder Wally Westlake, and $15,000. Cox, however, refused to report to the Indians. Commissioner Ford Frick ruled that the trade would stand, but the O's would have to return the cash to compensate for Cox's refusal.[35]

The trade pleased Pope and the fans. A utility outfielder for the Tribe, he could now play regularly, thereby increasing his pay. "You don't make any money as a utility player," Pope told the *AFRO*.[36] As an indication in the change of whites' attitudes toward African American players since Jackie Robinson's appearance in the city nine years earlier, 16,000 spectators at Memorial Stadium gave Pope a "tremendous ovation" when he first appeared in Memorial Stadium.[37] He batted a respectable .248 and remained the Birds' lone African American for the 1955 season.

Pope was the only African American on the team but not the only new face. Ever the strategist, Richards, through trades and calling players up from the minors, used 54 players during the season, earning himself a new nickname, "The Experimenter." Ten different players, for instance, none black, saw service at third base.[38] The "experiments" were of little value. The O's once again finished in seventh place with a 57–97 won-lost record, but a slight improvement over their 54–100 record the year before.

The team's sluggish performance prompted the Board of Directors to nudge Miles out of the presidency on November 7. Board members and shareholders found his executive skills lacking, while at the same time appreciating his political acumen in bringing the team to Baltimore. They nevertheless resented the fact that Miles and his law partner and Orioles' treasurer, Clyde Morris, had not consulted them on important financial decisions, chief among them being generous bonuses paid to untested players. The Board cited five "bonus babies" who did not pan out: Jim Pyburn, Wayne Causey (whose disappointing 1955–1957 seasons led to his trade to the Kansas City Athletics, where he found his stride), Bob Nelson, Tom Gastall, and Bruce Swango, as a chief cause of their displeasure. Morris wanted the club's finances to be kept under wraps. In June he had told a group of sportswriters, "I wish I could let you fellows in on what we're doing, but it is important to the club and will bear results later on."[39] Keeping secrets from the press is one thing. Miles' and Morris' refusal to tell stockholders how much money had been spent on the club sealed their fates.[40] In his resignation statement, the outgoing president strongly recommended his successor be "an experienced baseball executive."[41]

Instead, two weeks later, and to no one's surprise, the Board elevated the club's vice-president, James Keelty, Jr., the 43-year-old president of the building firm of James Keelty and Company, founded by his father, and a major Orioles stockholder, to the president's position. After lavishing praise on Richards and promising to bring first-class major league baseball to Baltimore's fans, the new president met with Ford Frick "for a social visit so that I could find out a little more about this baseball business."[42]

* * *

The Orioles returned to Arizona for spring training in 1956, but this year to Scottsdale, where Richards and his wife, Margie, owned a home. Situated 12 miles east of downtown Phoenix, Scottsdale, a small but growing town of 4,500, greeted motorists with a 12-foot-high sign warning them that horses had the right of way. Scottsdale claimed for itself the distinction of being the "Most Western Town in the West." "You almost expect to look up and see Gary Cooper come trudging grimly down the main street with a pistol in each hand," wrote Arizona historian Joseph Stocker.[43]

In addition to its western motif, mid-century Scottsdale presented the O's with a slowly changing but still segregated environment, as had Yuma two years earlier. On November 12, 1953, two Arizona assistant attorney generals, Herbert B. Finn and his black colleague, Hazel Burton Daniels, filed suit against Phoenix's Wilson Elementary School District, charging that school segregation was unconstitutional. Maricopa County

Superior Court Judge Charles C. Bernstein ruled in their favor. The School District appealed, but the Arizona Supreme Court delayed hearing the case while awaiting the outcome of *Brown v. The Board of Education*. Finn and Daniels had earlier won a similar case but on narrower grounds, necessitating the November filing. An emotional Maricopa Superior Court Judge, Fred C. Struckmeyer, had ruled in their favor in February 1953. "The man was crying," Daniels recalled. "He actually was crying when he wrote his opinion, and he said 'Fifty years of this is too long.'"[44]

The ensuing school desegregation went smoothly, but the rest of Scottsdale and nearby Phoenix remained segregated. Blacks sat in the back of streetcars and in the balconies of movie theaters. Most restaurants refused to serve them.[45] An African American nurse from Phoenix's St. Joseph's Hospital found herself not welcome at the Upton Candy Shop on West Thomas Road in April 1956. "Some Negroes are objectionable," explained Mrs. Dodgeso, the store's manager. "If we served one, we would have to serve them all," she added. Mrs. Dodgeso declined to define "objectionable" when asked to do so by the *Arizona Sun*, Phoenix's African American newspaper.[46] Kenny's Drug Store, at 19th Avenue and Western Boulevard, took a slightly different approach. A sign displayed over its lunch counter read "no Colored trade solicited." African Americans could fill prescriptions and pay their utility bills at the store, but Kenny's drew the line at blacks eating and drinking on the premises.[47] Another indignity confronting blacks in Scottsdale was the city ordinance requiring them to leave the town before sundown.[48] White players stayed at the new, 108-room Paradise Inn located in "this rapidly growing resort center." The Inn offered golf, swimming, tennis, horseback riding, and fishing.[49] Black players stayed where they could find lodging.

* * *

Five African American players reported to spring training in 1956 along with the rest of the team to the newly built Scottsdale Stadium. Pope had re-signed with the Birds in late January. Four others joined him, including Bob Boyd, a left-handed first baseman, born in Potts Camp, Mississippi, and nicknamed "The Rope" by Orioles pitching coach Lum Harris for his scorching line drives. The "scorcher" had played for the Memphis Red Sox in the Negro American League, had sporadic stints with the White Sox from 1951 to 1954, and hit over .300 in the Texas League in 1955. The others included Kelly Searcy, a southpaw pitcher, who had played with the Baltimore Elite Giants their last two years in existence, 1949–1950, and for semi-pro teams after that; and outfielders Ezell King, who signed as a free agent, and Willie Tasby, who had played for the Missions in 1955.[50]

Only Pope and Boyd made the trip east, which rejuvenated Boyd, who felt he had not received a fair chance with the Sox. "The White Sox kept me in the minors for the entire 1955 season," Boyd lamented, "and I began to wonder if I'd ever get a real shot with them."[51]

Rushing to meet the May deadline to finalize his roster, Richards, again through a trade with the White Sox, introduced six-foot, four-inch right-hander Clifford "Connie" Johnson, 33, a native of Stone Mountain, Georgia, to the Birds' pitching staff. Johnson, the first Orioles African American pitcher after Heard, could pitch brilliantly but often had control problems. Johnson had joined an elite group. With some notable exceptions, such as Don Newcombe, Joe Black, and Satchel Paige, few black hurlers had appeared on major league rosters.

A former Negro leaguer with the Kansas City Monarchs who had appeared in two Negro leagues East-West Games, Johnson gained a reputation as an affable person with an acceptable fastball, an explosive curve ball, and an illegal spitter which he achieved by applying perspiration from his cap to the ball.[52] "That fella's got five different pitches," observed Yankees manager Casey Stengel, "and they say, they say, mind you, I'm not saying it, that when it's hot he's got a little wet on the ball."[53]

* * *

Johnson's pioneering appearance came in the midst of strides toward integration in the city. Baltimore's City Board of Recreation and Parks, which had opposed integrating parks and pools on the grounds that state law held for segregated facilities, reversed course in light of a U.S. Supreme Court ruling on March 14, 1955. The Court held that state-imposed segregation was unconstitutional.[54] That same month, an African American physician persuaded Oriole Pontiac (a connection in name only with the team) to take the "for whites only" and "for colored only" signs off its restroom doors. He cited their existence as his reason for not buying a $3,000 convertible for his wife. "We've taken those old signs down. We feel they should have come down a long time ago. Please come back and buy the car you want," a salesman told the doctor a few days later. The doctor did.[55] Hecht's Department Stores in Northwood desegregated its cafeteria in the spring of 1956. Read's Drug Stores followed suit.[56] By secret ballot, the Bar Association of Baltimore City opened its membership to women by a less than overwhelming but nevertheless positive vote of 614 to 409, and, by a similar margin, to African Americans in June 1957.[57] Charles A.

Hooks, Superintendent of Parks, fined 26-year veteran Sgt. Ellsworth D. Johnson ten days' pay in June 1957, for saying to an African American parked in Druid Hill Park, "All right boy, move on."[58]

* * *

As challenges to Jim Crow continued to appear in the city, Richards dealt Pope back to the Indians after playing only 12 games in the 1956 season for outfielder Hoot Evers. Recovering from a beaning in spring training, Pope's batting average hovered below .200 and his defensive play suffered.[59] Boyd alternated between the outfield and first base, where Richards tried out five players during the season. Boyd performed well, hitting .311, good for second-best on the Orioles behind Bob Nieman's .322. The Birds now carried two African Americans on their payroll, Johnson and Boyd. Richards' scouts kept searching for others.

Jim Russo found baseball and football star Fred Valentine, 21, a six-foot, one-inch outfielder with speed, a lively bat, and a strong, accurate arm at Tennessee A & I, now Tennessee State University, an African American institution. Richards signed the Clarksdale, Mississippi, native and Memphis resident after a workout at Memorial Stadium in late July 1956.[60] The switch-hitting Valentine dazzled Richards with balls driven deep into the seats in spacious Memorial Stadium. "Oh, Jesus Christ, Mays [Willie] can't even do stuff like that," Richards exclaimed.[61]

Five teams had invited the slugger to work out, but Richards' approach "convinced me to sign with the O's," Valentine said 56 years later.[62] "I never will forget him and the way he talked to me. He brought me aside and told me I had a future in the game. He said, 'young fellow.' I said 'Yes, sir.' He said 'you have a lot of tools and there's a good chance you can get to the big leagues. There are a few things you have to work on. We can help you. I just want you to know I'm really impressed with what I've seen.'"

Boyd told the rookie that Richards treated everyone well, which clinched Valentine's choice. "I was so excited, just happy to be there,"[63] Valentine said of Richards' decision to assign him to the Vancouver (B.C.) Mounties of the Pacific Coast League.

Before Valentine inked his contract, Boyd got off to a fast start, batting .357 for the first five weeks and performing well at first base, but a fractured elbow in May kept him out of action until late August. He ended the year, nevertheless, with a .311 average to place him among the top American League hitters. Johnson managed his control problems well enough to win nine games and lose ten, and post the team's best earned run average, 3.43. In one of the team's rare overtures to Baltimore's black residents, the O's, assisted by Ted Kates, Maryland State Manager for Calvert Distillers, sponsored a "Connie Johnson Day" on August 28. The pitcher received many gifts, including a hunting rifle that teammate Bob Nieman presented to him. Mayor D'Alesandro, Jr., issued a proclamation commemorating the day as Connie Johnson Day. Sam Lacy read the scroll and presented it to the pitcher.[64]

Late September saw the arrival of a second African American pitcher from the Vancouver Mounties, Charlie Beamon, 21, a right-handed, sinker-ball hurler who hailed from Oakland, California.[65] The right-hander announced himself with a four-hit shutout against the Yankees to win 1–0 in his first start. His teammates mobbed him with back-slapping congratulations at the end of the game. *Sun* sportswriter Lou Hatter called the feat "one of the more sparkling rookie debuts in big-league baseball history."[66] The sinkerballer made one more appearance in 1956, pitching four innings in relief to pick up his second win against the Washington Senators on the last day of the season. Shortly afterwards, he took out a life membership in the NAACP at the Baltimore branch office, saying, "I don't know much about it but from what I've heard it's a good organization."[67]

The O's finished one place higher in the standings, sixth with a 69–85 record, than they had in 1954 and 1955. Fans had not seen many black faces. For most of the season, Johnson constituted the lone active African American Oriole. In other cities, eight more African Americans had joined major league teams, including two with the National League Cincinnati Reds, Curt Flood and Frank Robinson. Flood appeared in only five games, but Robinson, who played in 152 games, hit .290, led the league in runs scored with 122, and won the "Rookie of the Year" Award in the National League. Don Newcombe took the National League's Most Valuable Player Award.

* * *

Yet, no matter how well Johnson and Boyd, or other African Americans, performed on the diamond, they still could not register at a hotel in downtown Baltimore. The Hotel Association held firm in its segregation policy and forced the Sheraton Hotels, in May 1956, to rescind its short-lived integration policy "to assure," the *AFRO* reported, "the re-establishment of rigid colored barriers."[68] The Sheraton-Belvedere Hotel broke ranks when it agreed in March 1957 to welcome delegates attending a board meeting of the National Funeral Directors Association, an African American organization. Chicago undertaker Theodore R. Hawes told the *AFRO*, "I have been accorded every courtesy as a guest."[69]

An unlikely confluence of white players, Governor McKeldin, and the NAACP took up efforts to change the Hotel Association's policy. The Major League Baseball Players Committee agreed during spring training in 1957 to consider the hotel ban a player grievance. The committee, composed of one player from each team, brought player grievances to the attention of club owners. "Our group is in no position to force anything," Sherm Lollar, a catcher for the International League Orioles from 1943 to 1946 and now the White Sox's catcher and committee representative, confided to Sam Lacy, "but," he continued, "this is very definitely a problem, although many of us aren't aware of it. I think we can at least let the owners know this is a grievance we'd like to have them think about."[70]

Don Larsen, 25, a tall, lanky, right-handed pitcher who came to Baltimore in 1954 from the Browns and who gained lasting fame by pitching the only perfect World Series game in 1956, was one white player who did know about the hotel situation. "A lot of blacks couldn't stay in our hotels. I didn't like that. That wasn't right. But that's the way it was. We all had to live through that. You wanted to be a little bit of a family, get along with everybody the best you can," Larsen said.[71] McKeldin, in a move endorsed by Mayor D'Alesandro, Jr., sent a letter in May of 1957 to each American League owner, League President Will Harridge, and Commissioner Ford Frick, asking for their help.[72] Roy Wilkins of the NAACP had written Harridge three years earlier on April 9, 1954, asking Harridge to "use such persuasion as your office has at its disposal ... to insist on hotel and restaurant facilities for their entire teams regardless of race or color." Wilkins, as had McKeldin, pointed out that Baltimore was the only American League city to bar blacks from white-owned hotels and restaurants. Wilkins cast his appeal in economic terms. "The matter is not a 'social problem,' outside the interest and activity of baseball officials, but one that involves 'squad morale,'" he wrote. Clubs with Negro players could be penalized unfairly which could, he continued, "conceivably, in a close race, affect team standings and the financial rewards of players and owners."[73]

Wilkins' argument failed to elicit even a reply from Harridge, nor is there any record of club owners replying to McKeldin. But McKeldin finally managed to prevail with Harold I. Fink, president of the Hotel Association of Baltimore and one of the initial stockholders in the club. In July 1957 Fink, perhaps influenced by the Sheraton-Belvedere's decision several months earlier, announced that the hotels would now "admit tan visitors

in limited numbers." By limited numbers he meant "colored baseball players [professional and collegiate] and delegates to established conventions."
The question of admitting other "colored patrons," Fink said, "will be a
matter left to the discretion of the individual hotels."[74] "It was just a question of time. We all knew that," conceded Nelson Busick, president of the
Lord Baltimore.[75] A year later most downtown hotels allowed blacks to
register.

The Indians' African American players approached the new policy
gingerly. Al Smith told an *AFRO* reporter that he and infielder Larry Raines
would stay at the York Hotel for their one remaining visit to Baltimore
this season. "Right now, I don't know what the situation is down there,
and I am not too anxious to find out first-hand," Smith explained. "Next
season, we'll probably stay at whatever hotel they book our team in," he
added. Black players for the White Sox—Earl Battey, Larry Doby, and Minnie Minoso—on the other hand, immediately joined their white teammates
at the Lord Baltimore when the Sox next came to town.[76]

*　*　*

Shortly before the start of the hotel negotiations, Boyd, Johnson
(whom Richards now called "the best clutch right-hander in the league"
after winning two games in 1956) and Beamon had signed their contracts.[77] *Baltimore Evening Sun* sportswriter Paul Menton noted during
spring training that Beamon had all the tools but needed to learn to pace
himself. "If he doesn't learn to not throw his arm up the plate, he'll have
a short pitching life and it won't be a merry one," Menton predicted.[78] Perhaps he did not learn to pace himself. Beamon spent most of the season in
Vancouver and appeared in only four games without a decision for the O's.

Orioles players reported to spring training, again held in Scottsdale,
which Richards called "one of the garden spots of the world."[79] This year
the team stayed at the newly built and segregated Safari Hotel, "an opulent
tourist retreat, a six-acre, 108-room playground studded with luxurious
guest accommodations, jaw-dropping dining and dancing facilities, a
shopping arcade, beauty salon and even broadcast facilities for KPOK, the
town's first radio station," boasted *Phoenix New Times* reporter Dewey
Webb. In line with its name, "the Safari," Webb continued, "featured recur-
ring jungle motif typified by zebra-skin waitress outfits, taxidermied trophy heads, and the Safari mascot—a cartoonish silhouette of an African
tribesman on the warpath.[80] Black players found housing, Joe Durham,
recently discharged from the service, recalled, "at a motel off the high-
way."[81]

Richards continued his quest for African American players. By the end of February, 21 African Americans had signed minor league contracts; notably Fred Valentine, Willie Tasby, a native of Shreveport, Louisiana, and Lenny Green, a Detroit native. Echoing Richards' earlier assessment of him, Orioles coaches touted Valentine as a player whose talents could, with proper development, approach those of Willie Mays or Minnie Miñoso. "I'd like to have a roomful of his type," Coach Al "The Silver Fox" Vincent exclaimed.[82] Green would have been released had Richards decided not to accompany the "varsity" to an away game but instead stay back and catch a spring training game featuring the O's B-team players. He saw Green snare a sinking line drive off the tips of his shoes, pull in a 400-foot smash over his shoulder, and come through with two timely hits. "He makes it look too easy out there. The game just isn't that easy," Richards said with a grin.[83] Green and Tasby, both outfielders, opened the season as two of seven African American players with the Vancouver Mounties.

Valentine and shortstop Wayne Coleman spent their spring training with the Class C Aberdeen [South Dakota] Pheasants in Miami. The team left Miami in three station wagons for the three-day trip to Aberdeen. "There was snow on the field when we got there," Valentine remembered.[84] Along the way they encountered restaurants that would not serve blacks, thus forcing Valentine and Coleman to eat in the cars for the first couple of stops. "Then the white players decided they wanted the whole team together. They said we'll go in and order and then you and Coleman order. If they won't serve you, then once they put our orders in we'll get up and leave. That was all their idea. That was great. That really gave us a sense of unity there," Valentine said with feeling.[85]

While Valentine honed his skills in Aberdeen, Richards recalled Durham, who was batting a league-leading .391 for the San Antonio Missions, to join the team in Detroit for a mid–June series against the Tigers. Durham, in his first game back, "fielded sensationally" and lashed a single to right-center in support of Connie Johnson's near-shutout (4–1) win. "If Durham delivers against major league pitching," Richards told a reporter, "the centerfield job is his.[86]

As the season progressed, however, Durham's relationship with Richards soured. Durham thought he did deliver, but that Richards did not play him as often as Durham thought his performance warranted. Richards benched him for a game in Kansas City against the Athletics. "Two weeks prior," Durham said, "we played them here [Baltimore], against left-handed pitcher Alex Kellner. I had a double and a two run homer that won the game. At Kansas City's AAA park, considerably smaller than Memorial Stadium, with Kellner pitching again Richards didn't play me. So I asked why. He didn't give me a reason. I told him I'd lost faith in him and the ball club." Durham said he reminded Richards that "'You promised me in spring training, where I led the team in hitting, you'd send me to San Antonio for a couple of weeks, and if I'm hitting you'll bring me back.' He didn't call me until June 10 when I'm hitting .391. I knew right then my goose was cooked with him."[87]

Richards had assigned Durham to the Missions, the club's AA team, instead of the Rochester Red Wings, the AAA team, because, Richards told him, "the Red Wings roster was all full." "What did he mean?" Durham asked an interviewer. "He meant there were three black guys on the club, and he didn't want no more." Durham added that when the St. Louis Cardinals approached Richards about possibly acquiring Durham, "Paul told them I was an alcoholic, and I didn't even drink beer. There was nothing you could do in those days. No agents. You were all alone." (The Cardinals were not dissuaded. Durham played six games for them in 1959.) Summing up his feelings toward Richards, Durham said, "He was a Texan with a nasty attitude. Oh God I couldn't stand him. He would use racial epithets towards players on other teams while you're sitting there right next to him."[88] Durham stayed with the O's for the rest of the season though his batting average dropped to .185.

Still in search of an outfielder with power at the plate, Richards called up Lenny Green, who hit .309 in 132 games in Vancouver. Green's short stay did not pan out. He swung the bat at a mere .182 clip in 19 games.

Richards guided the Birds to their first .500 season (right on the button at 76–76), good for a fifth-place finish, the team's highest yet. African Americans led the way. Johnson topped the team's hurlers in wins with 14. Boyd led all American League first basemen in putouts with 1,073 and posted the team's highest batting average, .318, fourth highest in the American League behind some pretty fair ball players—Ted Williams, Mickey Mantle, and Gene Woodling.

Boyd's performance prompted Mayor D'Alesandro, Jr., and City Council President Leon Abramson to organize a second appreciation day for an African American Oriole. A committee of 30 prominent politicians, business people, and sports boosters honored Boyd at a pre-game ceremony during the last week of the season. After an introduction by teammate Bob Nieman and receiving gifts from local merchants and teammates, Boyd thanked the fans and those who organized the event. He singled out team trainer Eddie Weiner and two orthopedic surgeons, who had helped restore his elbow so he could continue his career, for special praise.[89]

* * *

By now, there could seemingly be no doubt in the minds of Orioles front office executives that African Americans could play the game as well or better than anyone. In addition to Boyd's and Johnson's performances, Richards no doubt knew that Hank Aaron, a Milwaukee Braves outfielder, led the majors that year in home runs with 44 to capture the National League's Most Valuable Player Award. With the help of two other African American outfielders, Bill Bruton and Wes Covington, the Braves beat the Yankees in the World Series.

Yet Richards' scouts were still unable to find a power-hitting outfielder. He turned again to the trade route. He gave up three players in return for four Chicago White Sox players, Jim Marshall, Russ Heman, Jack Harshman, and Larry Doby, 33. Richards hoped that Doby would be his power-hitting outfielder. For the previous ten seasons, including eight with the Indians, Doby had averaged 24 homers a year and knocked in over 100 runs in five of those seasons.[90]

A native of Camden, South Carolina, who grew up in New Jersey, Doby learned he had been traded on the morning of December 5, 1957. Eight-year-old daughter Christina, who heard about the trade on the radio, woke her father to tell him he was now an Oriole. While he may not have liked how he heard about the trade, he had no regrets about leaving Sox manager Al Lopez. He had clashed with Lopez in Cleveland and again in Chicago. "I can't have any respect for a man who lacks regard for a man because he's in a minority. I just don't care to play for him," Doby told a reporter from *Jet*.[91]

The new Oriole joined the Birds with a positive outlook after Minnie Minoso, a teammate with the Sox and a fan of Paul Richards, told Doby that Richards did not subscribe to Lopez's beliefs. "Minoso," Doby told a reporter at his home in Paterson, NJ, "has told me he'd rather play for Paul Richards than for anybody he knows."[92] Richards, whose wheeler-dealer reputation had been firmly established, sought to blunt rumors that he would soon trade Doby as part of a "shuttle deal" worked out before the trade. "Doby is the Orioles' center fielder for the next year," the O's skipper emphatically told the press. When pressed, Richards backed off a bit, saying, "This doesn't mean, necessarily that we won't trade him or anybody else if an opportunity presents itself to improve our club."[93]

Doby lived with the other black players in Scottsdale while the white players again stayed at the posh, segregated Safari.[94] Their wives entertained themselves with horseback riding, shopping, golf, tennis, and sunbathing. "Do we wives like spring training?" Mary Rose Dunn, Jack Dunn's wife, parried with a *Sun* reporter. "Do birds like to fly? Where else," she cooed, "could we get such relaxation, sun tan, and good clean fun."[95]

Doby did not have fun in Scottsdale. He managed only 11 hits in 50 at-bats, none of them a home run. Sam Lacy suggested that Doby's subpar performance resulted, in part, from his distaste for the segregated conditions. "Anyone of Doby's extremely sensitive disposition might well show his resentment even though it may not be his intention to do so,"[96] Lacy wrote.

The "opportunity" that Richards had referred to earlier presented itself. On April 1, the *Baltimore Sun*'s one-inch, block-letter headline read "Orioles Trade Doby for Gene Woodling."[97] His departure left members of the Friends of Larry Doby Club in Baltimore feeling "like the jilted bride." The group had sold 100 tickets for a welcome-home dinner.[98]

Richards, ever the "experimenter," kept trying. He called on Green to fill the still vacant power-hitting center fielder slot. Richards' choice of Green was a curious one as Green was not known for hitting the long ball. True to form, he responded with a mediocre .231 average and no homers over the course of 69 games in 1958. Richards then purchased Joe Taylor, 32, a free-swinging hitter, from the St. Louis Cardinals in late July. Though Taylor had hit 20-plus home runs for each of seven years in the minors, the Cards had used him as a pinch-hitter. Richards did the same. In 36 games Taylor hit a respectable .273 but managed only two homers.[99] Disappointed with Taylor, Richards turned to Willie Tasby, whose .303 batting average with the Louisville [Kentucky] Colonels ranked second in the AAA American Association. Only the second African American player to win the league's Rookie of the Year Award (George Crowe won the honor in 1951), Tasby joined the O's for an 18-game trial at the end of the season. He batted only .200 but won praise from Richards. "I don't mean to knock Busby [Jim, who was white and the starting O's center fielder following Green's mediocre performance]. He did a good job, but we think Willie Tasby will be able to do just as well for us ... and besides, he's a lot younger," Richards told the press.[100]

In the pitching department, Connie Johnson posted a disappointing 6–9 won-lost record. Beamon stuck with the O's for all of the 1958 season but won only one game while losing three in 21 appearances, marking the end of his major league career. *Sun* sportswriter Lou Hatter observed that

Beamon had to improve his speed and consistency "if he is ever to be regarded seriously as a big-time prospect."[101]

Beamon gave another reason for his losing record. "I saw enough to know that ability-wise, I had no problems," he told author John Eisenberg. Beamon complained that he rarely got a chance to pitch, and that other black pitchers in the majors such as Johnson, 36, Don Newcombe, 32, and Joe Black, 34, had more years on them than he did. Beamon turned 24 in 1958. "I don't know if it was the Orioles or Richards," Beamon continued. "He didn't respect me enough to talk to me. He had his coaches come over and talk to me when I was sitting right next to him. I think it was like the black quarterback thing. Teams didn't trust young black pitchers.... I'd rather forget about my time in baseball."[102]

While Beamon and other black players experienced as discriminatory Richards' use of coaches as intermediaries, white players got the same aloof treatment from the manager, even off the field. Anyone who found himself on an elevator with Richards rarely heard a word from the taciturn skipper.[103]

Boyd, seemingly unaffected by Richards' style, continued his mastery at the plate with a .309 average, second again among the Birds to Bob Nieman's .325.

The team rollercoastered through the 1958 season, moving between second place and the cellar before finishing sixth with a 74–79 record. A record number, six, African Americans had donned an Orioles uniform during the season, but only two, Boyd and Johnson, had major roles.

Even though black and white players were mixing more frequently within the confines of Memorial Stadium, they didn't do so outside of the stadium. "As long as we were at the ball park, in the clubhouse or the dugout, we were treated fine," Valentine recounted in 2012. "But when you left the ball park after the game, they went their way and we went ours."[104] "They [African Americans] pretty much associated with themselves. Eating habits, dressing habits and stuff like that, their own culture in other words you might as well say. Not that much integration at that time,"[105] said Chuck Diering, an O's outfielder from 1954 to 1956.

Don Larsen provided an exception that proved the rule. In 1954 he gave Durham rides between his apartment in northwest Baltimore and Memorial Stadium. "He had a brand-new '54 Oldsmobile, and he used to pick me up on Pennsylvania Avenue in front of the casino. And he'd drop me off there at night. Otherwise, I would have had to spend money on cabs. I couldn't afford a car," Durham told author Louis Berney.[106]

The same pattern held true for the players with the Baltimore

Colts. Star running back Lenny Moore, who took many handoffs and caught many passes from quarterback Johnny Unitas, regretted that he did not get to know him very well. "I wish I could tell you I knew Johnny better," he told author Mark Bowden. "As with the other white players on the team," Moore said, "we never mingled."[107]

Occasional instances of camaraderie between whites and blacks on the Colts did occur off the field, such as the time Alan "The Horse" Ameche, born of immigrant Italian parents in Kenosha, Wisconsin, and winner of college football's Heisman Trophy in 1954 as a fullback and linebacker at the University of Wisconsin, lambasted a movie theater owner in Westminster, Maryland, where the Colts trained at Western Maryland College (now McDaniel College). The owner had refused to admit cornerback Milt Davis. "Is this the land of the free, or are you an asshole?" demanded Ameche. But such support had its limits. Several years later, an embarrassed and ashamed Ameche asked offensive tackle Jim Parker and his wife to leave his Baltimore restaurant, explaining that black patrons were bad for business.[108]

CHAPTER 4

"Bring Pup Tents and Box Lunches"

By the end of the 1958 season, Richards was finding the dual roles of manager and general manager to be too much. "The job of managing and being a general manager has become too big a job for maybe any one man and certainly too big for me," the "Wizard" told a reporter from the *New York Times*.[1] He asked the Board to relieve him of his on-field duties. The Board, however, wanted a new general manager, one no doubt who would exercise greater restraint with the purse strings.

Lee MacPhail, a medium-built man with an oval-shaped face and known for his caution, patience, and politeness, left his position as director of player personnel for the Yankees, where he had developed one of the finest farm systems in the majors, to become the Orioles' general manager. MacPhail's Yankees had remained all white until 1955, when they signed Elston Howard, but the Yankees had not embraced integration eagerly. MacPhail's father, Larry, as co-owner of the Yankees, had opposed integrating the majors and made no secret of his opinion. He wrote to newly appointed baseball Commissioner A. B. (Happy) Chandler on April 27, 1945, saying the race issue is "increasingly serious and acute. If the issue is ignored," MacPhail continued, "we will have colored players in the minor leagues in 1945 and in the major leagues shortly thereafter."[2]

Yankees general manager George Weiss shared Larry MacPhail's sentiments. "Now Tom," Weiss told scout Tom Greenwald in 1947, whom he'd spirited away from Branch Rickey and who had scouted Jackie Robinson extensively, "I don't want you sneaking around any back alleys and signing any niggers. We don't want them."[3] Lee, therefore, did not bring impressive equal opportunity credentials with him. He did bring, though, in Jerry Sach's words, "much needed business acumen."[4]

Several months before MacPhail's arrival, Baltimore hosted the All-Star Game in July. The six black All-Stars, including Willie Mays, Hank Aaron, and Frank Robinson, registered at the Lord Baltimore, but visiting black spectators, of course, could not. *AFRO* assistant editor Jimmy Williams advised them to bring pup tents and box lunches. "The box lunches will be to ease the pangs of an aching stomach.... The pup tents will provide a place for them to rest their carcasses after the last door of the downtown hotels have been slammed in their face and the uptown hotels are filled." Williams predicted the visitors would leave town "just loving the quaint customs of Baltimore, which boasts of major league baseball and minor league businessmen."[5]

* * *

Other quaint customs that summer included ongoing discrimination in restaurants, taverns, and housing. A shortage of available housing forced African Americans to move into white neighborhoods, prompting whites to move out. Whites cited fears of diminishing property values, declining social status, crime, and intermarriage. Support within the City Council for integration was growing, but it was not yet strong enough to pass a wide-ranging anti-discrimination bill that had been introduced by Walter T. Dixon, the Council's only African American member. The bill would have required movie theaters, taverns, restaurants, and hotels to open their doors to everyone. But by a narrow margin of 11–9 in November 1958, the Council killed Dixon's bill. In its place the Council passed a resolution merely "suggesting" that public accommodations serve all comers.[6]

Councilman Jacob J. Edelman took loud exception to the Council's action. Born in Russia in 1896, he emigrated in 1912 by himself to Baltimore, where he eventually opened a law practice, became well-known throughout Maryland for his support of labor and civil rights, and served eight terms on the Council. Diminutive in stature, he cast his familiar bass voice into angry tones to decry that the day would be remembered "as a day of infamy in the annals of the Council which made Baltimore appear to the world as a bigoted hamlet instead of a great city."[7]

A similar bill had met a similar fate a year earlier. Thurgood Marshall, now chief NAACP legal counsel, recalled the demise of that bill in a January speech to a standing room only audience at the Bethel A.M.E. Church on the 95th anniversary of Abraham Lincoln's Emancipation Proclamation. He looked straight at Mayor D'Alesandro, Jr., a candidate for a U.S. Senate seat and seated behind him on the stage. Marshall then turned toward the audience and implored them, "Tell him whether or not he gets your vote will depend not upon what he promises to do when he's running for the U.S. Senate, but what he did when he had the opportunity to do something on this bill."[8] Most voters, the majority of them white and most likely few of whom had heard Marshall's speech, sided with D'Alesandro. The mayor won the May Democratic primary. He easily defeated five-time loser for elective office, George P. Mahoney. He cited "yeoman help from the city," as making the difference.[9]

The mayor fared less well in the general election, losing to Maryland's incumbent junior Senator, James Glenn Beall, who lived in Allegheny County in rural western Maryland. *Washington Post* reporter Laurence Stern attributed the mayor's loss to suburban voters who are "basically white, Protestant ... and innately suspicious of the racially and ethnic jumbled Big City that lies beyond its neat barricades of fence and hedge." One who attended a mayor's coffee hour "in well-mannered Bethesda" remarked, "He just doesn't seem to belong there. Somehow you sensed that he knew it, too."[10]

* * *

As D'Alesandro began his last year as Baltimore's mayor, MacPhail returned the O's to Miami for spring training in 1959. The new general manager hoped to cut transportation costs and generate revenue by enticing Baltimore fans, with the help of package deals, from the city's cold winters to Miami's sunshine and 10,000-seat stadium.[11]

White and black players still lived apart as they had in Arizona. The former bunked at the McAllister Hotel, a ten-story structure considered one of Miami's skyscrapers at the time. Blacks bedded down at the Sir John Hotel. Tasby, who would win the starting center field job during spring training, said, in retrospect, that the arrangement "was OK. It was owned by a Jewish white guy and had a pool."[12] Fred Valentine had fond memories of the Sir John. "The Sir John worked out well for us [African American players]. It was the only big black hotel in Miami. We saw a lot of the super entertainers [Count Basie, Ella Fitzgerald, Cab Calloway, Josephine Baker, Billie Holiday, Nat King Cole, and Aretha Franklin] because they had to live there. The players were more comfortable there."[13] White players did not bat an eye at the separate arrangements. Brooks Robinson told *Sun* reporter Alan Goldstein, "We'd run the bus by their hotel to pick them up when we played an exhibition game. You didn't think that much of it. You took it for granted. That was the way it was supposed to be."[14]

Black players, however, thought quite a bit about it, but few at the time went public with their feelings. One who did was St. Louis Cardinals first baseman Bill White. After he and his black teammates were excluded in 1961 from an invitation extended to white players to attend "A Salute to Baseball" function in St. Petersburg, White told UPI reporter Joe Reichler, "I think about this every minute of the day."[15] Later he told a reporter for the *Pittsburgh Courier*, a black weekly, "This thing keeps gnawing at my heart. When will we be made to feel like humans?"[16]

Toward the end of spring training in late March 1959, Durham, who also thought separate arrangements were a big deal and didn't mind saying so, registered another complaint about Richards, this time with Sam Lacy. The complaint turned out to be ill-founded, but the making of it demonstrated again the low regard in which Durham held Richards. Durham charged that Richards, in the spring of 1958, had summarily replaced Bob Boyd, who had an outstanding year in 1957, with Jim Marshall at first base. Lacy quoted Durham as saying, "I don't believe there's another manager … who would take away the first base job from Boyd and just give it to Jim Marshall," a rookie who came to the O's from the White Sox in the winter trade that involved Doby.[17]

"Are you kidding?" Marshall said in a tone of astonishment when asked in 2012 if he had indeed replaced Boyd. "Nobody," Marshall explained, "had a guarantee in those days; nobody felt secure. The whole structure of the game was different then. We alternated at first base." (The records show Marshall appeared in 85 games and Boyd in 125.) He added that "things were put where they should be" after Boyd clubbed seven hits in a doubleheader against Cleveland. The Chicago Cubs acquired Marshall for the waiver price in August. Marshall, unlike Durham, recalled no racial tensions on the O's. He "saw no problems, none whatsoever." As proof that he saw no racial problems, he offered that he had roomed with Connie Johnson.[18]

Johnson, however, had seen some racial issues. When a reporter insinuated to Richards that he might be prejudiced, Richards said, "If you want to believe that, okay," and then challenged the writer to check with Johnson and Boyd. It is not known if the writer followed up with Johnson and Boyd, but in a later interview with author John Eisenberg, Johnson said he admired Richards' knowledge of the game. But, Johnson added, "I don't think he liked blacks that much. He'd hide it in ways you wouldn't notice if you didn't come looking for it, but I noticed." Richards had recently pulled Johnson from the starting rotation, saying he had a sore arm. "My arm wasn't sore," Johnson said. "I don't think they wanted me to win too many games." Richards read Johnson's comment in the papers and told his pitcher, "Don't talk to sportswriters, they make things up."[19]

Boyd also encountered racial tension with Richards. Richards, Boyd said, always kept his word and helped him improve as a player but added, "He didn't like blacks. I was in enough team meetings where he would talk about the black players ... and he wouldn't say very nice things about them."[20]

Tasby, who also had some issues with Richards, arrived in Baltimore in April 1959, in the wake of positive press reports about his play in spring training. "He has all the qualities that go into making a top-flight major lea-guer. He can run, field, and has power," wrote Bill Nunn of the *Pittsburgh Courier*.[21] Lacy quoted Richards as saying, "Tasby will be the key to our situation. He can make us or break us. Up to now he has been great."[22]

Tasby played well in what would be his last full season with the Birds. He hit .250 with 13 homers and performed well in the field. Like Beamon and Johnson, however, Tasby felt he had experienced the sting of racism. Looking back at his time with the O's, Tasby said, "I have no use for the Orioles even though they send me a Christmas card every year. You had to be two-three times as good as white boys. They didn't bring me up 'til I was 26. They didn't like me speaking up. I had words with some of my managers in the minors, and if a black player speaks

Willie Tasby had mixed feelings about his three years with the Orioles and was one of the few African American players willing to speak out about and act on his discontent. He was also known for playing in his stocking feet any time a rain storm approached, fearing that lightning might strike his metal cleats (National Baseball Hall of Fame Library, Cooperstown, New York).

up he's a trouble maker. A white player is looking out for his own welfare."[23]

Tasby acted on his discontent in late April when the Orioles held their "Salute to the Orioles" luncheon at the Emerson Hotel. Boyd, Green, and Tasby all failed to appear. "They certainly knew about it and we'll expect some explanations," public relations director Jack Dunn, 3rd told the *AFRO*. Tasby told the *AFRO*, "I had to file my income tax. Lenny [Green] and I were at the lawyer's office." Boyd, currently residing at the York Hotel, told the paper he had an appointment with a realtor to see an apartment for his family.[24] The truth came out later when Richards asked why he skipped the event. Tasby told him "because I couldn't get in that hotel if it was just me. I could only get in because I'm on the team." Richards, Tasby said, said, "Okay, son," and left it at that.[25]

Tasby did, nevertheless, have some positive memories of the O's. He had kind words for teammate and fellow outfielder Gene Woodling, who helped him get a raise. "'Hey Willie,' he said to me one afternoon, 'go see Richards about a raise.' So I went to Richards, asked for a small raise. Richards said 'Okay son.' He set up an appointment for me with MacPhail, who had a new contract ready with a modest raise. Richards stood up for his ballplayers and," Tasby said with a hint of disbelief in his voice, "he was from Texas." Tasby commented that catcher-first baseman Gus Triandos "was a nice guy. The problems," Tasby concluded, "were with the organization."[26]

As Tasby garnered positive reviews in spring training, Connie Johnson, now 36, struggled with pain in his neck and shoulder that had affected him last season when his record fell to 6–9. His one stellar performance in Miami came when he held the Pittsburgh Pirates hitless in a four-inning relief appearance. Otherwise, he had been "lousy and appeared to have had it," Richards said. Nevertheless, he took Johnson north for what would turn out to be a brief final stay with the O's.[27] The aching hurler had already boarded the team bus at Memorial Stadium for the trip to Griffith Stadium for Opening Day against the Senators. Richards called him aside to tell him no other team would pay the $20,000 waiver price for his services. He would be going to the minors. "The tall, statuesque Great Stone Face from Stone Mountain, Georgia," as *Sun* reporter Lou Hatter described Johnson, departed Baltimore convinced that, if allowed to pitch regularly, he would soon be back in a big league uniform.[28] Father Time, however, had caught up with the right-hander, who finished his career in the minors.

With the exception of Boyd and Tasby, African Americans again played minor roles with the 1959 Orioles. Richards called on Green, this time primarily for defensive purposes, often inserting him in the lineup late in the game.[29] But after only 27 games with Green batting a more than respectable .292, he found himself traded to the Senators in May for Albie Pearson, who was hitting an inauspicious .185. Pearson had won Rookie of the Year honors the year before. Green went on to play nine more years with five major league teams. Pearson stayed with the O's for one more season before moving on to the expansion Los Angeles Angels and retiring in 1966. Richards later admitted the trade had been a mistake. "I lay awake at nights and bleed every time I think of letting Lenny Green get away from us," Richards told Lacy two years later.[30]

Joe Taylor maintained his utility role, although at .156 not what Richards had expected. Taylor further disappointed Richards on July 26 by failing to show up at Comiskey Park for a doubleheader, claiming to

Lenny Green (right), the player who kept Richards awake at night, ruing the day he traded the outfielder to the Washington Senators in 1959, is shown here, probably in 1958, with Hall of Fame pitcher Hoyt Wilhelm, whose knuckleball baffled Orioles opponents from August of 1958 through the 1962 season. A photograph of a white man and a black man together smiling was a rare sight in the late 1950s (National Baseball Hall of Fame Library, Cooperstown, New York).

have overslept. "He will make his next appearance for Vancouver," Richards told a reporter with a tinge of anger in his voice.[31]

Switch-hitting Fred Valentine finally got a call from the parent club on September 1, the date when major league clubs could expand their rosters from 25 to 40 players. He had hit .250 for the AAA International League Miami Marlins and showed power with 22 doubles, 11 triples, and 11 homers. In 19 at-bats for Richards, he swatted the ball for a promising .316 average.

* * *

While thrilled to be in the majors, Valentine considered his proudest moment to have come a year earlier in 1958 with the Class B Wilson [North Carolina] Tobs, where he led the league in hitting, received the Most Valuable Player Award, and excited fans with steals of home. Jim Crow prevailed in Wilson as it did in his home town of Memphis. "We had our sections of town, our shopping areas," Valentine reminisced. "I came up in a segregated environment, all the way through school, so I knew what to expect."[32]

In Wilson he could do something about it. Segregated seating prevailed at Wilson's Fleming Stadium. Whites sat in the covered grandstand while blacks sat on open-air, wooden benches. One hot, Sunday afternoon the

Fred Valentine: The switch-hitting, speedy outfielder saw action with the Orioles and Senators for all or part of the 1963 through 1968 seasons. He carried the nickname "squeaky," given by his aunt for the noises he made as a toddler. At his suggestion, whites and blacks sat together in a minor league stadium for the first time when the blacks' stands collapsed. Along with Chuck Hinton and other former major leaguers, Valentine founded the Major League Baseball Players Alumni Association in 1982 (National Baseball Hall of Fame Library, Cooperstown, New York).

packed wooden stands collapsed. Fortunately, no one suffered a serious injury, but African American fans now had no place to sit. Tobs general manager Jim Mills sought out Valentine, the team's oldest black player, for advice.

MILLS: "Valentine, we have a problem."
VALENTINE: "Yeah, I can see that."
MILLS: "We got all these people. I don't know what we're going to do with 'em."
VALENTINE: "You see all those seats over there (pointing to the grandstand). Why don't you let 'em sit up there. Everybody in this little town knows everybody."
MILLS: "I don't know if it'll work."
VALENTINE: "Try it."

"So, everybody got up there in the seats talking to people they knew. Never did build those stands again. People still talk about it when I go back there for a visit,"[33] Valentine said with pride in his voice and a smile on his face.

Life off the field in Wilson came as no surprise to the outfielder. Businessmen offered players cash, meals, pizza, and free services such as a month's dry cleaning for home runs and stellar plays in the field. "When I won something," Valentine said, "which I did often, I couldn't go in the front door. I'd have to go around back. If it was a meal, they'd box it up for me."

Asked if he encountered any racial problems among teammates, he recalled only one instance, in 1965. A white player for the Hawaii Islanders, a farm team for the Washington Senators, confided to other white players, "I don't mind playing with blacks but I don't want to live with 'em." The Islanders housed all the players in the same complex. "Of course, that got back to us," Valentine said. "My wife never will forget that."[34]

Fans at minor league games were another matter. A frequent base stealer, he often heard taunts from white fans such as "We got ourselves a rabbit out there," or "Hey coon, let's see how fast you can get to second base." "I didn't hear anything like it in Baltimore," Valentine continued. "The people in Baltimore treated me fine."[35]

* * *

Boyd, who continued to hold down first base, had an off-year. His batting average dropped below .300 for the first time in four years. "I could do nothing right.... I'm just hoping I get the chance to play myself back into the line-up," Boyd told Lacy during spring training in 1960.[36] He did not get his chance. Richards, following a hard-fought spring training competition between Boyd and Jim Gentile, Walt Dropo, and John "Boog" Powell, awarded the 1960 starting first base job to Gentile and demoted Boyd to pinch-hitting status. While getting only 82 at-bats, he elevated his average to .317 with nine RBI but no homers. Gentile came through for Richards with a .292 average, 98 runs batted in, and 21 round-trippers.

Tasby lost his starting center field job during spring training in 1960 to Jackie Brandt, who had played previously with the Cardinals and the New York and San Francisco Giants. Knowing that Woodling had left field nailed down, Tasby looked to right field as his salvation even though it was his least favorite outfield position. "Almost everything hit out there is sailing or curving. It's like trying to catch Hoyt Wilhelm [masterful knuckleball pitcher]," Tasby told *Sun* reporter Lou Hatter. "But it's ok with me. I'll play anywhere…. The important thing is to play," he added.[37] Tasby did play but only in 39 games before MacPhail traded him in early June 1960 to the Red Sox, leaving the O's with one part-time African American, Boyd, on the roster.

* * *

Not only were African American players in short supply in Baltimore and the American League generally, but all African American players, regardless of team or league, got the short end of the bonus money stick. Sam Lacy published an eye-opening column in August 1958 that reported wide discrepancies in the amount of bonus money paid to white and black prospects. In the first seven months of the year, major league baseball shelled out more than $5 million in bonuses. Only $95,000 of that amount went to "colored players." Black players since 1947 had received modest to paltry amounts. Jackie Robinson's $3,500 signing stipend topped those received by Roy Campanella, Willie Mays, Joe Black, Don Newcombe, Sam Jethroe, and Frank Robinson. Mays kept the balance of a $350.00 travel expense check. Hank Aaron received $250.00 and a new suit of clothes. Ernie Banks got $20 "spending money" when he boarded a plane to join the Cubs organization. One African American, Earl Robinson, whom we'll meet later, received $30,000 from the Dodgers but the transaction was not reported, a highly unusual event.

Whites fared considerably better. In the first eight months of 1958, 17 California prospects received between $5,000 and $90,000. The Phillies bought a house for the parents of brother prospects Ritchie and Robert Haines, the equivalent of $65,000. The Braves paid $100,000 each to pitcher Tony Cloninger and shortstop Denis Menke, and $125,000 to catcher Bob Taylor. The top bonus paid by the Orioles to Joe Durham, Charlie Beamon, Willie Tasby and Lenny Green amounted to the $5,000 dispensed to Joe Pulliam, a Baltimore native and graduate of Dunbar High School. On the other hand, the O's outbid 14 other clubs to sign Dave Nicholson, an untried white high school player from St. Louis, for $110,000. (Nicholson confirmed the amount in a phone call with the author.) "How," Lacy asked, "do big league clubs acquire for little or nothing" the African American players they did? Lacy's answer? "Owners have an unwritten agreement not to bid against each other for their services, an agreement as iron-clad and as vicious as was their common view against the use of colored players before Branch Rickey."[38]

CHAPTER 5

"Why So Few Blacks?"

The Orioles carried fewer black players during their first seven seasons than did most teams. Orioles executives maintained their practice of assuring disenchanted black fans that they sought players solely on the basis of talent. African Americans were not buying it. Why, then they wondered, could so many other teams find black superstars and the Orioles could not? The Orioles certainly weren't being outspent in terms of bonus money. In addition, *AFRO* readers asked for more playing time for the African American players the Orioles did have on their roster. "Richards won't let the colored boys play," and "I don't see why he doesn't play Bob Boyd more often," said two in August 1960 when the Birds were in the thick of the pennant race.[1] Bob Brown, who joined the O's as assistant public relations manager in late 1957, offered "as a guess" that Richards was a large part of the reason so few blacks appeared on the team.[2] Sam Lacy, on the other hand, never one to shy away from critical comment in the realm of racial matters, did not think so. Noting that some fans have said, "he [Richards] has prejudices that influence his handling of the team," Lacy wrote, "There are some folks I don't like; and far be it from me to argue that I am free of prejudice. I like what he has done," Lacy concluded. "I hope he stays, despite what he may think of me, and I of him ... personally." Lacy assured his readers that managers of other teams did not let their personal feelings toward a player get in the way of "what he considers to be the most advantageous handling of the team." Lacy did not say how he knew how other managers managed their feelings.[3]

Yet we get a decidedly mixed verdict from the African American players themselves; some thought Richards treated all players the same and some did not. Valentine and Minoso had positive things to say about Richards. Tasby was more critical of the organization than Richards.

Durham, Boyd, Beamon, and Johnson thought Richards had a negative attitude toward blacks.

Richards, as we have seen, did sign black players, though no superstars. He did not publically make overtly racist comments like the one made by Tom Yawkey, owner of the Boston Red Sox, the last team to sign an African American. "Anyone," Yawkey told a reporter, "who says I won't hire blacks is a liar. I have about 100 working on my farm down south."[4] Or like the remarks George Washington Williams had previously directed to the Supreme Court's *Brown v. Board of Education* decision.[5]

On the other hand, Richards did nothing to support black players' concerns about their second-class status. When Tasby told Richards the reason for himself, Green, and Boyd not attending a welcome home lunch, Richards missed the chance to find out more about the players' issues. His patronizing response, "OK, son," simply cut off any more discussion. He did not advocate for them in the way Branch Rickey did for Jackie Robinson. He did not form close bonds with them as Veeck had with Paige, who, as we have seen, would follow him to Afghanistan. Veeck also earned Larry Doby's gratitude. When the two first met in Veeck's office in Cleveland, the owner insisted that Doby call him "Bill" and not "Mr. Veeck." "I had never said 'Mister' to anybody else and got that kind of response," Doby recalled. Veeck sat the 23-year-old down for a heart-to-heart about what he could expect as the first black player in the American League. "He told me the same thing that Mr. Rickey told Jackie," Doby later told an interviewer.[6] There is no evidence of Richards or any other Orioles executive having a similar conversation with an African American player.

Nor did Richards do anything to challenge the Jim Crow customs that forced his black players to live apart from their teammates. His choice of language on occasion showed a lack of respect for African Americans.

Several sports writers who covered the O's in their early years could recall no instances of prejudice on Richards' part or that of the organization. "Oh God, no!" Bill Tanton, a Baltimore native and sportswriter for the *Evening Sun* said when asked if he had seen anything racist in the Orioles organization. "I never heard anybody in the front office, managers, coaches, scouts say we don't want to have them," he continued. By the same token, however, Tanton said tellingly that he never heard anyone say "we should get African American players. It was," he added, "so obvious that all the black players were in the National League."[7] Vince Bagli, who covered Baltimore's professional sports from 1949 to 1995, said, "I've lived in Baltimore all my life and know there have been some changes in peoples' attitudes towards the blacks." But during the Orioles' early years, Bagli said, he did not remember any racism. The lack of black players "just never occurred to me. I had no opinion on it at all."[8] "No one ever said 'let's not sign him because he's black.' I don't recall any conversations about it." Said Bob Maisel, former sportswriter for the *Sun*, "The O's didn't have anything against them. They did have a couple like Heard but he just didn't have it." Maisel added, "I don't remember there were many around. I mean where the hell would you get them?"[9]

Richards likely received little support to find and cultivate African American talent from the Orioles' Board of Directors. Prominent real estate, hotel, ship building, aviation, investment banking, and manufacturing executives sat on the Board. That Board in 1956 consisted of Joseph A. W. Iglehart, investment banker and chairman; Robert J. Gill, attorney and secretary; Howard S. Jones, executive of an envelope manufacturing company and treasurer; and members Thomas F. Mullan, real estate executive; John W. Willis, president and general manager of Bethlehem Steel's Baltimore Division; Harold I. Fink, president of the Hotel Association; Zanvyl Krieger, attorney; William H. Callahan, Jr., president of a contracting firm; W. Wallace Lanaham, Jr., investment banker; Henry A. Parr, III, insurance executive; William F. Schluderberg, head of a meat packing firm; and Miles, who was retained as a member after resigning earlier as secretary.[10] Keelty's former Board position as vice-president was not filled, leading some to think an experienced baseball person, as Miles had suggested, might be brought in to assist Richards. Organizations represented by members of the Orioles' Board of Directors, and others like them in Baltimore, were often the targets of civil rights protestors seeking fair employment opportunities for African Americans.

For whatever reasons, Orioles management, unlike Rickey and Veeck, did not deem it advantageous to the team to make a concerted effort to find, sign, and develop outstanding black players. Perhaps Richards and MacPhail thought the team was doing well enough as it was. The 1960 Birds contended for the pennant until the last weeks of the season but finished second to the Yankees. Richards had finally achieved his goal of a first division finish and won "Manager of the Year" honors for so doing.

* * *

As Richards and MacPhail talked about talent as the sole criterion for signing players, other employers in Baltimore had no compunction against hiring employees on the basis of skin color, gender, marital status and perhaps talent as well through the late 1950s. The Calvert Hotel and

Dominique's Café, for instance, advertised for "white" barmaids in the *Sun*. Harry W. Checkit and Co. wanted a "young, white, single lady" for a clerk-typist position.[11]

Such hiring practices were of concern to the newly formed Equal Employment Opportunity Commission (E.E.O.C.). That body pushed the issue of fair employment into the public arena by announcing in March of 1959 the possibility of convening an informal conference of insurance and banking executives to discuss "hiring by merit" with city employers. A planned television spot would feature Orioles players and point out that several African Americans played for the O's.[12]

First, however, the Commission had to deal with a City Council divided over whether the Commission should even exist. In March 1959, the council rejected, 12–9, a bill to expand the agency's jurisdiction and enforcement powers. The bill would have made it city policy to foster employment of people to their fullest capacity and provide equal access to public places. Courts could order violators to comply. Knowing they had the votes to defeat the bill, the Council had short-circuited the usual procedure of referring the bill to committee for discussion before the vote. The bill's sponsor, Walter Dixon, called the council's action "a discourtesy shown to me, a personal affront." He promised to reintroduce the bill "until we find someone who has the decency, manhood, and courage to consider it."[13] On June 8, Dixon did just that. Incensed by the strong language in Dixon's new bill, council members from the 1st District introduced a bill a week later to abolish the commission. The council sidestepped the issue by referring both measures to the city's Commission on Human Relations for recommendations. In the summer of 1960, following elections in the spring, a newly constituted council voided the need for a recommendation from the Commission by passing Dixon's bill, 14–7, a clear signal that change was in the air. However, in a manner reminiscent of the School Board's endorsement in principle only of *Brown v. the Board of Education*, the council's action provided no penalties for non-compliance.[14]

The year 1960 also saw another step on the road toward integration in the city. The Restaurant Association of Baltimore circulated a survey in April "among leading restaurants" asking owners' opinions about serving African Americans. The survey came on the heels of major department stores opening their eateries to all. Several owners interviewed by the *AFRO* declined to predict what would happen. Peter Colyn, city manager for the White Tower Restaurants, gave a more definitive reply, saying, "The only objection we have is that we don't want to be first. We serve colored persons in Philadelphia and Washington but here we are sort of in between."[15]

Integrated restaurants would have pleased Monte Irvin, Hall of Fame left fielder for the New York Giants. Baltimore's segregated restaurants during the 1940s, when he came to town with the Negro National League's Newark Eagles, remained fresh in his memory in 2012. "We knew where we could go and where we couldn't, so we usually went where we could," Irvin recalled. "But this one time we tried to go to Obrycki's Restaurant." Obrycki's, established in 1944, started as a bar in Baltimore's historic Fells Point neighborhood and soon became well-known for its steamed crabs and crab cakes. "They saw us coming," Irvin said, "and as soon as we got to the front door this guy blocked the door and told us, 'You can't come in here, we don't serve colored.'" Irvin, with a soft chuckle in his voice, said he replied, "We don't want colored, we want some of your famous crab cakes. Well, the guy gave us a faint smile and said 'Nice try.'"[16]

* * *

The O's returned to Miami in 1961 for their third year of spring training in the Sunshine State. Major league teams and their minor league affiliates had trained peacefully for years in Florida before Jackie Robinson and pitcher John Wright appeared at the Dodgers' and Royals' 1946 spring training camp in Daytona Beach. Wright's blazing fastball for the Kansas City Monarchs had prompted Branch Rickey to sign him to a Montreal Royals contract shortly after Robinson signed his contract. Robinson's and Wright's presence caused several Florida cities to cancel Royals exhibition games, some without giving a reason. "We know what's going on," Montreal secretary Mel Jones said. "Let 'em cancel all of them. We're sticking by Robinson and Wright. They're members of the team and they go where we go."[17] Other cities, like Jacksonville, were quite direct. George G. Robinson, executive secretary of the Playground and Recreation Committee, told Jones that city ordinances stipulated "Negroes and whites cannot compete against each other on a city-owned playground." The city owned the stadium where the game was to be played.[18]

For the next 15 years, teams with black players, with the exception of the Dodgers, who held their 1947 spring training in Havana, Cuba, before converting an old air force base at Vero Beach into "Dodgertown" for spring training, arranged separate housing for black players, either in hotels or private homes. Integrated squads avoided communities such as Jacksonville, Deland, and Sanford, Florida.[19] *The Sporting News*, in its traditional cautionary stance toward integration, editorialized that "common sense" coupled with "calmness and diplomacy" would solve the issue of segregated housing. "There is an obligation on the part of both baseball and the Negro players," the paper intoned, "to be aware of what at any time could be a delicate situation."[20]

Physician and president of the St. Petersburg chapter of the NAACP, Ralph Wimbish, broached the delicate situation. Buoyed by several successful court decisions in St. Petersburg, Wimbish announced on January 31, 1961, that he would no longer seek housing for the New York Yankees' black players. Yankees president Dan Topping suddenly issued a statement saying black players "mean as much to our ball club as any other players and we would very much like to have the whole team under one roof."[21] Unable to persuade the management of the Soreno Hotel to integrate, Topping moved the Yankees the following spring to the more receptive city of Fort Lauderdale. Not wanting to appear to have been pushed out, Topping assured the *St. Petersburg Times* that the move "has nothing to do with the problem of segregation."[22]

Two months later, Milwaukee Braves players Hank Aaron, Billy Bruton, and Wes Covington, breaking with black players' custom of suffering segregation silently for fear of reprisals, disagreed with the team's executive vice president, George "Birdie" Tebbetts. The Braves VP told the press that black players had no problems with their housing. "It's about time you all realize we're a team and we need to stay together," Aaron told Tebbetts, who had called Aaron into his office.[23] Tebbetts eventually found a hotel willing to accommodate all players.

MacPhail, in the first move of its kind by an Orioles executive, sought integrated facilities for the Orioles in the fall of 1960. He quietly initiated talks with DeWitt Coffman, the McAllister Hotel's general manager,[24] "in furtherance of our desire to have any colored players on the squad stay at the same hotel.... They have been very friendly and cooperative talks,"[25] MacPhail told a *Sun* reporter in February of 1961. By this time the McAllister had agreed to allow all the Orioles to stay there. Decisions by the Yankees and the White Sox to cancel reservations at the McAllister for exhibition games with the O's in favor of the nearby, integrated Biscayne Terrace Hotel may have bolstered MacPhail's negotiating power.[26] Civil rights advocate and long-time critic of major league baseball's whites only policy, *Pittsburgh Courier* sportswriter Wendell Smith cited MacPhail as "a fair-minded man" for his efforts.[27] At the same time, the O's did away with segregated seating at Miami Stadium, becoming the third team to integrate its Florida ball park.[28] By spring training 1962, 15 of 20 teams in the majors had integrated housing facilities. The five teams who did not were all in Florida: Detroit at Lakeland, Minnesota at Orlando, Kansas at West Palm Beach, Washington at Pompano Beach, and Pittsburgh at Fort Myers.[29]

Jim Crow still ruled, however, beyond the hotels' confines. Most beaches, restaurants, race courses, golf courses, and theaters remained segregated. These conditions influenced the O's only black player on the final 1961 roster, Earl Robinson, 24, to choose to stay at the Sir John. Born in New Orleans but raised in Berkeley, California, Robinson excelled at basketball at the University of California, Berkeley. He led the team to conference titles in 1956, 1957, and 1958. He also led the Cal baseball team to the 1957 National Collegiate Athletic Association (NCAA) championship with a .352 batting average.[30] Robinson explained his decision to stay at the Sir John to Lacy, who termed his choice "unfortunate." Life at the McAllister would, Robinson thought, distract him from his primary purpose, making the team. Robinson told Lacy, "I would have spent most of my time in my room ... because I have little in common, socially, with the other players.... If I were downtown and felt the need of some social life, I would have to pay taxicab fare to get across town where I am to find my friends. What they need to know about me as an athlete and a person," Robinson continued, "they can learn on the diamond and in the locker room."[31] Both MacPhail and the hotel's new general manager, Fred Gee, confirmed to Lacy that Robinson had been invited to stay with the team. MacPhail went along with Robinson this year, saying, "we do not wish to impose any kind of hardship on a young athlete. That is why we allowed Earl his choice."[32] Robinson told Lacy he might decide differently next year.

The amenities at the Sir John enjoyed earlier by Tasby and Valentine may also have influenced Robinson's choice. Located in Miami's Overton district, known as "The Harlem of the South," the Sir John offered its guests, in addition to a pool and top-flight entertainers, linen tablecloths and silver utensils, cocktail parties, and hot dog roasts. By contrast, the McAllister offered only card games, reading, and checkers as diversions. Miami police further complicated the situation by barring blacks from walking around parts of white Miami without a written note from their boss.[33] Robinson ended up with a roommate at the St. John—shortstop Mickey McGuire, 20, a native of Dayton, Ohio, and recently signed by the O's as an amateur free agent. McGuire had no choice. "They didn't ask me where I wanted to stay," McGuire told *Pittsburgh Courier* sportswriter Bill Nunn, Jr., "I was told to stay at the Sir John."[34] Nunn concluded the O's wanted McGuire more as a companion for Robinson than as a player. Nunn may well have been correct. McGuire spent the season in the minors and would appear in only six games for the Orioles in 1962 and ten in 1967. MacPhail did not give Robinson a choice of residence for 1962 spring training. He told the *AFRO* after the end of the 1961 season, "We expect Robinson to be at the McAllister next spring."[35] Robinson called the McAllister home in the spring of 1962.

* * *

The Birds arrived back in Baltimore in April 1961 with but one African American, Robinson, on the team. In January the Birds had traded Boyd, 35, and four other players to Kansas City in exchange for two white left-handed-hitting outfielders, Whitey Herzog, 29, and Russ Snyder, 26. Boyd's arrival in Kansas City broke a two-year drought of black players there.

Orioles management, aware of not only the small number of black players on the team but also the low turnout of African Americans at games, continued to wonder aloud why more blacks didn't come to Memorial Stadium. Richards and MacPhail, for example, addressed a June 1961 sports luncheon sponsored by a prominent black dentist, Dr. John Woodland. "I don't know what we can do to prove to the colored people that we want to see them at Memorial Stadium," MacPhail told the 100 people in attendance. Richards regaled his audience with the exploits of Minnie Minoso and Lenny Green. "These are the kind of players anyone in baseball likes to have, and it doesn't matter if he's Chinese, Indian, colored or white, so long as he can play baseball," Richards said."[36] Some eyes in the audience may have rolled. Lacy suggested the obvious, "that the absence of a bona fide colored player … may be largely responsible for the aloof attitude of tan fans." He also wondered aloud why the O's had been unable to sign a star black player "of which there is an abundance at the moment." By the end of May 1961, 66 black players had won jobs on major league teams. The National League had the edge, 36 to 30. The San Francisco Giants had the most of any club with eight. Only the Birds and the Los Angeles Angels carried but one.[37]

Lacy's observation seemingly made no impact on MacPhail and Richards, who limited their efforts to recruiting black fans to making speeches. Jerry Sachs recalled, "I don't think we did anything to promote the team in the African American community other than approach large companies such as Bethlehem Steel and encourage them to have a 'Bethlehem Steel Night' at the stadium." African Americans who worked at the plant attended those games. "Otherwise," Sachs said, "I can't remember any effort we made specifically in the African American community."[38]

Others pondering the O's paleness pointed to the city's professional football team, the Baltimore Colts. Black stars Lenny Moore, Jim Parker, and Eugene "Big Daddy" Lipscomb had led the Colts to successive National Football League Championships in 1958 and 1959.

Playing before few African Americans, the Birds again achieved a first division finish, third place, with a 95–67 record. As the season progressed, Richards began negotiations with the newly formed Houston Colt .45s in the National League to be their general manager. The Orioles' Board of Directors did not appreciate Richards' talks with George Kirksey, Houston's executive vice-president. They gave him an ultimatum in late August to decide by Friday, September 1, whether he would stay or go. Richards decided to go. Houston was only 220 miles from his home in Waxahachie, and it was reported he had negotiated a $10,000 raise for himself throughout a five-year contract. He offered to manage the team "for the rest of the season if they [Board of Directors] want me."[39] They didn't. Coach Lum Harris managed the team for the month of September.

CHAPTER 6

"What's All the Mystery About?"

Lee MacPhail wasted little time in filling the vacant manager's job. By October 1961 he had tapped Billy Hitchcock, 45, six-foot, one-inch tall and weighing 185 pounds, from Inverness, Alabama. A well-traveled utility infielder for the Browns, Senators, Red Sox, Tigers, and Athletics, Hitchcock had managed the Vancouver Canucks, an Orioles farm club, in 1961 after six years as the third base coach for the Detroit Tigers. Described by *Sun* sportswriter Douglas Brown as "educated, astute, diplomatic, thorough, patient, and considerate,"[1] Hitchcock's easy-going manner would, MacPhail thought, give players a respite from Richards' authoritarian style. "Hitchcock is not a controversial outspoken type of person. He has impressed me with what I might best describe as quiet determination," MacPhail said of his new hire, who had been named "Manager of the Year" in the Pacific Coast League the year before.[2]

Hitchcock's appearance in Baltimore drew varied reviews from the *AFRO* staff. An *AFRO* editorial asked, "Why can't they find managers from somewhere else besides the segregation belt?" Taking his colleague to task for violating the "innocent until proven guilty" maxim, Lacy promised Hitchcock his support "until he proves to me he has prejudices based on complexion rather than skill."[3]

Several blacks, including outfielders Earl Robinson, Joe Durham, and Sam Bowens along with infielder Osvaldo Joseph (Ozzie) Virgil, went to spring training in 1962. Virgil, the first player from the Dominican Republic to play in the majors when he broke in with the New York Giants in 1956 and the Detroit Tigers' first black player (1958), had a disappointing year in 1961. He hit only .137 for the Tigers and Kansas City Athletics. Hitchcock, however, had coached Virgil in Detroit and thought he had the skills to help the O's.[4] Bowens, a native of Wilmington, North Carolina, had been signed by the same scout, Jim Russo, who signed Valentine and Tasby, and was from the same black university, Tennessee A & I, that produced Valentine.[5] The outfielder had played two years in the Birds' farm system with the Bluefield Orioles of the Appalachian League and the Leesburg Orioles of the Florida State League.

Hitchcock brought only Robinson north from Miami. Hampered by injuries, he appeared in only 96 games but hit a respectable .266. A re-injured elbow in early July prompted MacPhail to sell Robinson to the Rochester Red Wings, the O's AAA farm club, leaving the O's without an African American player until late August, when the O's dipped into their Rochester roster to bring up Mickey McGuire. The rookie appeared in only six games, going hitless in four at-bats.[6] The Birds returned McGuire to Rochester after the season. Ozzie Virgil disappointed Hitchcock. He made the briefest possible appearance with the Birds in 1962, one turn at bat that resulted in a walk.

By this time 56 black players, 26 in the American League and 30 in the National League, had taken the field on Opening Day for 18 of the now 20 major league teams. Only Kansas City and the Red Sox fielded an all-white team.[7] The Orioles, while not totally bereft of black players, had precious few, a fact not lost on Frank McDougald, now a member of Baltimore's Citizens Interest Group. He called on MacPhail to meet with the group to discuss the absence of "tan" players or face a boycott. "The Orioles policy may not be anti-colored, but try to tell this to the disillusioned colored fan from Baltimore," McDougald told an *Afro-American* reporter in July 1962.[8] Neither the meeting nor the boycott took place.

Others, however, took up the cause. Richard Hobson of North Warwick Avenue charged in a letter to MacPhail that race had driven the decision to sell Robinson to Rochester. Not so, MacPhail replied. The O's, MacPhail said, could have placed Robinson on the disabled list, but then he could not have played for 30 days. By going to Rochester he could play within ten days should his elbow improve, MacPhail explained. The general manager also noted that even though they sold Robinson to the Red Wings, the O's still had first call on his services.

Once again MacPhail found himself assuring people that race was not a factor in his personnel decisions. "It is not good business for us not to have a colored boy on our club," he told Hobson.[9] He noted that the O's had "several good colored players" in the minors. The GM echoed Ehlers' comments on the subject eight years earlier by issuing the now-familiar refrain that "they will be advanced just as fast, no faster or slower, as their abilities and experience warrants. I can only hope," MacPhail concluded in his reply to Hobson, "that any fans we lose now will accept our future actions as proof that their feelings were unfounded." Hobson, unconvinced, told friends: "They could find some who are as good as the white boys they are getting or the difference would be so slight it wouldn't matter."[10] Hobson had a point. The 1962 Orioles carried only two .300 hitters, right fielder Russ Snyder (.305) and Brooks Robinson (.303). Three O's, catcher Gus Triandos, infielder Ron Hansen, and outfielder Dave Nicholson, all with more than 170 at-bats, failed to crack the .200 level at the plate.

Though unable to dispel Hobson's doubts, MacPhail managed to convince Lacy of his sincerity in a telephone call. After the call, Lacy wrote in "A to Z" (the title of his column), "A to Z is not nearly so irked by this [lack of black players] as it would be if the Baltimore front office should move to pacify its critics by placing on the roster a player of dubious ability but definite complexion."[11] Robinson finished the season in Rochester. His elbow did not improve.

Nor did the practically all-white O's improve on their promising third place finish of the previous year, falling to seventh place with a 77–85 record in 1962. *Sun* reporter Bob Maisel chalked up the Birds' tailspin to the Army's call to pitcher Steve Barber and shortstop Ron Hansen, injuries to pitchers Milt Pappas and Jack Fisher, a shortage of enthusiasm teamwide once the first division seemed out of reach, the lack of a top-notch catcher, and, lastly, the oft-cited need for a "big man in the outfield."[12]

In yet another attempt to fill the outfield gap, MacPhail bought Joe Gaines in January 1963, from the Cincinnati Reds. A native of Bryan, Texas, Gaines brought a .231 batting average and speed to the 1963 spring training camp in Miami. The GM also obtained outfielder Al Smith, at 35 eight years older than Gaines, from the Chicago White Sox. As a two-time All-Star selection, MacPhail looked to Smith to provide timely hitting while knowing he had lost a step on the bases and would have to be rested periodically. The O's planned to use Gaines in left field, Smith in right, and Jackie Brandt in center. Robinson's elbow had improved to the point where he reported to spring training, but he failed to make the team and returned to Rochester.[13]

Another promising African American outfielder, Paul Blair, 19, joined the team for spring training in 1963. The youngster made an impressive showing but not impressive enough to make the "big club's" roster. Blair spent the season with the Class A Stockton Ports in the California League. There he led all O's minor leaguers in runs scored, total bases, and stolen bases while batting .324 and driving in 77 runs. He would be heard from again.

Blair's experience with discrimination differed from that of many of the O's African American players who hailed from and played in the South. Raised in Los Angeles and a product of minor league ball in California and New York state, Blair said in 2012, "I never experienced any of the bad stuff and hostilities."[14] Earlier he had told author John Eisenberg that since blacks and whites now stayed at the same Miami hotel during spring training, he never thought about blacks and whites. "I never thought of that. I never did.... Times were changing and things were fine. It was just baseball, the same game for everyone."[15]

* * *

The dog days of August found the Orioles flirting with second place. Valentine had been brought up from Rochester to join Gaines and Smith. Bigger changes were taking place beyond Memorial Stadium. The fight for civil rights took the national stage. On August 28, 1963, Dr. Martin Luther King, Jr., led the March on Washington for Jobs and Freedom. Two hundred thousand people heard his "I Have a Dream" speech delivered from the steps of the Lincoln Memorial. Four days earlier, in a column titled "Everybody Belongs in D.C. 'March,'" Lacy urged black players from those teams in Washington and Baltimore at the time (the Washington Senators, Minnesota Twins, Kansas City Athletics, and Orioles) to participate. He reminded African American players of their debt to earlier civil rights struggles. "Surely, no argument needs to be raised to remind Al [Smith] that rights demonstrations are current in every city he has called home. Nor is it necessary to remind Gaines of life in Bryan, Texas," Lacy wrote. He lamented the fact that many professional athletes were indifferent to civil rights activities because they "have made it," and that others shied from such events for fear of reprisals.[16]

When asked about the march, Gaines said that no one had approached him about participating. "I don't recall the march happening when I was there," Gaines said in 2012. He added, "I would think you would have had to be careful getting too much involved in that kinda stuff. You might have had some problems."[17] No record could be found of any professional baseball players attending the March.

* * *

As the 1963 season began to wind down with the Birds in danger of finishing out of the first division, MacPhail called Sam Bowens up from

Rochester in September. Seen as a "prize prospect" by *Sun* reporter Lou Hatter, Bowens, 25, had hit for a .289 average at Rochester. In 15 games with the O's, Bowens hit an impressive .333.[18] The O's now suddenly had four African American players: Bowens, Smith, Gaines, and Valentine, outfielders all who shared playing time with white outfielders John "Boog" Powell, Russ Snyder, and Jackie Brandt.

The presence of four African Americans muted some of the criticism directed at the Birds by disenchanted black residents who, nevertheless, did not overlook the fact that most Orioles African American players had been "flychasers." With a few notable exceptions, in a practice commonly known as "stacking," blacks had been assigned to the outfield while white players filled the positions calling for the most decision-making skills— pitcher, catcher, and infielder.

The number of black outfielders fell by one when the O's sold Valentine to the Senators after the 1963 season. Jim Russo, who had developed a knack for finding promising African American players, offered Al Vincent's stinging criticism of Valentine as one reason Valentine did not stick with the Birds. When both were with the International League Miami Marlins in early 1963, Vincent, the Marlins' manager, who earlier had said he would like a "roomful" of Valentines, yelled at him after a strikeout or an error in the field. Valentine would hear such loud and public comments from Vincent as "You're dead meat, Valentine. Dead meat. Jesus Christ, are you dead."[19] Would encouragement have brought better results? Russo wondered.

The Birds did manage a first division finish, fourth place, with an 86–76 record, up three notches from their seventh-place 1962 finish. MacPhail decided, however, that he needed a new manager, "one who will be a little tougher ... not a policeman or a disciplinarian, but someone a bit more aggressive."[20] Brooks Robinson said of Hitchcock's managerial style, "Billy was the nicest guy you ever wanted to meet, but we didn't play very well under him."[21]

MacPhail's gaze landed on Hank Bauer, who had served as the third base coach for the O's in 1963 following an illustrious 12-year career as a Yankees outfielder. The two first met and became friends shortly after World War II, when Bauer played for the top Yankees farm club, the Kansas City Blues, and MacPhail worked as the club's general manager.[22] Bauer played in nine World Series and three All-Star Games. A U.S. Marine in the South Pacific during World War II, where he won 11 campaign ribbons, two Bronze Stars and two Purple Hearts, and worked as a pipefitter before his Yankees days, Bauer, at six feet, 202 pounds, made his presence felt. "When Hank comes down the base paths the whole earth trembles," said Red Sox infielder Johnny Pesky. Bauer said of himself, "It's no fun playing if you don't make somebody else unhappy. I do everything hard."[23] MacPhail had his "a bit more aggressive" manager.

Blair returned to spring training in 1964 and again performed superbly in the field. "The 20 year old long range jet," *Sun* reporter Lou Hatter said of Blair, "caught everything but pneumonia in the Grapefruit League this spring."[24] Needing to work on his hitting, the fleet-footed Blair spent most of the season with the Elmira [NY] Pioneers. He got his first taste of major league baseball when MacPhail called him up for eight games in September.[25]

Dissatisfied with Al Smith's performance in 1963, the O's traded him back to Cleveland for African American Willie Kirkland, six years younger than Smith and with more power at the plate. Bauer platooned Bowens and Kirkland in right field. MacPhail signed another African American outfielder, Lou Jackson, a native of Riverton, Louisiana, who hit for a .315 average and blasted 31 round-trippers the previous year for the Toronto Maple Leafs of the International League. Jackson had a bit of major league experience, having played in 30 games for the Cincinnati Reds in 1958–1959.

The O's opened the 1964 season with four African American players, again all outfielders: Kirkland, Jackson, Bowens, and Gaines. By mid–May, MacPhail had sent Jackson to Rochester and Gaines to the National League Colt 45s in exchange for $20,000 and minor league outfielder Johnny Weekly, who went to Rochester. In Houston, Gaines met Paul Richards.[26]

Gaines much preferred Baltimore. When asked his opinion of the former O's manager, Gaines said, "I don't even want to tell you what I thought of Paul Richards. He was really a redneck. Baseball was different then," he said. "They owned you. Whatever they said went."[27] He had a better experience in Baltimore than in Houston. "Fair," he said when asked in 2012 how he had been treated in Baltimore. "You didn't forget who you were, but I never had any problems."[28]

* * *

In 1964 white and black players still went their separate ways after the game. Gaines recalled that "we [he and Al Smith] lived in the black part of town. We didn't try to go anywhere else. You could have all the fun you wanted in places we could go,"[29] he added.

Pennsylvania Avenue in northwest Baltimore provided Gaines and Smith with many places to go. They had their choice of Eddie's Café,

Woolf's Café, the Dreamland Café, Inc., and the Alhambra Grill—advertising itself as "Baltimore's Finest" at 1520 Pennsylvania Avenue, as well as clubs that carried the names of Sphinx, Frolic Café and Lounge, Ubangi, and Moonglow. The two could play a game of pool at several Pennsylvania Avenue establishments, including the Belmont Billiard Parlor and the Royal Pool Parlor. Those who drank too much could find themselves spending the night locked "under the Clock," a lofty clock adorning the Northwestern Police Station. Women went to the Charm Center for top-of-the-line New York fashion, where they tried on clothes which they were not allowed to do in Baltimore's downtown's stores. Gaines and Smith could take their wives or girlfriends to the Green Room Restaurant in the York Hotel, a block off the Avenue, at 1200 Madison Avenue, for fine dining. Soul food could be had at the Clarke Hotel, a block south of the York on Madison. Jazz artists Dinah Washington and Nat King Cole held forth at the Casino Club or the Royal.[30]

Frederick Lonesome, who grew up near Pennsylvania Avenue as one of 11 children, said he, like Gaines and Smith, enjoyed the social life along the Avenue. "On Saturday night," he said, "I'd make sure I had my best clothes on and I'd get on the Avenue. I'd walk north all the way up to the North Avenue where the Met [the white-owned Metropolitan movie theater] was; that was the end of the black territory, and then I'd walk back down on the other side of the street." Lonesome favored the Royal Theater, which dominated the 1300 block of Pennsylvania Avenue and featured big bands and jazz combos. "That was really great for me. You had the whites like

A two-time All-Star selection before joining the Birds for the 1963 season, Al Smith shored up the outfield for his only season with the Orioles and befriended fellow, younger African American players Joe Gaines and Sam Bowens (National Baseball Hall of Fame Library, Cooperstown, New York).

Tommy Dorsey, Benny Goodman, and Charlie Barnet and of course Duke Ellington, Count Basie, Cab Calloway, and Louis Armstrong."[31]

Lonesome missed the trolley rides on Pennsylvania Avenue the most. "We could ride the cars all night on Saturday night. It was nice and cool on those hot nights."[32]

Gaines had fond memories of his time with Smith in Baltimore. "He was OK people," Gaines told an interviewer. "Sometimes you get to the majors and someone's been up making money and don't spend much time with a rookie. Not Al Smith."[33]

* * *

Bauer had the team playing exceptional baseball throughout the 1964 season. Thanks to back-to-back homers by Brooks Robinson and Sam Bowens, the Birds beat the Chicago White Sox, 4–2, on August 21 at Comiskey Park to reclaim first place in the American League. African American outfielders continued to come and go. A week earlier MacPhail had sold Kirkland, who in 65 games had hit only .200, to the Washington Senators. Earl Robinson re-surfaced from Rochester in mid–July to appear in 39 games, mostly as a pinch-hitter. As extra insurance for the pennant run, MacPhail returned Lenny Green to Baltimore in early September by purchasing him from the Los Angeles Angels. Green, however, provided little insurance with a .190 batting average in 14 games.[34]

This Robinson had an on-again, off-again relationship with the Birds from 1961 to 1965. In an unusual move for African American players in the 1960s, Earl Robinson preferred the all-black Sir John Hotel during spring training in Miami to the newly-integrated McAllister Hotel (National Baseball Hall of Fame Library, Cooperstown, New York).

In a down-to-the-wire, three-way race for the pennant between the O's, the White Sox, and the Yankees, the Birds, after spending 83 days in first place and 61 in second, crossed the finish line in third, only one game behind the Sox and two behind the pennant-winning Bronx Bombers. A happy MacPhail rewarded Bauer with a two-year contract extension and a raise.[35] Not as well pleased with several of his African American outfielders, MacPhail demoted Robinson, Jackson, and Green to Rochester. Bowens' and Blair's contracts stayed with Baltimore.[36]

Meanwhile, African American players continued to excel in the National League. The St. Louis Cardinals, led by pitcher Bob Gibson and outfielders Curt Flood and Lou Brock, beat the Yankees, who now fielded three black players—Howard, Al Downing and Hector Lopez—in the 1964 World Series.

* * *

The Earl Robinson saga continued into 1965. Bauer assigned him to lead the team in calisthenics during spring training, a job usually done by coach Billy Hunter. Displeased and seeing the writing on the wall, Robinson asked MacPhail to trade him. If returned once again to the minors, Robinson asked that he be sent to the Pacific Coast League to be closer to his family in Berkeley. Robinson hastened his departure with an unauthorized attempt to steal home during an exhibition game. Home umpire Nestor Chylak called him out by two feet. "I thought I made it. I thought I could make it. I had a good lead," Robinson told *Sun* reporter Jim Elliot. "It was a bad play," said Bauer. Asked by Elliot if third base coach Billy Hunter may have given Robinson the green light, Bauer retorted, "Well, if Hunter sent Earl in, Hunter's going back to Rochester too."[37] Robinson ended up with the Salt Lake City Bees who, as he had requested, played in the Pacific Coast League.[38] His major league career had ended.

The start of the 1965 campaign saw two African American players in the O's starting lineup, outfielders Sam Bowens and Paul Blair. MacPhail returned Blair to Rochester in July when his batting average dropped to .211 and recalled him in August when his average with the Red Wings reached .336. At the same time, MacPhail demoted Bowens to Rochester in light of his .145 batting average, leaving Blair as the sole African American on the roster.[39] Bauer guided the O's to a third-place finish, one game behind the White Sox and eight behind the Minnesota Twins.

Black players once again played a major role in the World Series. Led by Maury Wills, Junior Gilliam, Willie Davis, and Lou Johnson, the Los Angeles Dodgers bested the Milwaukee Twins, four games to three. The Twins featured Mudcat Grant, Tony Oliva, Earl Battey and Zoilo Versalles,

of Cuban heritage, who won the American League's Most Valuable Player
Award.

* * *

Controversy of another nature involving the Orioles erupted in Baltimore in September over white players not appearing at black-sponsored
functions. An increasingly hostile exchange of letters between the Birds'
publicity director, Jerry Sachs, and civil rights activist and President of
the Baltimore Chapter of the American Labor Council, Troy Bailey, over
what Bailey saw as the reluctance of the O's to sanction appearances of
white players at black-sponsored events, led Bailey to charge the O's with
prejudice.

Sun columnist Bob Maisel took issue with Bailey's charge. Referring
no doubt to the Sachs-Bailey letter exchange, Maisel reported that "a gentleman who is respected and influential in the colored community" had
accused the O's of prejudice. Following his investigation, Maisel concluded
that the charge lacked merit. "There was," Maisel wrote, "a difference of
opinion over a luncheon and a rather strong letter written by an Orioles
official, but I am convinced it had nothing to do with race. It was more a
clash of personalities." Maisel did not explain how he came to his conclusion. Maisel further said he had investigated similar charges in the past
and had found them all to be baseless. He did add, however, that the
scarcity of black spectators resulted from the O's poor job "of public relations in the colored community." To bolster his point, Maisel cited
MacPhail at length. "I'll have to agree with you," MacPhail told Maisel,
"that we haven't done a good job of promoting in the colored community."
MacPhail promised the O's were "going to do something about it."
MacPhail, once again trying to blunt charges of prejudice, reiterated to
Maisel the O's oft-expressed statement that "we do our best to sign good
ball players.... We don't care who they are." MacPhail noted that the Birds
had spent more than a quarter of a million dollars over the past four years
to sign "colored players," not including salary.[40]

Maisel did echo Lacy's earlier observation that "a star Negro per-
former ... should certainly improve these figures [attendance] and the
Birds know it."[41] Baltimore resident and future Pulitzer Prize-winning his-
torian Stephen E. Ambrose, who was enrolled as a graduate student at
Johns Hopkins University, made the same point. In a letter to the *Sun*'s
editor, Ambrose asked rhetorically, "What's all the mystery about poor
Oriole attendance? Nearly half this city is unrepresented on the ball field.
Why should Negroes attend the games?"[42]

Why indeed. If the Orioles were free of prejudice, then they were not free of rank ineptitude. As Orioles management continued to talk about the need for quality black players, while signing precious few and none of star quality, National League teams were continuing to find and sign stellar African American players. These players dominated the Most Valuable Player Awards from 1954 to 1965. Hank Aaron, Ernie Banks (twice), Roy Campanella, Willie Mays (twice), Frank Robinson and Maury Wills took the honor in eight of the 12 years. Among all black major leaguers under a major league contract at one time or another during the O's first six years in town, only nine appeared in an Orioles uniform, and none won any awards. A better record than some teams such as the Red Sox, Tigers, and Yankees, but the gap between rhetoric and results continued to widen, putting the O's credibility, with at least the African American community and some whites, on the line.

AFRO columnist George W. Collins expanded the discussion beyond the diamond. "One who makes an occasional visit to the stadium," Collins wrote in 1965, "sees nothing even faintly resembling tan faces in allied departments of the organization—ticket takers, ushers, and minor officialdom." Collins reminded his readers of "not-so-distant conditions" which gave rise to many blacks feeling that most whites carried "an anti-us" attitude toward them. These included blacks being forced to see baseball at Bugle Field, and not Oriole Park, "if they wanted to be comfortable," few blacks in city jobs, and segregated restaurants, movie theaters, hotels, and department stores. Collins noted these conditions "have been washed away by the tides of time … but that 'anti-us' image hanging over the Orioles has demonstrated incredible durability."[43]

Collins, however, saw promise on the horizon in the person of Jerold C. Hoffberger, and for good reason. A Baltimore native and president of the National Brewing Company, Hoffberger was now the new owner and president of the O's. He had been an O's shareholder since 1954 but acted as a silent partner who continued to buy stock in the team. By June 1965 he had acquired enough stock to have a controlling interest.[44] Among his many civic activities was his co-chairmanship, with Mayor D'Alesandro, of the National Alliance of Businessmen in Baltimore. Dubbed "the businessman's WPA," the group's objective was to provide job opportunities to the "hard-core unemployed," i.e., "a poor person, school dropout, handicapped, ex-convict or member of a minority group." Hoffberger enlisted Baltimore businessmen to approach other businessmen to ask them to set aside two percent of their job openings for the "hard core."[45] It was Hoffberger's statement that "The successful operation of a baseball team, like any other business, requires common sense," that gave Collins hope that the "anti-us" attitude would soon dissipate.[46]

Inroads into the "anti-us" feeling were not, in fact, far off. MacPhail left Maisel with a tantalizing comment just before leaving for the annual owners' meeting in Chicago in October 1965: "We're working on something right now that we think will help," MacPhail told the reporter, "although I'd rather not go into too much detail at this time."[47]

CHAPTER 7

"You Can't Be Enemies and Win"

Lee MacPhail, after returning from the owners' meeting, tendered his resignation as general manager to accept a position as assistant to newly appointed Baseball Commissioner William D. "Spike" Eckert, a retired Air Force general. His resignation came amidst a shake-up in the Orioles' front office. In June, Jerold Hoffberger, 46, president of Baltimore's National Brewing Company, whose National Bohemian beer was enjoyed throughout the mid–Atlantic states, and a Baltimore native, had become chairman of the Orioles' Board of Directors and club president. He brought a company executive with him—Frank Cashen as executive vice-president to replace MacPhail. He promoted Harold Dalton, who for five years had directed the operations of the team's seven minor league teams, to director of player personnel.[1] MacPhail stayed on in an advisory capacity until December 15, when Hoffberger threw a champagne-laced going-away party for him.[2]

During the latter part of 1965, MacPhail had established the groundwork for a trade that, when announced, ignited the imagination of Orioles players and fans, black and white alike. World Series fever swept the city. Pre-season ticket sales soared by 150 percent. Las Vegas odds-maker Jimmy "The Greek" Snyder made the Birds 3–1 favorites to win the American League pennant. On December 9, 1965, in a trade that stunned the baseball world, Cincinnati Reds General Manager Bill DeWitt, with 28 years under his belt as either general manager or assistant general manager with the Browns, Yankees, Tigers, and Reds, handed over African American outfielder and slugger extraordinaire, Frank Robinson, 30. The Birds gave up pitcher Milt Pappas, 26, who had amassed an admirable 110–74 won-lost record from 1958 to 1965, relief pitcher Jack Baldschun, and minor league outfielder Dick Simpson. Defending his decision, DeWitt said Pappas would replenish a depleted pitching staff. Asked by reporters why he would trade Robinson who "was only 30," DeWitt infamously replied "Yes, but he's an old 30."[3]

Reds fans referred to DeWitt as "Dim Witt." Black weeklies had a field day. "The Big Wigs of the Cincinnati Reds are either out of their cotton picking minds or just plain daffy," wrote William Jackson, sportswriter for the *Cleveland Call and Post*."[4] The *Pittsburgh Courier* put Robinson in a class with Willie Mays and Hank Aaron "as untouchables—being by far the greatest slugger in the Redlegs 90-year history."[5] "Ordinarily, you don't get rid of a player like this unless he writes dirty words in electric lights on the scoreboard," observed *Chicago Daily Defender* sportswriter A. S.

"Doc" Young.[6] The trade gained renewed notoriety in the 1988 movie *Bull Durham* when Susan Sarandon's character, Annie Savoy, said, "Bad trades are a part of baseball; I mean who can forget Frank Robinson for Milt Pappas, for God's sake?"[7]

Robinson, a native of Beaumont, Texas, grew up in Oakland, California. The youngest of ten children, he developed into a slender, six foot, 180-pounder. His biceps approached the size of duckpin bowling balls. He had won "Rookie of the Year" honors in 1956 and "Sophomore of the Year" in 1957. In 1961 he was named the National League's Most Valuable Player. In ten years with the Reds, Robinson averaged 32 homers and 100 runs batted in a year. He pounded the ball at a .303 clip.[8]

Jerold Hoffberger was the first Orioles executive to demonstrate by his words and actions an understanding of the challenges faced by African American players. The Birds became a truly integrated team and a force to be reckoned with during his ownership of the team from 1965 to 1979 (National Baseball Hall of Fame Library, Cooperstown, New York).

Yet, for all his power, players and fans alike also knew Robinson for his take-no-prisoners approach to the game. He would just as soon take out a second baseman or shortstop at second base to break up a double play as he would be to park a ball in the bleachers. As early as 1961, Philadelphia Phillies manager Gene Mauch fined pitchers for throwing at Robinson. Such tactics only made him more aggressive. Several American League managers followed suit once he arrived in Baltimore. "Pitchers did me a favor when they knocked me down," Robinson said. "It made me more determined. I wouldn't let that pitcher get me out. They say you can't hit if you're on your back. But I didn't hit on my back. I got up."[9]

"Cannons at the corners," exulted Dalton, who drooled over the prospect of Robinson in right field, Brooks Robinson at third base, "Boog" Powell at first base and Curt Blefary in left field.[10] Orioles pitcher Dick Hall shared Dalton's enthusiasm. "We had pretty good pitching, a good infield, and we'd won ninety some games the season before, and we were on our way," Hall said in 2013, "so when Frank came we knew he'd get us over the hump."[11]

Some issues remained, however, before the trade could become final. Along with his baseball credentials, Robinson brought a reputation which gave MacPhail pause during his negotiations with the Reds. A hard-charging player who played through injuries and expected the same of others, Robinson had been the undisputed leader of

The only player in the game's history to be named the Most Valuable Player in both the National and American leagues, Frank Robinson's arrival in Baltimore in 1966 opened the door for more African American players to follow, initiated the team's dominance of the American League for years to come, and helped chip away at the notion shared by many in Baltimore that the O's carried an "anti-us" attitude toward African Americans. He demonstrated his leadership on the field, as both player and manager, in the clubhouse, and in the Orioles' front office (National Baseball Hall of Fame Library, Cooperstown, New York).

the Reds. People knew him as one intense ballplayer. Robinson could be assertive. If he disagreed with a management decision, such as to platoon him against right-handed pitchers or with DeWitt calling him "lazy," he spoke his mind. As a result, articles in the Cincinnati papers implied he could be moody and hard to manage. Echoing Willie Tasby's earlier comments, Robinson told Sam Lacy soon after arriving in Baltimore, "I guess a ballplayer is not supposed to refute anything management says. If you do, you're a trouble maker."[12] He could be cavalier. During a game in his rookie year, May 22, 1956, he figured he would save himself the trouble of running in from the outfield in the bottom of the seventh inning and hung out in the bullpen instead while his mates batted. They did better than he expected. Manager Birdie Tebbetts had to summon him to the plate for his turn at bat. He promptly smashed a home run, his eighth of the season.[13]

The gun episode caused MacPhail the most concern. Robinson had bought an Italian Beretta .25 caliber, a small hand gun, during spring training in 1960. Before marrying his wife, the former Barbara Ann Cole, he carried large amounts of cash and "wanted to feel safe." Following a fight one winter night in 1961 in Cincinnati involving Robinson, two friends and three whites, all patrons of a sandwich shop, the white chef drew his right index finger across his throat while looking at Frank as if to say, "I'll slit your throat." Robinson glared back and yelled, "You wanna fight. Come on!" The chef advanced toward Robinson brandishing a butcher knife. Robinson showed the gun in his left palm. The chef stopped in his tracks and yelled, "Hey, this guy's got a gun!"[14] Someone called the police, who arrested Robinson. He paid a $1,000 bail bond and found his case bound over to the Hamilton County [Ohio] Grand Jury. The jury reduced the charge from a felony to a misdemeanor. Robinson changed his plea from not guilty to guilty for carrying a concealed weapon and paid a $250 fine.[15] "I'm sorry it happened. I want to apologize to baseball fans in general and especially to the young fans," Robinson told the court.[16] MacPhail's concerns faded after he checked with a former colleague, Reds pitching coach Jim Turner, whom MacPhail knew from his Yankees days. Turner gave Robinson a glowing recommendation.[17]

MacPhail left the final decision to Dalton and headed for the commissioner's office. Dalton had similar reservations but overcame them after Orioles scout Jim Russo, who again played a major role in bringing a black player to the team, this time by bringing initial word about the trade possibility from DeWitt to MacPhail, convinced Dalton to overlook the reputation. "Forget about his reputation. Just call DeWitt and make the God-damned deal," Russo urged Dalton.[18]

Before Dalton made the call, Cashen had to deal with Bauer's reservations. Bauer did not want to lose his best pitcher. Nor did he want to break up the team's chemistry. Dalton acknowledged the trade represented a "gamble." Cashen agreed but, in sharp departure from the actions of previous O's executives, thought the gamble should be taken "to change our image, to be a more exciting club, to win more friends in the Negro community. Not at the expense of winning, of course, but it is true we considered these fringe things in making the deal," he told Doug Brown, a reporter for *The Sporting News*.[19] Elaborating on his decision in a 2012 interview, Cashen reiterated that he thought his job included improving the O's image. "Turning down the National League's Most Valuable Player was not the way to go," Cashen said. Having made those decisions, Cashen persuaded Bauer and told Dalton to make the call to DeWitt.[20] The "first Grade A Negro," as *The Sporting News* referred to Robinson, had arrived in Baltimore.[21]

* * *

Like Satchel Paige before him, Robinson arrived in town with some unpleasant memories of Baltimore. The slugger had played pre-season games in Baltimore as a member of the Reds. During his first visit to Baltimore in 1958, he recalled years later, "I went to a movie, put up the money, and the lady threw it back. I put it up again and she threw it back again. She said, 'We don't serve your kind here.' I said, 'I don't want to be served. I just want to see the movie.'"[22] He knew that players could now register at the downtown hotels but "was unsure how my family would be treated." That the trade might attract more black fans to Memorial Stadium sat well with him. He knew that African Americans came to see him in Cincinnati. He told Cashen, though, that he did not want to make appearances before African American groups. "I don't want to be used as a tool,"[23] he said. The new VP honored his request.

Once in the Monument City as an Oriole, Robinson, spurred on by DeWitt's "old 30" comment, was determined to make good in his new setting. DeWitt's choice of words "turned me around as a player and as a person," Robinson told *Sun* reporter Ken Nigro in 1982. "I felt I had something to prove and coming to Baltimore was the turning point in my life."[24]

Frank McDougald remembered Robinson's arrival. McDougald listened to Orioles games on the radio, but did not follow them closely. He did recall, however, "They didn't have many black guys…. Oh, yeah!, Oh, yeah! I'd heard of him," McDougald said of Robinson. "He was a sparkplug, a tremendous player, and he wouldn't take a whole lot of guff from nobody.

I always imagined he probably got in arguments with himself in front of the mirror. I wanted to be like him," McDougald said in 2012.[25]

* * *

Not only had the Orioles' new group of executives brought an African American player of stature to Baltimore, they further distinguished themselves from former O's executives by taking an active interest in him and his family's well-being. Cashen and Dalton personally promised Robinson he would be treated fairly. "We have one set of rules for everyone," they told him over dinner at the Belvedere Hotel soon after his arrival. "That's fine with me," Robinson replied, "but if I find out later that certain guys get privileges, you will have problems."[26] Robinson appreciated Hoffberger's personal touch with him. After a game, Robinson told the audience at his Hall of Fame induction in 1982, "He would come over and slap you on the back and say 'nice game.' ... The first words out of his mouth were 'How are you? How's your family? Is there anything I can do for you?'"[27]

The new Orioles president helped the Robinsons find a house. After Robinson left Baltimore for spring training, Barbara Robinson went house hunting in Baltimore. She immediately came face to face with Baltimore's housing mores. The Robinsons maintained a luxurious year-round home in Los Angeles and had become accustomed to renting homes of their choosing in Cincinnati. Such was not to be in Baltimore. In a telephone call to a John Hopkins University professor with a house to rent, she introduced herself as "Mrs. Barbara Robinson." She told the professor, "my husband plays for the Orioles." When they met, he refused to rent the house to her. "He must have thought," she said, "I was Mrs. *Brooks* Robinson." Similar rebuffs prompted Frank to tell Hoffberger, "If my family can't find a place to live in Baltimore, there's no sense in my tying to play with this ball club." Hoffberger, again taking a novel step for an Orioles executive, personally helped the couple find a house in a black neighborhood, though it needed fumigating. Even with Hoffberger's support, it would take the Robinsons five years to find a house to their liking in Baltimore. That house happened to be in a white neighborhood where the neighbors did not welcome black neighbors. "Black stars were cheered only on the field in Baltimore then," Robinson recalled years later.[28]

* * *

As Frank and Barbara and their two children, Frank Kevin, 3, and infant Nichelle, settled into the new home and Robinson began the 1966 season, the battle for fair housing galvanized city politics and framed Maryland's 1966 gubernatorial campaign. Whites had been fleeing the city in droves for the suburbs since 1954. In the city proper, blockbusting, which took its name from the huge World War II bombs the Allies rained down on German cities, helped along by the *Baltimore Sun* newspapers, did what covenants used to do.[29] Once one block became "broken," i.e., a black family had moved in, the area could be described as "Colored" in the *Sun's* real estate classified ads. The ads panicked many white home-owners into selling, often at significantly below market prices, and joining the white exodus to the suburbs. Realtors then re-sold the homes to African American families, often at inflated prices, reaping handsome profits in the process. The *Sun* refused numerous requests to drop the "Colored" label from the ads. The racial makeup of neighborhoods "was news," contended *Sunpapers* president William F. Schmick, Jr., and know-ing it, he maintained, served the best interests of his readers.[30]

Opposed to Schmick's stance, civil rights groups such as the Congress for Racial Equality (CORE), the Contemporary Trends Housing Commit-tee, and the Negro American Labor Council pressed McKeldin, now Bal-timore's mayor, and city council president, Democrat Thomas D'Alesandro 3rd, son of D'Alesandro, Jr., to get a strong fair housing bill passed by the city council. The two co-sponsored a bill in January 1966, that would ban discrimination in the rental and sale of homes save for two-family homes in which the owner of one home rented out the other.

The tumultuous public hearing on the bill and its aftermath demon-strated just how strongly people felt on both sides of the fair housing issue. More than 2,000 people jammed into a three-hour hearing at the War Memorial Building on January 15. Sixty people spoke for and against the proposal. Cardinal Lawrence Shehan spoke first in favor of the bill. Born in Baltimore in 1898, the son of an operator of a tailors supply business, he graduated from St. Mary's Seminary in Baltimore.[31] In place of the Cardi-nal's resplendent red robes, he wore the plain black garb of a priest that night. Boos, hisses, and catcalls greeted the Cardinal's comments. Other clergy-men received similar treatment. Several in the audience spat at Shehan. Other opponents, led by Robert V. McCurdy of the Real Estate Board of Greater Baltimore, argued, more civilly than some, that the bill, if passed, would deprive all citizens, regardless of race, of their right to manage their property as they please.[32] Police ensured the crowd's and speakers' safety.

Knowing they had the votes to force an immediate vote on the meas-ure rather than keep it in committee, where advocates could add amend-ments, council members opposed to the bill yanked it out of committee at the council's meeting two days later. A bitter debate ensued. Councilman John A. Pica compared the bill to "Hitler in 1938 and Fidel Castro now." "The bigots of yesterday are in here as the liberals of today," he yelled across the chamber. Councilman Reuben Caplan, who favored the bill, said he resented the implication that he belonged to the "lunatic fringe." Once the speeches and accusations subsided, the council killed the bill by a 13–8 vote.[33]

Baltimore residents weighed in. Jimmer M. Leonard applauded the council's vote. "Government control over private property is appropriate in a Fascist or Communist country, not in the United States," he wrote to the *Sun*'s editor. Evelyn Frick, making a case for ecumenical racism, took the *Sun*'s "biased reporting" to task for not mentioning that participants, herself included, had booed all clergymen, not just Cardinal Shehan. Beverly S. Moe, in her letter to the editor, acknowledged that prejudices of all kinds exist but "cannot be eliminated through laws, because no one can legislate love."[34] Three days later McKeldin called on "all responsible citizens to dissociate themselves from this wretched affair so we can wipe off the stain that a witless and unruly few have put upon us."[35]

Baltimore's finest managed to prevent any physical outburst during the contentious hearing, but burgeoning complaints of police brutality toward African Americans had prompted Democrat Governor J. Millard Tawes to call for Police Commissioner Bernard Schmidt's resignation in January 1966. A 600-page report by the National Association of Chiefs of Police had found the department failed to investigate citizen complaints thoroughly, maintain internal discipline, and establish a viable program of community and public relations. "This report points clearly to the need for a new police commissioner and upper echelons of management," the report concluded. Tawes favored relaxing the law that required a person to have lived or worked in the city for three years prior to being appointed commissioner.[36] In September, the governor appointed Donald D. Pomerleau, former Public Safety Director in Miami, Florida, and Kingsport, Tennessee, to the commissioner's position. Pomerleau set out to modernize and professionalize the force.[37]

During Tawes' search for Schmidt's successor, CORE, which had been active in Baltimore for several years, in mid–April declared Baltimore its "target city" for 1966. "Why us?" asked a puzzled McKeldin, a perennial favorite with Baltimore's African Americans. "Because," Floyd B. McKissick, CORE's national director, replied, "Baltimore is segregated in all areas. Unless someone does something positive, segregation is never going to be changed."[38] CORE made open housing its top priority.

In mid–May CORE took to the streets. Members picketed the segregated, luxury Horizon House Apartments. The complex featured a rooftop pool, sauna, 24-hour secretarial service, restaurant, pharmacy, valet, and hairdresser. The Ku Klux Klan set up a counter-protest. Dressed in colored robes, they carried signs attached to extra-heavy, wooden sticks, shouted racial epithets, and led German Shepherd dogs on leashes. Hearing that CORE planned to demonstrate until the Horizon House integrated, the Klansmen vowed to return the following week with double their number. A mostly silent crowd of 200 people looked on while police stood nearby.[39]

A week later, McKeldin had verbal promises from nine luxury apartment building owners to integrate their properties on the condition that all nine apartment owners sign on. Like the restaurant owners before them, no one owner wanted to go it alone. CORE said they would stop picketing pending the outcome of McKeldin's efforts. The Klan promised to demonstrate only if CORE did. Three weeks later McKeldin had written pledges to integrate from all nine owners.[40] Subsequent efforts by CORE and McKeldin to elicit voluntary integration from nine more luxury apartments failed, but the governor and CORE kept talking.[41]

Demonstrations, like those at Horizon House, had so far been free of violence. That changed on July 28, 1966, at "an anti–Negro rally" sponsored by the States Rights Party. Connie Lynch, 53, from California and spokesperson for the States Rights Party, set up a sound truck outside Patterson Park. In invective directed at a crowd of over 1,000, mostly white teenagers, Lynch accused Supreme Court justices of treason and said they should be hanged. McKeldin, in his words, "was a super pompous jackassie Nigger-lover."[42] Police broke up a group of whites who shoved black bystanders. Some white youths broke away and entered a black neighborhood, where they were met with a hail of bricks, stones, and bottles. Two required hospitalization. Some whites and police officers traded blows. Officers in helmets and plastic face shields, reinforced by dogs, subdued the fighting. The courts indicted Lynch and four others on charges of rioting and incitement to riot. James Pettyman, of the Civil Interest Group, advised members to buy guns. Not that he advocated shooting whites, Pettyman told his members, but he advised them, in case of a repeat of the Patterson Park fracas, "you know what to do."[43]

* * *

The housing issue dominated the 1966 Democratic gubernatorial primary. Voters had several choices. U.S. Representative Carlton B. Sickles, strongly supported open housing. Thomas B. Finan, Maryland's Attorney

General, promised to put blacks into high state government positions and make inroads into employment, schools, police conduct, and welfare. Clarence Miles entered the race but few gave him much of a chance. George P. Mahoney, a real estate developer and frequent but unsuccessful seeker of elected office, opposed open housing. The youngest of 11 children and the son of an Irish police officer in East Baltimore, Mahoney ran on his infamous slogan "Your home is your castle, protect it!" Many perceived his slogan as racist and divisive. James H. (Jack) Pollack, head of the city's most powerful political association, backed Mahoney.[44]

The perennial candidate (Mahoney ran for senator or governor and lost ten times), who had predicted a 50,000-vote margin of victory, squeaked by Sickles by less than 2,000 votes out of half a million cast. In the all-white suburb of Essex, Mahoney led the vote count by 10–1. In the city, Mahoney prevailed in Polish, Italian, Irish, German, and Bohemian wards. Sickles carried the mostly Jewish neighborhoods. Sickles led Mahoney by 7,000 votes before the Baltimore vote count had been completed. He deemed "the Negro vote" in Baltimore "very disappointing."[45] Finan finished third and Miles a distant fourth. Mahoney would face Baltimore native and Baltimore County Executive Spiro Theodore Agnew in the general election. Agnew favored open housing but only for new developments.

The gloves came off early and stayed off. The principals shed any pretense of decorum. At a Baltimore County rally, Mahoney referred to Agnew as "that big slob." Explaining why he would not join Agnew and Hyman A. Pressman, a Jewish independent candidate and Comptroller of Baltimore City, in a televised debate, Mahoney told a crowd he "wouldn't dare go on television with those two nuts."[46] Mahoney referred to some of Agnew's backers as "Greek millionaires." Agnew was the son of a Greek immigrant.[47] Agnew pounded Mahoney as "a menace to the state representing a two pronged devil's pitchfork of bigotry and incompetence."[48] "Now," Agnew proclaimed at every stop, "is not the time to let George do it."[49]

Mahoney hired sound trucks to broadcast his slogan state-wide. His message hit home with a white Baltimore cab driver who told *Post* reporter Dessoff he favored Mahoney. "He'll keep the _____ in their place." Asked what else he knew about Mahoney, the driver responded "Know? What's to know? Mahoney. Mahoney. That's all I know." A middle-aged white woman in Baltimore's affluent Homewood neighborhood made the same choice. "We've lived here 19 years. We don't want any trouble. What would you do?"[50] she asked Dessoff.

African American Assemblyman Clarence M. Mitchell III, the nation's youngest black legislator when elected in 1963, organized a drive to get Baltimore's blacks to the polls. He urged blacks and Jews to support Agnew. Had Mahoney not been in the race, Mitchell and his followers would have supported Pressman, a strong advocate for open housing and a popular figure among Jews and blacks. Concern that Pressman and Agnew might split the vote, enabling Mahoney to win, prompted Mitchell's move. The *AFRO*, normally Democratic leaning, endorsed Agnew. Mitchell did not ask the city's most popular Republican, Mayor McKeldin, for assistance. He feared that while the mayor could wrap up the black vote, his role in doing so might further alienate whites, to Mahoney's benefit.[51]

African American the Rev. Herbert O. Edwards, retiring director of the State Interracial Commission, contributed to the campaign's intensity. He delivered a stinging and bitter statement just days before taking a similar position in Rhode Island. In a late October press conference he blamed Tawes, McKeldin, the press, moderate black leaders and African Americans in general for the lack of civil rights progress. He singled out Mahoney and his slogan, calling it "an indefensible attempt to inflame the passions of the people for selfish ends, and just as lawless as the act of a rioter in Watts (a black community in Los Angeles, California) or someone who snatches a purse in East Baltimore."[52]

Agnew won the election handily, beating Mahoney by 82,000 votes out of over 900,000 cast. The Republican governor-elect's margin of victory, in a state where Democrats held a 3-to-1 edge in voter registration, demonstrated the limited state-wide appeal of Mahoney's message. In Baltimore Agnew beat Mahoney 47 percent to 37 percent, with Pressman getting the remaining 16 percent. Mahoney, true to predictions, outpolled Agnew in suburban Baltimore County, 47 percent to 39 percent.[53]

* * *

While the campaigns raged on, the 1966 season got under way. Some wondered if the African American slugger would clash with the O's on-field leader, 11-year veteran Brooks Robinson, who won the American League MVP Award in 1964. The third baseman hailed from rigidly segregated Little Rock, Arkansas. He described his "culture shock" to *Sun* reporter Alan Goldstein upon arriving in York, Pennsylvania, fresh out of high school to join the York White Roses in 1955. "I'd never competed with or against a black in my life before," he said.[54] Robinson had, however, played playground ball against black teams in Little Rocks as a kid. According to his childhood friend Buddy Rotenberry, Brooks was "friendly with the black kids, the same as with everyone else."[55] Being friendly, however, didn't blind him to the realities of segregation in Little Rock. In 1957, two years after he graduated from Little Rock Central High School, President Dwight D. Eisenhower ordered U.S. Army troops to escort nine black students into the school. More than 1,000 angry whites shouted their disapproval. "It was quite a traumatic experience for my younger brother [Gary]," Robinson recalled.[56]

Those concerned about a clash between the two Robinsons need not have worried. Brooks had lent a helping hand to Bob Boyd and Connie Johnson. "Those fellows," said Troy Bailey, now a Maryland State Delegate, who himself helped black players when they arrived in town, "loved Brooks. He did more to make it easier for them than anyone else."[57] Pope concurred. "He was a friend to all of us on the team. Something the blacks really appreciated in those days."[58] Quay Rich, an African American who would later help integrate the Orioles' front office staff, had fond memories of Brooks as a teenager. Waiting for player autographs with friends after a game at Memorial Stadium, Rich told an interviewer, "Frank would just push right by us on his way to his car. Blair signed some and so did Boog [Powell, first baseman and outfielder]. But Brooks," Rich said with admiration, "now he was just like family. He signed 'em all."[59]

Frank Robinson credited Brooks with helping him and his family feel comfortable. "He," Robinson wrote in his autobiography, "made it a lot easier for me to adjust to playing in Baltimore."[60] The two had lockers next to each other and never exchanged a cross word. Robinson remembered that Brooks "never really invited me but, on road trips, he often asked where I was going after the game. I'd say I wasn't sure and he'd say 'some of us are going to so and so restaurant.'" Paul Blair and Sam Bowens, the only other blacks on team in 1966, and Frank Robinson often ate with Brooks and other teammates at the restaurants Brooks mentioned.[61] At home, Frank Robinson recalled less mingling. "White and black players never got together at home," he said. "Not once did we have a meal together in a Baltimore restaurant or get together at a player's home. The O's were close but not that close."[62]

Paul Blair recalled the situation differently. Some players, white and black, gathered to play cards together occasionally at one another's homes as "we didn't have the money to eat out," he said. But regardless of who socialized with whom, Blair stressed that "As a matter of fact, from 1964 [when Blair first joined the O's] on there were no problems. We were a team. We mingled. There was no separation. It wasn't allowed. Bauer told us 'you can't be enemies and win.' If you weren't part of the family they just got rid of you. We had one rule. If you can't swing you ain't staying. If you can play you can stay no matter what color you are, black, green, purple, yellow." Blair also remembered, "You couldn't wait to get to the park every day 'cause we won. I liked my teammates. I liked the atmosphere. I liked the fans."[63]

For his part, Frank Robinson, a self-described loner, decided to loosen up with his new teammates. "I wasn't," he said, "going to stop knocking the shortstop off his butt when sliding into second," but he did decide to be more outgoing, relax a bit, and smile more.[64] His teammates liked the new persona. Nicknames sprouted in the clubhouse. Frank's skinny legs earned him the moniker "Pencil." Players knew reliever Eddie Watt as "Squatty Body." Pitcher Moe "The Footer" Drabowsky kept players guessing by giving everyone, including owner Jerry Hoffberger, a "hot foot" and scaring people with snakes, real and plastic. Frank Robinson, with a mop on his head, presided over a "Kangaroo Court" in the locker room after every win. There he levied small fines to mates who made a bad play. He proclaimed later, "So I was the leader of the Orioles on the field and in the clubhouse."[65]

He also led the way in ribbing players. He mocked Boog Powell for having the legs of an elephant and for being named after a piece of snot, and nicknamed him Crisco for his large size. "Robby" referred to certain white players as "pale face." Brooks Robinson, whom players nicknamed "Brooks McKeldin" for his welcoming efforts toward Frank, Bowens, and Blair, recalled, "we were pretty open about things. We got on one another and everyone had a

Sam Bowens, one of the early African American outfielders for the Orioles. He played for the team from 1963 to 1967 before playing for the Senators in 1968–1969. He had his best season in 1964, when he batted .263 with 22 home runs and 71 RBI (National Baseball Hall of Fame Library, Cooperstown, New York).

good time."[66] 1966 was a threshold year for integration among the Orioles, players as well as executives.

* * *

On the field in 1966, Frank Robinson was all business. He not only led the O's, but the entire American League, in batting average (.316), home runs (49), runs batted in (122), slugging average (.637), and, for good measure, total bases (367). He showed power never before seen in Baltimore. On May 8, 1966, in the second game of a doubleheader against the Cleveland Indians with Luis Tiant on the mound, he became the first and only player to hit a fair ball out of Memorial Stadium, "451 feet on the fly, 540 feet on the roll."[67]

Led by Robinson, Bauer's Orioles won the American League pennant

in a walk, finishing nine games ahead of the Minnesota Twins. They swept the World Series in four straight games against the Los Angeles Dodgers, who boasted eventual Hall of Fame pitchers Sandy Koufax and Don Drysdale.

Meanwhile in Cincinnati, Milt Pappas turned in a so-so 12–11 record for the Reds, who fell from fourth place in 1965 to seventh in 1966. DeWitt continued to swing in effigy in the Queen City.

* * *

Throughout the World Series, Birds fans crowded into Al Kirson's Bar to watch the action. Mrs. Jamie Cope and her husband, a Johns Hopkins University professor, cheered from bar stools. Retired Navy veteran Dick Ambose kept saying "They're fabulous. They really are." John Wascavage

Paul Blair camps under Los Angeles Dodger Lou Johnson's fly ball to end Game 4 of the 1966 World Series and give the Orioles their first World Championship (National Baseball Hall of Fame Library, Cooperstown, New York).

posted the game totals on the bar's chalkboard. Sparrows Point steel worker Bill Russell displayed his ticket to Game 5, saying "They gotta lose one." A Frank Robinson triple moved one patron to exclaim "Man, that Robinson!"[68]

Had Robinson, Blair, or Bowens—the O's only African Americans, the fewest carried on any major league team that year and, again, all outfielders—wanted to join in the merriment at Kirson's, Jim Crow customs would have stopped them at the door. The same fate would have befallen the eight African Americans on the Dodgers' roster. McKeldin pleaded with tavern owners to serve African Americans during the Series. "I find it a distasteful piece of irony," he said, "that I must make this plea in the light of the fact that without Frank Robinson we would probably have no World Series."[69] Chamber of Commerce President L. Mercer Smith joined with McKeldin, warning that "any unpleasant incidents will be magnified many times by the news media, giving the entire nation a false impression of Baltimore."[70] "How can the truth give a false impression?" wondered the Rev. Herbert O. Edwards. "It would just show people what Baltimore really is."[71] The Liquor Commission ignored the governor's plea.

Sam Lacy underscored the irony of black players bringing glory to Baltimore while being shunned by its white citizens. "Unfortunately," Lacy wrote, "ours is a 'capital' where Frank Robinson can win the all-round championship, yet cannot buy a home to his liking; where Sam Bowens cannot send his children to play or swim in certain areas, and where Paul Blair needs a special plea from the mayor to spare his friends embarrassment in establishments not forced by law to serve them."[72] Complexion still trumped skill in Baltimore.

Jim Crow made an unfortunate appearance on the field at the end of Game 4. Immediately after Blair's routine catch of the Dodgers' Lou Johnson's fly ball to give the O's their first world championship in modern times, police and stadium personnel could be seen pushing, grabbing, and roughing up African American children as young as ten to 12. The kids had raced onto the field along with hundreds of other fans. No one else received similar treatment. "There was," said Bijan Bayne, a baseball historian who reviewed videos of the scene, "no reason to put their hands on those kids."[73]

The Series did, however, give Blair a chance to even the score with a restaurant in a hotel where he had been refused service two years earlier. Frank Peters, a white teammate of Blair's in Elmira and working out with the O's but not on the roster,[74] suggested they eat there one September evening in 1964. Once inside, "this guy comes over and tells me I can't eat here," Blair said. "'We don't serve blacks.'" After Blair's 430-foot, solo shot off Dodgers pitcher Claude Osteen gave the Birds all the runs they needed to win Game 3 of the Series, the same restaurant invited him to sign autographs for a $1,000 fee. "I refused," Blair said. "I wouldn't go in there."[75]

* * *

Frank Robinson found himself showered with many honors before and after the Series. A week before the Series started, McKeldin led 200 to 300 fans and neighbors in a celebration on the street where the Robinsons lived, Cederdale Road. The governor renamed the street Robinson Road but only for the day, as another Robinson Road already existed.[76] McKeldin failed in his attempt to have the Park Board name a city park after Robinson. Concerned about encouraging a steady stream of such requests, Board President Samuel Hopkins explained that while the Board admired Robinson greatly, similar requests to name a park after Johnny Unitas and Babe Ruth had been denied. "If we start this," said board member Mrs. M. Richard Farring, "we'll have many, many similar requests."[77]

The Baseball Writers' Association of American made him the unanimous choice for MVP in the American League. No other player before or since has won baseball's highest accolade in both leagues. The Triple Crown went to Robinson for leading the league in batting average, runs batted in, and home runs. In 1956 Mickey Mantle had been the last player to take both the Triple Crown and MVP honors in the same year. Only two other players have repeated the feat. Carl Yastrzemski, Hall of Fame outfielder for the Boston Red Sox, won both the following season, 1967. Forty-five years later Miguel Cabrera, a native of Venezuela, captured both honors in 2012 with the Detroit Tigers. Not to be overlooked was the red, convertible Corvette he won as the most outstanding player in the Series for belting two homers off Don Drysdale, the first non-pitcher to win the award in six years.[78]

"The first one is always a big thrill," Robinson told reporters in November at the Hotel New Yorker by telephone from his home in Los Angeles. "But this [his second MVP award] is even bigger than the first one. I'm the first player to do it in two leagues. It's something that's never been done before."[79] It has never been done since. The MVP plaque pleased Frank's wife Barbara as well. "He's happy. I'm happy and the children are happy. The year can end tonight," she told Sam Lacy in November.[80]

The year did not end then nor did the honors. Robinson won the Hickok Belt,™ awarded annually to the top professional athlete of all sports, as voted on by a panel of 300 sportswriters across the country.[81] The

National Newspapers Publishers Association (representing more than 100 African American newspapers) in March 1967 named Robinson one of eight winners of the Russwurm Award, named for John B. Russwurm, founder of the nation's first black newspaper, *Freedom's Journal*, in 1821. The association gave the award annually to those it deemed to "enrich the democratic concept or uphold the high traditions of the American way of life." Other recipients included Massachusetts U.S. Senator Edward Brooke, the nation's first black U.S. senator since Reconstruction; Charles Evers, Mississippi's field director for the NAACP, who led the civil rights efforts in that state before being felled by a sniper's bullet; Bill Cosby and Robert Culp for co-starring in the TV show *I Spy*, which enabled Cosby to break through the barrier that kept blacks from star roles on network television; U.S. Commissioner of Education Harold Howe II, for his support of desegregating public schools; Mr. and Mrs. Stephen R. Currier, for contributing millions of dollars to civil rights causes; and Charles L. Weltner, a former Georgia congressman who declined to run for re-election rather than support fellow Democrat Lester Maddox for governor.[82] A picture of Maddox and several friends wielding axe handles to turn three black activists away from his restaurant in 1964 cemented his reputation as a die-hard segregationist.

Awash in honors for his remarkable accomplishments and pleased to have been treated well on the banquet circuit where, he told *Sun* reporter Doug Brown, "I encountered no racial prejudice," Baltimore's pre-eminent professional athlete could still not escape discrimination in the city's housing market. After the house he had rented was sold, a friend looked for another house for the Robinson family. Only after many people with a house to rent declined upon learning who would occupy it, saying they "had to think about their neighbors," did the Robinsons find a house. "It doesn't matter what you do," Robinson said, "they just look at the color of your skin."[83]

CHAPTER 8

"Love Time Is Here"

"Forgettable" best describes the O's 1967 season. Expectations ran high all winter for, if not a repeat world championship, at least for a serious run for the pennant. Bauer's charges, however, fell flat. They failed to break the .500 mark and dropped to sixth place in the standings. Frank Robinson, Blair, and Brooks Robinson continued to anchor the team but none had the success at the plate they had the year before. Bowens saw limited duty. Bauer shuttled two African American rookie outfielders, Curt Motton and Dave May, between Rochester and Baltimore. Motton managed only a .200 average while May did slightly better at .235. Neither could stem the O's slide. Bauer called McGuire up from Rochester for two weeks in July to fill in for shortstop Mark Belanger during his Air National Guard duty. McGuire, a veteran of seven-and-one-half years in the minors, and who had four at bats with the O's in 1962, played ten games at short-stop. He became the first African American infielder to play in ten games for the O's since Bob Boyd alternated between first base and the outfield from 1956 to 1960.[1]

* * *

While fans continued to see few African Americans at Memorial Stadium, the first effort to break up baseball's all-white culture above the playing field surfaced in November 1967. Cleveland Browns running back Jim Brown, considered by many to be one of the best football players ever to don a helmet, held two meetings in November, one in Miami and one in New York City. African American athletes from professional baseball, football, and basketball attended. Brown's objective was "to have each club name a Negro to an executive position at the assistant general manager level." At the time there were none in major league baseball. *Cincinnati Post and Times Star* sportswriter Earl Lawson, reporting from the major league baseball winter meetings in Mexico City, said no one in the commissioner's office had any comment, and that "a lot of top club officials, alarmed and resentful, are doing a lot of talking among themselves." Orioles VP Harry Dalton said he knew nothing about the meetings. Baseball Commissioner Spike Eckert did promise to hire an African American as a liaison between the Commissioner's office and black players.[2] A year later, true to his word, he appointed Monte Irvin, Negro leagues star and Hall of Fame outfielder with the New York Giants, to a new position, assistant director of promotions and public relations for baseball.[3] Irvin would be the sole African American in the commissioner's office until Bowie Kuhn, Eckert's successor, added Emmett Ashford, baseball's first African American umpire, to the public relations staff in 1971. Irvin and Ashford served together until Ashford's death in 1980. Nothing more came of Brown's efforts, but the issue was far from dead.

* * *

Opening Day 1968 took a back seat to a national tragedy. On Thursday evening, April 4, a single bullet from a 30.06 Remington pump-action rifle fired by James Earl Ray, a white drifter and ex-convict, killed Dr. Martin Luther King, Jr., as he stood on a balcony outside Room 306 of the Lorraine Motel in Memphis, Tennessee. King had gone to Memphis to lead a protest of striking sanitation workers, mostly African Americans. King's assassination from an ambush by a white man burst the boil of anger and frustration that had increasingly festered among African Americans nationwide and a growing number of whites since his "I Have a Dream" speech five years earlier.

The fight for civil rights had picked up considerable steam in the early 1960s, much of it under King's leadership. Freedom Riders, in the face of violence and physical harm, challenged the South's ban on mixed groups riding on interstate busses even though the Supreme Court had ruled such bans unconstitutional in *Irene Morgan v. Commonwealth of Virginia* (1946) and *Boynton v. Virginia* (1960). In January 1963, newly elected Alabama Governor George C. Wallace declared in his inaugural address, delivered at the state capitol in Montgomery, "I draw the line in the dust and toss the gauntlet before the feet of tyranny, and I say segregation now, segregation tomorrow, and segregation forever."[4] In May, pictures of children being attacked by police dogs, high-pressure water hoses, and electric prods under the orders of Birmingham's ironically titled Director of Public Safety, Bull Conner, sickened millions across the country.[5] Helmeted Mississippi state troopers carrying riot guns and nightsticks in

Jackson beat over 600 school children before hauling them off to jail in garbage trucks. The students were conducting sit-ins and prayer sessions.[6] Birmingham again made national headlines when, in September 1963, just a month after King's speech, four young girls died in a dynamite bomb explosion. White men had hidden the bomb in the 10th Street Baptist Church.[7] On March 7, 1965, Wallace ordered state troopers to stop people, "using all necessary means," attempting to march from Selma, Alabama, to Montgomery to protest to Wallace the denial of voting rights. Using bullwhips, lengths of rope, and tear gas, the troopers stopped the march and inflicted broken arms and legs and severe head gashes on 50–60 of the marchers.[8]

Baltimore saw many civil rights demonstrations during the same period. Activists frequently picketed amusement parks, taverns, restaurants, and apartment houses. Fortunately, while tensions between whites and blacks remained high, McKeldin and other civic leaders were able to maintain an uneasy calm during 1966–1967 in the city that had been spared the violence like that occurring in Mississippi and Alabama. McKeldin used a style all his own. He showed up everywhere in the city, campaigning for racial justice. Dressed immaculately and stepping out of his city-owned limousine, he'd wade into crowds of blacks with a disarming grin, a pumping handshake, and the greeting he offered to every black man, "Hello, my brother." He called a spade a spade. He derided Lynch's Patterson Park speech as "a name calling, disruptive, un–American tirade."[9]

Photographs of Dr. King lying in a pool of his own blood pierced the calm. Rioting in Baltimore broke out at 5:30 p.m. the next night, Friday, April 5, in "the Gay Street ghetto area," quickly spread throughout African American neighborhoods and spilled into other parts of the city.[10] Three days of rioting and looting, mostly by young African Americans, left six dead and more than 600 people injured. Rioters set 1,150 fires. More than 5,000 people were arrested, mostly for curfew violations. Over 11,000 U.S. Army and National Guard troops and city and state policemen struggled to contain the violence.[11]

Two Orioles players served with National Guard units, shortstop Mark Belanger with the Maryland Air National Guard in Baltimore, and relief pitcher Pete Richert in Washington, D.C., where he had pitched for the Senators the previous three seasons.[12] The rioting made a distinct impression on the pitcher. "I saw some things you wouldn't believe," the lefty told *Sun* reporter Lou Hatter. "The burning, the looting the violence … two entire streets of 15 blocks and another 22 blocks of streets were leveled. It was an awful thing. Firemen would be fighting fires and there were these arsonists throwing Molotov cocktails at the fire trucks. I feel sick just thinking about it." Richert added, "there had been some hand-to-hand exchanges," but declined to elaborate.[13]

King's death found the O's in Atlanta at the start of a three-game exhibition series against the Braves to wrap up spring training. Even though news of King's death had reached his home town well before game time, the O's and the Braves played on Friday. The O's won, 4–3, in ten innings. Reporter Jim Hennenman, in Atlanta to cover the games, recalled sitting at the bar in a restaurant after the game. The mood in the city was, he said, "surprisingly calm." He had a sense the mood would soon change. After someone in the restaurant announced that King was dead, "the band," Hennenman remembered, "started to play *Dixie*. That crossed the line," he said, "and I thought it a good idea to get back to my hotel."[14] A forecast for near-freezing temperatures and a soggy field resulting from an overnight downpour, coupled with the realization that "the emotional climate [in Atlanta] may have been considered potentially hazardous for public assembly," as *Sun* reporter Lou Hatter put it, forced cancelation of Saturday night's game.[15] After President Lyndon Johnson declared Sunday a national day of mourning, all major league teams canceled their Sunday exhibition games.[16]

Word of rioting in Baltimore quickly reached Atlanta. "I heard somebody yell, 'My God, Baltimore is burning!'" Jerry Sachs, who had left the Orioles for a front office position with the Braves, recalled in 2012. "My wife and our two young children were in Baltimore visiting with my parents. The O's said I could ride to Baltimore on their plane that night. My wife couldn't pick me up because no one was allowed into the airport." Lou Hatter took Sachs to his house. Sach's wife picked him up the next morning on the way to look at his parents' store, The Doll and Hat Shoppe, a millinery store that specialized in women's hats and gloves, located on Gay Street north of Blair Market. The Shoppe was like most businesses attacked by the rioters, small stores and shops owned by whites who lived in other parts of the city. "The windows had been broken," Sachs recalled, "but everything else was intact. It was an absolutely eerie experience going down there and seeing National Guardsmen with rifles on the roofs of buildings all along Gay Street; very frightening!"[17]

It would take the city years to recover from the effects of the riot, a process made more difficult by Governor Agnew's public castigation of leading African Americans. Eighty African American leaders had accepted an invitation from Agnew, extended, ironically, a day before the riots began, to meet "to discuss steps to be taken to guard against rioting in Baltimore." He wanted to prevent riots from occurring in Baltimore like those the summer before in Detroit and Newark. His effort blew up in his face.

The governor charged those at the meeting with disunity for "breaking and running" in the face of criticism from younger black militants. He blamed civil rights activist Stokely Carmichael for urging the rioters on. "The looting and rioting," Agnew told the increasingly angered group, "did not occur by chance. It's no mere coincidence," he continued, "that a national disciple of violence, Mr. Stokely Carmichael, was observed meeting with local black power advocates and known criminals in Baltimore" on April 3, 1968, three days before the Baltimore riots began. Several in the audience stood up and shouted, "Let's have a black caucus" and "It's an insult." "He's got to be out of his mind," Troy Bailey said on his way out of the room."[18]

* * *

The riots and Agnew's ham-handed response underscored the need to address issues of concern to blacks. Lack of adequate housing had long been a sore spot for African American ball players, including switch-hitting Don Buford, born in Linden, Texas, and raised in Los Angeles. Like Barbara and Frank Robinson three years earlier, Buford found "It was hard for a black athlete to find a place to live in Baltimore." He and his wife "did not find anything appealing to rent through the listings in the paper." After many fruitless inquiries they found an apartment on Cold Spring Lane, not far from Memorial Stadium, only because a woman whom he knew had moved into her mother's house after her mother died. The infielder and his wife "ate mostly at home," but when they did eat out they did so at "minority restaurants in the black part of town."[19]

The Maryland Assembly had passed a fair housing act in March 1967, but it was full of exceptions. The legislation excluded single houses built by an owner or sold by the last occupant, developments which acquired their building permit before June 1 (the date the act was scheduled to take effect), condominiums and cooperative apartments, and multiple-unit developments of 12 or fewer units if the developer occupied one of the units. Not until Congress passed the 1968 Fair Housing Act on April 10, 1968, only six days after Dr. King's assassination, did Baltimore have a fair housing law with any substance. The federal act exempted only owners of single-family homes who rented or sold their home without using a broker and without relying on discriminatory advertising.

Four of Maryland's eight congressmen opposed the measure. On the day before the vote, Hervey Machen, representing Southern Maryland, and Rogers Morton, representing the Eastern Shore, spoke out against the bill. Machen pronounced himself "disgusted with the rioters and looters." Morton intoned, "If civil disobedience becomes a legislative lobby, there are parallels in history—the fall of the Roman Empire and the establishment of the police state." None of Baltimore's three congressmen publically tipped their hand beforehand, but two voted no, Edward Garmatz and George Fallon. Samuel Friedel voted "aye."[20]

The newly passed laws did little, however, to stem whites' prejudice against blacks. Complaints charging discrimination against African Americans seeking to rent or purchase a home or apartment were commonplace and on the rise. Lack of city funds to enforce the laws and complicated procedures resulted in few fines or convictions. "We should have four times as many housing investigators," complained Treadwell O. Phillips, executive director of the state's Human Relations Commission, the agency responsible for investigating all claims of bias.[21] By July 1972, only four of 200 housing complaints had been settled, by which time those filing the complaints had found other accommodations.[22]

At the same time, Jews continued to experience housing discrimination due to what writer Antero Pietila, a native of Finland and *Sun* reporter who spent 30 years covering the city's neighborhoods, politics, and government, called Baltimore's "embedded aversion" to Jews. The aversion took the form of a three-tiered housing market in the city. In the early 1970s, most cities had two well-developed housing markets, one for whites and one for blacks. Baltimore, however, still maintained a three-tiered system. The third catered to Jews through a separate multiple-listing service.[23]

* * *

Segregation still held sway in the schools as well. The National Education Association (NEA) in Washington, D.C., took the School Board to task in April for its "tragic neglect" of inner city schools. The NEA called for a crash program "to eliminate ancient and dangerous buildings and unproductive courses." A Johns Hopkins University report in September 1967 concluded that "virtually all progress made in de-segregation has been wiped out by re-segregation," caused largely by white flight and a proliferation of private schools.[24] Little happened on the federal level until February 1974, when the Department of Health, Education, and Welfare

(HEW) gave the city a month to come up with a plan to do away with "the clear vestiges of a dual school system" or lose millions of dollars in federal aid.

School Superintendent Roland N. Patterson, 44, a Washington, D.C., native, the eighth superintendent in nine years and the city's first African American superintendent, had not waited for HEW's warning. He initiated far-reaching changes immediately following his 1973 appointment. The new superintendent replaced the system's monolithic top-down structure with nine school districts, each with its own superintendent. He abolished the 19 jobs directly below his, telling those now jobless that they would have to compete with candidates from across the country for their old jobs. Patterson re-assigned another 200 administrators. He ordered all instructional personnel, coaches, shop and music teachers, and guidance counselors, in addition to classroom teachers, to provide reading instruction.[25] His efforts did not sit well with John Waters, president of the school administrators union. Flabbergasted and upset by Patterson's bold moves, Waters criticized Patterson "for not doing it in what we call the Baltimore way. It is being rammed down our throats," he complained.[26]

Patterson's bussing plan, endorsed by HEW, engendered more howls of protests from whites. Parent Betty Wiley denounced the plan for placing children "in high crime areas." Councilman John A. Schaefer, who earlier had urged the Board to refuse federal funds if the system had to comply with de-segregation, now questioned HEW's authority to enforce the plan. Others denounced HEW as "an enemy of the people" and labeled the plan "communistic" and "un–American." Some saw the plan as a slippery slope, fearing the plan's "infringement on civil liberties" would soon spread to religion and employment. Several city politicians, including Mayor Donald Schaefer, who hoped for smooth opening of schools in September, urged acceptance of the plan.[27]

Schools opened on schedule in September 1974, but with spotty attendance. Patterson met with Schaefer on Labor Day as pickets surrounding City Hall called for an end to bussing. The two men accomplished nothing and ended up shouting at each other.[28]

Patterson's style rankled not only Schaefer and Waters but the School Board that had hired him as well. In May 1975, the Board met to dismiss him. Patterson's supporters in the audience accused white members of being racists. Before a motion could be made to fire him, supporters flooded the stage, ripped out microphones, and pounded on tables. The meeting ended on that chaotic note.[29] Patterson kept his job until the July meeting when, by a 7–2 vote, the Board fired Patterson, ending 12 months of battles with racial overtones between the superintendent and the Board. The Board appointed Dr. John Larry Crew, a member of Paterson's staff and an African American, to replace Patterson.[30]

Crew enjoyed a smoother tenure than Patterson largely because he replaced bussing with "attendance zones," a gerrymandering procedure used to make schools as integrated as possible without bussing. HEW reduced its pressure for de-segregating the schools, concluding that substantial racial balance had been achieved given the city's highly segregated housing patterns and the lack of bussing.[31]

* * *

Inside the confines of Memorial Stadium, smoother progress toward integration was being made. The O's, as did all major league teams, opened their 1968 season on April 10, a day later than scheduled out of respect for Dr. King's funeral held the day before in Atlanta. Twenty-two thousand fans, 17,000 fewer than attended the previous year's opener, filed into Memorial Stadium to see the Birds beat the Oakland Athletics 3–1. *Sun* reporter Robert A. Erlandson, with smoke and tear gas still in the air, pointed out that "three of the first four Orioles at bat got on base and all were Negroes, Don Buford, Paul Blair, and Frank Robinson, while first baseman Boog Powell, who is white, drove Buford home with the season's first run." Erlandson reported he overheard a fan remark, "That's the way it should be all the time. What a difference in here and out there on the streets."[32]

Don Buford split his playing time between the infield and the outfield. With Boog Powell at first, Davey Johnson at second, Mark Belanger at short, and eight-time Gold Glove Award winner Brooks Robinson at the hot corner, Buford said his infield play consisted of "spelling Brooks and Mark once in awhile."[33] In a major step toward integrating the team, rookie catcher Elrod (Ellie) Hendricks, a native of the Virgin Islands who had played minor league ball in Mexico, became the O's first catcher of color. Hendricks would share playing time with Andy Etchebarren for the next eight seasons. Dave May and Curt Motton again saw playing time in the outfield with the big club, but neither could lift his batting average over .200. In June, after four years with the Senators, Fred Valentine rejoined the Birds, but he saw limited action, appearing in only 47 games to close out his major league career.

Valentine never achieved the prominence once envisioned for him by Paul Richards and Al Vincent. Jim Russo, as we have seen, suggested that Vincent's criticism of Valentine's play in Miami earlier in 1968 may have been a factor. When asked about Russo's observation in 2012, Valentine replied, "During the years after signing with the Orioles there was a lot of talent in the Orioles system. There were good old and young outfielders and my chances of starting were slim. I was blessed with abilities to get to the majors, and I have no regrets. I may not have been the favorite of some managers and coaches because I did not drink, smoke, play golf or socialize with some. I will leave the statements as they are."[34]

* * *

Even though the Birds finished second to the Tigers, albeit a distant second, in 1968 after having finished in sixth place in 1967, Dalton thought a change of manager was needed.[35] Bauer did not take kindly to the move. As the first base coach at the start of the 1968 season, Earl Weaver, a former minor league player and manager in the Orioles system, was seen by many as Bauer's heir apparent. Bauer had not liked Weaver sitting in the wings. "I didn't want him around," Bauer said after being replaced. "I was knifed in the back once before," Bauer told a *Washington Post* reporter (referring to 1962, when Kansas City Athletics owner Charlie Finley had replaced him with pitching coach Eddie Lopat).[36]

The move, however, worked out well for the Orioles and for Weaver. The five-foot, seven-inch, chain-smoking St. Louis native attained a level of success seen by few others in his profession. His winning percentage as the O's manager, .583, ranks ninth in major league history. From 1969 to 1979 Weaver piloted the O's to five 100-win seasons, four American League pennants and one World Series championship. He brought personality as well as competence to the dugout. The "Earl of Baltimore" argued incessantly with umpires. He turned his cap around so he could go face-to-face with them without bumping them with the bill of his cap. He argued with his own players, most famously Hall of Fame pitcher Jim Palmer. The pitcher got in his own shots at Weaver. "The only thing Earl knows about a curveball," Palmer once told a reporter, "is that he can't hit one."[37] On Weaver as a manager, Palmer said he "was a black and white manager. He kinda told you what your job description was going to be and kinda basically told you if you wanted to play for the Orioles, this was what you needed to do.... I don't think anyone other than his wife, Marianna, would describe Earl as a warm and fuzzy guy."[38] The "Earl's" vociferous rants and penchant for kicking dirt on umpires' shoes earned him 97 ejections, third on the all-time list.[39] African American Orioles outfielder Pat Kelly once complained to Weaver that he did not give Kelly enough time to hold a prayer meeting before games. "Earl, don't you want us to walk with the Lord?" Kelly asked. "I'd rather you walk with the bases loaded," Weaver snapped.[40] But histrionics and quips aside, the man could manage.

Weaver's accomplishments were helped along in no small measure by an increasing number of players of color. Under Hoffberger's leadership, Orioles executives did not give speeches to African American audiences; they found and signed African American players of major league caliber.

By 1973 it had been well accepted that minorities contributed mightily to making the O's the American League East's most successful team. The 40-man 1973 roster included two Cubans, pitchers Mike Cuellar and Orlando Pena, and ten African Americans: pitchers Grant Jackson and Jesse Jefferson, catchers Ellie Hendricks and Earl Williams, and outfielders Paul Blair, Don Baylor, Curt Motton, Don Baylor, Al Bumbry and Rich Coggins. The O's had traded Frank Robinson to the Los Angeles Dodgers after the 1971 season.

Players now mixed more readily off the field as well as on. Following Weaver's first season, a dozen players who lived year-round in the Baltimore area formed a basketball

Shown here in a relatively civil stance toward an umpire, Earl Weaver managed the Orioles to six League Championships and four World Series appearances (winning one) over the course of 17 seasons from 1968 to 1986. Many attributed his success to his meticulous use of statistics that he recorded on index cards. If a player complained about not starting or playing, he'd say, "Sorry, it's not in the cards" (National Baseball Hall of Fame Library, Cooperstown, New York).

The bond between Frank Robinson and Brooks Robinson remained intact after the Orioles traded Frank in 1972 to the Los Angeles Dodgers, who then traded him to the California Angels the next season. Here the two All-Stars are seen sharing a light moment before the start of the 1974 All-Star Game at Pittsburgh's Three Rivers Stadium (reprinted with permission of the DC Public Library, Star Collection, © *Washington Post*).

team. Players included Joe Durham, who maintained contact with the O's by throwing batting practice, Dick Hall, Paul Blair, Pat Kelly, Jim Palmer, Brooks Robinson, and minor league player and Baltimore native Joe Pulliam. Hall, an O's pitcher from 1961 to 1966 and again from 1969 to 1971, said Pulliam "was really our star." Between the day after New Year's Day and the start of spring training, the team played games in Frederick, Maryland; Maryland's Eastern Shore; Harrisburg, Pennsylvania; and Newport News, Virginia, Durham's hometown. "We'd play in charity games," Hall said, "and we'd play at high schools where we'd beat the pants off of the faculty. The kids really loved that." Hall recalled the team losing only one game and having a great time in the process.[41]

Helped by the camaraderie on the basketball court, African American players now felt more at ease than had many of their predecessors. They offered positive comments about their time with the Orioles. Rookie Coggins, raised in Indianapolis, told *Sun* reporter Bill Rhoden, the *Sun*'s first

African American sportswriter following a stint on the *AFRO*, a week after Opening Day in 1973, "This is a very, very close knit ballclub. They're just a very good bunch of 'cats.'" Bumbry, a native of Fredericksburg, Virginia, a decorated Vietnam War veteran and a rookie, added, "Everything's been great since we've been here. Up here you're accepted as a ball player first."[42] Bumbry, echoing Paul Blair's earlier comments, said, when an interviewer asked him about discrimination on the O's during his career, 1972–1984, "I'm going to be a short interview. From my perspective," he added, "regarding how I was treated, I don't recall anything with the O's. I never felt there was any discriminatory situations, comments, or remarks directed at me personally or as an African American."[43] When established slugger and eventual Hall of Famer Reggie Jackson reported to the O's from the Oakland Athletics in May 1976, he did so with a gentleman's agreement between himself and Hank Peters, newly hired general manager to replace Frank Cashen, but without a signed contract. Peters impressed Jackson, as he did most players, with his "soft-spokeness, ego-free personality, and astute baseball knowledge."[44] "I decided to report," Jackson told *Washington Post* sportswriter Tom Boswell, "because of the consistent humanness and sensitivity toward me on the part of Hank Peters.... I want to be part of an organization that has nice people, good people."[45]

Jackson found the city of Baltimore less welcoming than the team. He reported encountering "constant racial tensions that are very noticeable here [Baltimore]." Those tensions kept Jackson close to his suburban, two-room hotel suite. "I feel them [racial tensions] everywhere I go," the slugger told the *Sun*'s Michael Janofsky. One incident in particular grated on him. A stadium guard approached his girlfriend while she waited for Jackson by standing next to his car after a game. After learning whom she was waiting for, the guard asked, "Why are you waiting for a nigger ballplayer?" "Nothing like that ever happened in Oakland," Jackson said.[46]

Even though racism still permeated the city, newspaper reporters, black as well as white, no longer identified African American players as "colored," "Negro," "tan," or "black," as they had in the 1950s and 1960s. Sam Lacy, in January 1973, identified African American rookie catcher Earl Williams simply as "the new Bird catcher"[47] in his article introducing Williams to *AFRO* readers. Lacy's colleague on the *AFRO*, William (Bill) Rhoden, referred to Bumbry and Coggins as "two of the Orioles' newest faces."[48] *Sun* reporter Ken Nigro, in an August 1972 article about promising players on the Red Wings, described Bumbry as "a little guy they call the Bumble Bee."[49] In May 1976, *Washington Post* sportswriter Thomas Boswell referred to Reggie Jackson as "the man whose first coming has been awaited here like that of a Messiah."[50] Unfortunately for the O's, Jackson, who led the American League in slugging percentage during the 1976 season, went on to the Yankees in 1977.

Fortunately for the Birds, Peters had his eye on a 21-year-old, switch-hitting African American first baseman from Los Angeles, Eddie Murray. After hitting .298 and driving in 46 runs for the Charlotte [North Carolina] Orioles in the Southern League during the first half of the 1976 season, the O's promoted him to Rochester. There he continued his superb play with a .294 batting average and 40 runs batted in. For good measure, Murray swatted the ball at a .323 clip in winter ball in Puerto Rico. "Murray is the guy we want to get a good look at this spring,"[51] Peters told the *Sun's* Seymour Smith at the start of spring training. "On paper you would ticket him for Rochester but you never know."[52] Peters, on the advice of Weaver, eventually decided that Baltimore was the better fit.[53] It proved to be a wise decision. Murray hit 333 of his 504 career homers and won three Gold Glove Awards over the course of the next 12 seasons with the Birds. Chants of "Ed-dee, Ed-dee" rained down on him from every corner of the stadium. "And not," in the words of former Orioles public relations director Bob Brown, "just out of black mouths."[54]

Fan support for Murray did not go unnoticed by Mike Schmidt, the future Hall of Fame third baseman for the Philadelphia Phillies. Schmidt, during the 1983 World Series, which Baltimore won from the Phillies four games to one, told Brown, "Ya know, I get booed in Philadelphia when I strike out, but here when Eddie Murray strikes out he walks back to the dugout and the fans cheer him with 'Ed-dee, Ed-dee.'" Brown, who had been in the O's front office since November 1957, remembered thinking at the time that the O's biggest accomplishment was not winning three World Series (1966, 1970, 1983) but the fact that "what with Baltimore being a racially sensitive city, it just didn't matter anymore if you were black or white."[55]

Dave Ford, who pitched for the O's during parts of the 1978–1981 seasons, agreed. "I was the only white guy on my basketball team in high school [in Cleveland] so I could care less if a guy was black," Ford said. Ford, however, like many of his white counterparts, had not seen the discrimination encountered by blacks. He said he was "kinda surprised" to hear from several black teammates on the Charlotte Orioles that they did not want to go to certain parts of Birmingham, Alabama, and Columbus, Georgia.

Black and white players not only played together in increased numbers, they now lived together. During Ford's time with the O's he and "eight or nine" players lived within "100 yards of each other" in Cockeysville, Maryland, a northern suburb of Baltimore. African Americans Al Bumbry, Eddie Murray, Lee May, and Pat Kelly bought townhouses near white players Ford, Mike Flanagan, Gary Roenicke, and Kiko Garcia (of Mexican-American descent). When asked if they socialized, Ford replied, "Absolutely! We had cookouts. Lee May was master of the ribs and kept the clubhouse in order. It was a great family atmosphere. It was a tight knit team that bonded together, and we thoroughly enjoyed each others' company on the field as well as off."[56]

By the mid–1980s the Orioles were an integrated team and had been for years. Gone were the days of only one or two African Americans on the roster for an entire season, of black outfielders making a series of cameo appearances, of management redoubling its talk about unsuccessful efforts to find black players and scratching their heads over the lack of black fans in the stands. Sam Lacy, ever the straightforward critic of the O's relationships, or lack thereof, with African American players and fans, found favor with the 1985 Orioles. Black fans finally "could satisfy their hunger for a legitimate reason to love their baseball Birds," proclaimed Lacy. After recalling the names and accomplishments of African American players since 1954, pointing out that blacks now held down the first five spots in the batting order, and noting the presence of two African American coaches, Frank Robinson and "the delightful Ellie Hendricks," Lacy proclaimed "love time is here." He added, "I would be reluctant to call it mere coincidence that black attendance has increased to a marked degree."[57]

CHAPTER 9

"All Brawn, No Brain"

Love time on the field perhaps, but not in the front office. By 1974 African American players had been enshrined in Cooperstown, elected to All-Star teams, performed in World Series, and selected by the Baseball Writers' Association of America to All-Major League teams. Yet only a handful of blacks had landed jobs other than players, and these were all below the managerial level as coaches and scouts, including the O's Joe Durham, a scout. None had landed jobs as managers or even been interviewed for a manager's job, to say nothing of general manager or assistant general manager positions. This situation did not go unnoticed.

A. S. "Doc" Young, sports editor for the African American weekly *Chicago Daily Defender*, found it striking that only whites had made the transition from player to manager. On August 5, 1971, Young reported on the latest example. The Cleveland Indians had just fired Alvin Dark. Dark started managing in 1961, immediately following a 14-year playing career as an infielder with the Giants, Cardinals, Phillies, Cubs, and Braves. Young acidly predicted that Dark would not be out of work for long, even though the Indians "were playing some of the worst baseball in history, drawing fewer fans than pornography, and exuding more unhappiness than divorce court." Why? Because, Young stated, "he's white—the first requisite of major league managing." After a three-year layoff, Dark did return to manage the Oakland Athletics for two years and the San Diego Padres for one.[1]

A whiff of potential progress surfaced three days after Young's column appeared. *New York Daily News* columnist Dick Young predicted a precedent-shattering event, that Frank Robinson would replace Dark. Indians president Gabe Paul denied Young's crystal-balling. Robinson said no one had approached him, but, if they did, he would consider such an offer carefully.[2] Paul chose journeyman infielder and minor league manager

Johnny Lipon, whose managing career included a stint with the Selma [Alabama] Cloverleafs in the Cleveland system, to replace Dark.

Lipon's selection raised no eyebrows, but it did add to the frustration experienced by African American players who saw no future in baseball for themselves after their playing days. African American stars including Frank Robinson, Roy Campanella, Hank Aaron, and Larry Doby had voiced suspicions as early as 1968 that no African American would be tapped to manage.[3] "The white players," Robinson told John F. Steadman, sports editor of the *Baltimore-News American*, in March of 1968, "get the chance to remain in all phases of baseball and it should work the other way too. The Negro should have the same opportunity to teach the game and its skills if he's a coach or a manager. Baseball has been standing still in this respect." Robinson did note to Steadman that a few jobs as coaches and scouts exist for "Negroes," and that there was one African American umpire Emmett Ashford in the American League. Of Ashford, Robinson said, "This is a token thing like on television when a Negro is used to make a commercial or have a part in a program."[4]

A year later, 1969, Robinson announced his interest in being the first black manager, but he wasn't holding his breath. "The old-line club owners won't name a Negro," he told *Washington Post* sportswriter Shirley Povich. "The move," he said, "will be made by liberal-thinking newcomers."[5] Not everyone struck as moderate a tone as did Robinson. Future Hall of Fame St. Louis Cardinals pitcher Bob Gibson, for instance, told *Time Magazine* sportswriter Leonard Shecter, "The time is right to stop all the bull. It's time for a Negro manager. They've been avoiding the issue too long."[6]

However, before the opportunity to manage in the majors came his way, Robinson accepted an offer to manage the Santurce Crabbers in the Puerto Rico League during the 1968–1969 winter. Earl Weaver recommended him for the job. "I wanted to see if I had the temperament to manage," Robinson told Povich after the season, "and I think I proved to myself that I do."[7] Writers responsible for electing the Puerto Rico League's Manager of the Year agreed. They awarded him that honor for winning the pennant with a 49–20 record.[8] Now he had to prove his managerial mettle to a major league team owner.

Rumors of Robinson managing the Indians persisted, fed by Robinson's well-known friendship with Gabe Paul, whom Robinson had played for in Cincinnati, where Paul was the team's general manager. As he had for the Puerto Rico manager's position, Weaver endorsed Robinson for the Cleveland job, saying "I know Frank is qualified and I think he's ready." The Earl of Baltimore even suggested the Monument City would be "the ideal place" for Robby to start managing. "People here like Frank, and I know our owner [Jerold Hoffberger] is no bigot," Weaver told the *Sun*. He quickly added, "But, I sure hope the Baltimore job isn't open for awhile."[9]

Rumors sometimes ripen into reality. Five years after Robinson's interview with Povich, Cleveland Indians General Manager Phil Seghi, a native of Cedar Point, Illinois, a graduate of Northwestern University, a former minor league player and long-time assistant to Paul in Cincinnati, presented Robinson to a crowded press conference on October 3, 1974, as the team's player-manager for 1975. A "smiling, jovial, and proud" Robinson put more importance on being a manager than being the first black manager. "Managing is the important thing with me. Of course being first is special, but it's not the most important," he said. The Indians' African American utility player Tommy McCraw begged to differ with his new boss. "Frank is not just managing a ball club," McCraw told the assembled reporters. "He is managing for all black people, and the future of all blacks depend on how good a job he does."[10]

Others also noted the moment's significance. Baseball Commissioner Bowie Kuhn said it was the first manager announcement he had attended. Lee MacPhail, now American League president, sat with Barbara Robinson during the ceremony. Robinson's appointment stood as "welcome news to baseball fans across the nation and a tribute to you personally," read a telegram from President Gerald R. Ford.[11]

* * *

The Orioles, meanwhile, had showed no signs of integrating their front office, but, as was their practice, they had talked about doing so. In 1965, members of the O's management continually assured the "colored fans" that "the entire working staff was being overhauled" with a view to achieving integration at all levels.[12] Yet by 1974 no African American held a decision-making job at Memorial Stadium. The O's had offered Fred Valentine, after his retirement in 1968, an opportunity to coach in the minors. Valentine wanted to work out of the front office in public relations. "They told me they had no need for that service at this time, which is one way of saying they didn't have anything for me," Valentine said.[13] Valentine went on to a successful career in the construction industry.

Sam Lacy kept the spotlight on the O's all-white front office. He celebrated the 1975 yuletide season by giving a "Merry Christmas" wish to Hank Peters and to Earl Weaver. Lacy wished the two "would look around them and recognize the lily-whiteness ... in the above the field operation of the Baltimore Orioles."[14] Two years later, in August 1977, he had criticized the O's decision not to fill the coaching vacancy created when third base coach and former Orioles shortstop Billy Hunter left town to manage the Texas Rangers. Lacy thought Robinson would be the ideal replacement. Robinson, recently fired by the Indians in mid-season after two-and-one-half seasons at their helm, was available. Peters squelched such hopes two weeks after Hunter left when he announced the O's would go with four instead of the five coaches they had the prior season, and that Cal Ripken, Sr., would replace Hunter as third base coach, traditionally the last stop before becoming a manager. The GM cited Ripken Sr.'s stellar performance the past two weeks at third base as the rationale for not adding a fifth coach. Lacy then pointed out that Tigers catcher Milt May had recently stolen two hit-and-run signs flashed by Ripken and gunned down Orioles Mark Belanger and Al Bumbry attempting to steal second base with called pitchouts. Lacy, in a parting shot, noted that the O's were one of just six teams that did not carry an African American in a position above the playing field level. "Bringing Frank Robinson back would have spoiled that record," Lacy pointed out.[15]

Peters spoiled the record in early December 1977 when he signed the Birds' first coach of color, Elrod Hendricks, to fill the vacancy created when Brooks Robinson resigned from the coaching staff. "At long last—and they are among the last—the Orioles have desegregated their coaching staff," the *AFRO* exclaimed.[16] "Earl [Weaver] liked him as did the other coaches," Peters recalled in a 2012 interview. "He knew baseball and had a great personality, so we gave him the job. We didn't hire him because he was black, he happened to be black."[17]

Peters had Hendricks' appointment in mind as early as June 1976 when the catcher, toward the end of his playing career, went to the Yankees in a trade. "I told him then," Peters said, "'we'll have you back next year,' because I knew the Yankees wouldn't keep him."[18]

As 1977 drew to a close, Robinson told Harry Dalton, former general manager of the Angels after leaving Baltimore and now the Milwaukee Brewers' GM, in a phone call, "Harry, I'm out of work. I'm looking for something. Keep me in mind."[19] Dalton kept him in mind but did not hire him.

Peters, however, did. In early February 1978, Peters re-opened the fifth coaching position and filled it with "old No. 20," Robinson's number during his Baltimore playing days and the first O's number to be retired. "I'm very pleased," Robinson said on his return to Memorial Stadium as the O's second African American coach. "I know I'll be helping wherever I can with a little bit of everything."[20]

Wherever turned out to be Rochester, New York, but not as a coach. By choosing to manage in Rochester rather than coach in Baltimore, Robinson became the second manager of color in the International League (Hector Lopez had managed the Buffalo Bisons in 1969). "We'd like to see him continue with the organization," Peters said. "It [the Red Wings job] helps fill in the voids that have existed in his baseball background."[21] The voids, Peters explained later, consisted of "learning how to handle players and how to evaluate talent."[22]

Dave Ford thought Robby excelled at Rochester. "We played hard for him," Ford said in 2013. "Frank was all business and pretty tough and probably favored hitters over pitchers, but he would work with you. We had a run-in one time when I was pitching, but after that we had no problems." Ford played for Robinson in Puerto Rico as well as Rochester. "I had nothing but respect for Frank," Ford added.[23]

Robinson's move to Rochester left Hendricks as the only coach of color at Memorial Stadium. Africans Americans, on the other hand, accounted for four of the starting nine on Opening Day; Murray, May, Bumbry, and outfielder Ken Singleton, raised in Mt. Vernon, New York, and a graduate of Hofstra University who played for the Orioles from 1975 to 1984.

Robinson expressed no regrets about his year at Rochester, even though the team flubbed its way out of playoff contention during the last two weeks of the season. He continued to push for more black managers in an end-of-season interview with *Sun* reporter Bryan Burwell. He noted "there was something wrong" with the situation, that of 26 major league managers only one (Larry Doby, hired by the White Sox in mid-season) had a dark complexion. Robinson dismissed the oft-heard statements that black players needed minor league managerial experience before taking over a major league post. He ticked off the names of white managers who had gone directly from the playing field to the manager's office. "Somewhere down the line we will have some more black managers," he said. "I just don't know when, and it's coming entirely too slow."[24]

Peters offered Robinson a choice of assignments for the 1979 season. Robinson could continue as the Red Wings' manager or return to Baltimore as a coach.[25] "No. 20" opted for the latter and spent the 1979 and 1980 seasons coaching for the Birds. Seeing that the outfield needed a little shoring up in 1979, he coached the "flychasers." The following year he was the team's hitting and first base coach.[26] Though he did not comment on it publically, Robinson saw two O's white coaches move into manager jobs. George Bamberger, O's pitching coach, who appeared in ten major league games over three seasons with no decisions, took the Milwaukee Brewers' manager job in 1978. Jim Frey, who like Weaver had played in the minors but not the majors, signed a contract to manage the Kansas City Royals in 1980.

Sam Lacy joined the conversation about African American managers after the Pirates beat the Orioles in the 1979 World Series. Each team, Lacy pointed out, fielded at least five African Americans in their starting nine, but he pointed out there were no black managers in the majors. (The White Sox had fired Doby and hired two white managers during the 1979 season, Don Kessinger and Tony LaRussa, each for half a season.) The reason for the lack of black managers, Lacy said, lay with "[the owners'] judgment [that] blacks in baseball are all brawn, no brain."[27]

Hank Peters, of course, did not own the Orioles, but he did have a voice in who played for and who managed the team. He did not share Lacy's assessment of white owners' attitudes toward black managers, at least as it pertained to Robinson. "Should Weaver resign," Peters told *Sun* sportswriter Bob Maisel in October 1980, "he [Frank Robinson] is one of the first I'd consider.... He has obvious leadership qualities ... has certainly paid his dues ... has many desirable qualifications, but for some reason teams needing managers don't seem to be considering him."[28] No one, Peters told Maisel, had asked Peters' permission to talk to Robinson, the necessary first step for any team even considering Robinson as its manager.

Two months later San Francisco Giants president Bob Lurie, a San Francisco real estate magnate, placed such a call to Peters, who enthusiastically gave Lurie the go-ahead. Lurie hired Robinson in January 1981 after considering former white major league players and managers Dick Howser, Bob Lemon, Del Crandall, and Gene Mauch. "I talked to a lot of people, but Frank Robinson was the best for the job. He knows how to win, he knows how to communicate. I believe he will have the ability to earn the respect of players and fans in a very short time," said Lurie, explaining why he chose Robinson, now the National League's first African American manager.[29]

Robinson had no easy task. He had to rally a team whose stars had openly clashed with former manager Dave Bristol. Pitcher John Montefusco, since traded, engaged Bristol in a fist fight. The Giants' new manager had left Cleveland with a reputation for being a demanding and difficult boss.[30] Robinson himself admitted, "I wasn't ready to manage then.... Now I am. I tried too hard before." Trying too hard included punching a pitcher for the Toledo Mud Hens, an Indians' farm team, who complained to

Robinson about not making the Indians' roster. Robinson grabbed an occasional jersey in anger and, in response to statements that he had problems communicating with players, said, "I communicate with them. I just tell them things they don't want to hear."[31] On taking the job with San Francisco, Robinson told the press, "the one thing you have to do in this game to survive is to learn."[32] One Giants player thought Robinson had learned how to communicate with players. "He can step on your toes without messing up your shoeshine," is how Joe Morgan, the Giants' African American future Hall of Fame second baseman, described Robinson's approach to managing after just three months on the job.[33]

The Giants, however, did not win enough games to suit Lurie. He showed Robinson the door toward the end of the 1984 season. In the six-team Western Division of the National League, Robinson led the Giants to a fourth-place finish in 1981 and a third-place finish in 1982, but the Giants fell to fifth place in 1983 and last place in 1984. "I know it's a difficult situation. Do what you have to do," Robinson told Lurie after Lurie said he would have to make an announcement. Robinson then said, "Thank you," and walked out of Lurie's office.[34]

* * *

After Robinson had spent two years in San Francisco, the Baltimore job opened up in 1982. Following 14½ seasons at the helm, six pennants, and four World Series appearances, the Earl of Baltimore packed it in. He wanted "some time for myself" and rounds of golf at the Country Club of Miami where his home overlooked the seventh green.[35] Weaver's last game left a bitter taste in his mouth as the Milwaukee Braves overwhelmed the Birds, 10–2, to take the American League East flag. A sell-out Memorial Stadium crowd of 51,642 fans stayed after the last out for two hours to cheer the manager they had come to love. Weaver called the players back on to the field to join in the adulation, embraced them, and shed a few tears.[36]

Robinson seemed an obvious candidate to replace Weaver. Peters, however, did not talk to the newly inducted Hall of Famer whom Cooperstown had just welcomed into membership in July. "No," Robby told a reporter in October 1982, "Hank has said nothing to me. He hasn't even asked permission of the Giants to talk to me." Lacy characterized the lack of contact between the two men as "a mystery" and "difficult to understand."[37] Peters decided, instead, on Joe Altobelli, at the time a coach with the Yankees, who had previously served 11 years in the Baltimore farm system as a coach and manager.

Altobelli got off to a great start. He took the O's to their third world championship. He did so with starters that included four African Americans (Dan Ford, Eddie Murray, John Shelby, and Ken Singleton), Mexican native Leo Hernandez, Dennis Martinez from Nicaragua, and four whites, Cal Ripken, Jr., Rich Dauer, Gary Roenicke, and Rick Dempsey. If managers of color were not to be found in the majors (and only one, Robinson, was), the same could not be said for Orioles players. Players of color were now firmly entrenched with the Orioles.

The stars did not shine as brightly on the 1984 team, which finished in fifth place. After a disappointing start to the 1985 season, Peters fired Altobelli. Cal Ripken, Sr., won the single game that he managed. Back from the Miami Country Club came Earl Weaver to finish the season. The O's finished in fourth place that year.

Again the question arose, why not Robinson? True to his word about wanting to keep Robinson in the organization, Peters had hired him as a coach soon after he left San Francisco and had left it up to Altobelli to determine Robinson's duties.[38] But by not hiring Robinson as the O's manager, "did the O's 'shaft' Frank?" Lacy asked. This time Lacy found no mystery. "An objective look at the situation" led the *AFRO* sports editor to answer his own question in the negative. To promote any one of the four coaches—Cal Ripken, Sr., Ray Miller, Jimmy Williams, and newcomer Robinson—over the other three would, Lacy concluded, create hard feelings on the part of the three not selected. To keep the peace, owner Edward Bennett Williams, who had purchased the team from Hoffberger in August 1979, Lacy opined, went outside the existing personnel to rehire Weaver just as he had gone outside earlier to hire Altobelli.[39]

Weaver stayed on for 1986, a season that proved most unkind to him. In second place in August and closing in on the league-leading Red Sox, the team suddenly fell apart, finally landing in the cellar of the American League East. Weaver's 1986 record, his only losing season as a major league manager, came to 73–89. One of the most successful managers the game has ever known (1,480 wins and 1,060 losses), announced his retirement in early September. With the team in free fall, this goodbye lacked the passion of 1982's.[40] He left Baltimore "without tears, without regret ... just some flowers."[41]

Weaver's retirement again led to speculation that Robinson's moment to manage the O's had at last arrived. Robby did not think so. "I'm an afterthought," he dejectedly told *Sun* reporter Tim Kurkjian, "and, yes, it does bother me." Cal Ripken, Sr.'s name had surfaced in many discussions on Weaver's successor. To Robinson's surprise, Peters did call him in for

Orioles owner Edward Bennett Williams, shown on the field with a bat on his shoulder, imparts some words of advice to Manager Earl Weaver, who seems not to be giving his boss his full attention. Washingtonian Room (reprinted with permission of the DC Public Library, Star Collection, © *Washington Post*).

a talk. "I feel good about the meeting," Robinson said afterwards. "It was very sincere.... I have no idea one way or another what will happen." Ripken got the nod. Robinson agreed to stay on as a coach.[42]

* * *

Eddie Murray's slump had added to Weaver's woes during the manager's last year at Memorial Stadium. Murray, who pulled down $2 million a year, real money in those days, ended 1986 as the O's leading hitter with a .305 batting average, in line with his previous five seasons where his average ranged from .316 to .297. His home run production, however, had fallen to 17, noticeably below his average of 31 per season the four previous years. He had also missed 25 games due to injuries for the first time in his career. Considered the best player in the majors the past five years but slowed by injuries this season, Murray discovered that racism could still be found in Baltimore. He heard boos for the first time at Memorial Stadium. The vitriolic comments fans hurled at the first baseman forced parents to keep their children away from the box seats near first base.

African American Judge William "Billy" Murphy, Jr., heard the abuse heaped on Murray first-hand. "You could get into the games free after the fourth inning so that's when I went with my four boys," he said in 2013.

"We'd sit behind home plate and we could hear occasional epithets, including the 'n' word. It was disgraceful and shameful. White fans," the judge added, "couldn't take that [not running out meaningless ground balls and pop ups] from a black man, even one who carried the team on his back with incredible hitting for long stretches of time, given the stereotypical way whites viewed blacks in the era."[43]

Sun sports columnist Mike Littwin added to the criticism directed Murray's way by zinging Murray in his August 26, 1986, column. Ridiculing Murray's request to be traded, Littwin asked, "How does our hero confront his problems? ... Murray intends to cut and run." After suggesting that Murray felt the team and fans did not sufficiently appreciate his injuries, Littwin intoned, "All together: 'Awww.'"[44] A week later *The Sun* published 50 responses from readers to Littwin's column. They ranged from "Leave Eddie alone, get rid of Mike 'The Jerk' Littwin," to "Criticism comes to all of us. How one handles it tells if the person is mature or a crybaby."[45] Talk show hosts joined in with daily barbs directed Murray's way. Never one to talk to the media, let alone voice his feelings to them, Murray quietly told Peters in September that he had enough and asked Peters again to trade him. Peters refused, saying he had picked a bad time to ask because "we're in a pennant race."[46]

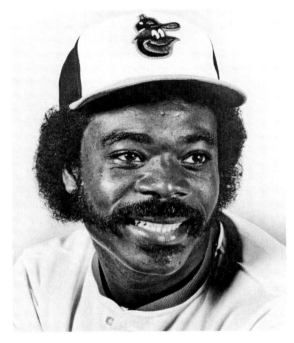

One of baseball's all-time great players and one of only five major leaguers to attain 500 home runs and 3,000 hits, Eddie Murray's quiet and generous nature left a mark on Baltimore beyond the confines of Memorial Stadium and Camden Yards. The Carrie Murray Nature Center, founded and initially funded by Murray and named for his mother, introduces thousands of children and adults each year to animals and the outdoors through a series of educational programs (National Baseball Hall of Fame Library, Cooperstown, New York).

Edward Bennett Williams had inflamed

the situation earlier by publically criticizing Murray. Frustrated by the realization that the O's were headed for their first losing season in 19 years, Williams thought a public rebuke would motivate Murray. From his swivel chair in his private box during a rain delay on August 21, 1986, he told the assembled reporters, "Murray hasn't given us a good year. He faces a challenge next season because he's at the age where he has to work hard to get ready for the next season."[47]

Not surprisingly, players and coaches sprang to Murray's defense. "People who know the game, know what he's done around here for ten years," Hendricks said. "He's been the leader, the brunt of the attack, in the middle of everything for ten years." "He feels slighted," added pitcher Mike Flanagan. As for talk that rookie Jim Traber should replace Murray at first base, Hendricks said knowingly, "if anybody thinks that boy is going to do what Eddie did over the past 8–10 years, they're crazy."[48]

Murray had not been the only victim of Williams' public criticism. The attorney once called third baseman Floyd Rayford, also African American, "Fatso."[49] Orioles public relations director Bob Brown recalled that Williams did not confine such comments to his swivel chair. "He," Brown said, "had a knack for going to a cocktail party, having a few drinks, and shooting his mouth off."[50]

Williams, a nationally acclaimed trial attorney, some said on a par with Clarence Darrow, defended the infamous. His clients included Sen. Joseph R. McCarthy, Jimmy Hoffa, syndicated crime boss Frank Costello, Rep. Adam Clayton Powell, Jr., and President Lyndon Johnson's aide, Bobby Baker. Those credentials, however, did not endear him to Peters. "Let me tell you a little bit about Edward Bennett Williams," Peters said in 2012. "He was a difficult guy to work for. Great lawyer and orator but courtroom skills didn't apply to running a ball club and motivating players, but he thought they did. Like a lot of guys, he couldn't zip his mouth shut when he should have. He thought if he said something critical it would be a motivator. It had just the opposite effect on Murray who was a very sensitive guy."[51]

Refusing to be mollified by an apology from Williams, the Orioles' star turned his back on Williams when the owner showed up in the O's dugout during spring training in 1987 to deliver one of his many pep talks.[52]

Williams' rebuke stung Murray particularly hard because Williams rarely criticized a player but "often lambasted the team," Peters said. "He always wanted to address the team when things were not going well. I'd say, 'Ed I don't think that will help the team,' but it was his ball club." Asked how the players reacted to his talks, Peters said, "they just rolled their eyes."[53]

Sam Lacy cast the Williams-Murray controversy in a slavery framework. Lacy portrayed Murray as the "uppity" first baseman who "had the gall to complain to overseer Peters" and Williams as "Massa Ed Williams who came over from the big house and lamped into him [Murray]." After explaining that "all the foregoing is written in a facetious vein" and that he had no intention of comparing the Orioles "to an early Dixie estate," Lacy told his readers that "the temptation to do so is there but not the inclination."[54] Lacy, nevertheless, had made his point.

* * *

The year 1987 marked 40 years since Jackie Robinson became the first African American major leaguer. By now, black players were commonplace. Baseball's Hall of Fame had inducted 18 African American players, nine from the majors and nine from the Negro leagues. Orioles minority players continued to feel comfortable in Memorial Stadium because the organization treated them as ball players, not black ball players. Former outfielder Ken Singleton, who had played with the New York Mets and Montreal Expos before coming to Baltimore, said, "Baltimore is one of the most comfortable places to play."[55]

Still, the majors had seen no black general managers or assistant general managers and but three black managers, none with a talented group of players and only one, Robinson, with tenures of any significance, three seasons with the Indians and four with the Giants. Larry Doby managed the White Sox for 87 games in 1978. Maury Wills, who held down the shortstop position from 1959 to 1972 for the Los Angeles Dodgers and Pittsburgh Pirates, piloted the Seattle Mariners for 82 games during parts of the 1980 and 1981 seasons. Of more than 800 front-office positions among 26 clubs, African Americans and other minorities held three percent of them. Of that number, more than half occupied secretarial or "community relations" positions. Of 45 Orioles employees, one, a secretary, had dark skin.[56] A public, if unintended, explanation for the dearth of black managers and executives in Baltimore and elsewhere would soon be forthcoming.

CHAPTER 10

"May Not Have the Necessities"

Ted Koppel, anchorman for ABC's TV evening news show *Nightline*, invited Jackie Robinson's widow, Rachel; Roger Kahn, author of *The Boys of Summer* (1972), a best-selling book about the Brooklyn Dodgers, and Al Campanis to appear on *Nightline* April 6, 1987, Opening Day for major league baseball. Campanis was a last-minute stand-in for Don Newcombe, African American teammate of Robinson with the Brooklyn Dodgers from 1949 to 1956, whose plane to New York had been delayed. Campanis, in his 20th year as Los Angeles Dodgers' vice president and general manager, had played seven games at second base for the 1943 Dodgers and had played alongside Robinson with the Montreal Royals.

Koppel conceived of the segment as a "wet kiss to Jackie Robinson and to some extent major league baseball," to celebrate Robinson's historic debut. The *Nightline* host designed the piece to last a few minutes and end with Campanis "putting a cherry on the top of the sundae." Koppel then intended to turn to what had been considered the night's big story, the Sugar Ray Leonard-"Marvelous" Marvin Hagler middleweight title boxing match. The piece lasted longer than Koppel expected and far over-shadowed the fight.[1]

Rachel Robinson led off with remembrances of her husband and a statement regretting the lack of black executives in baseball. Only one African American held an executive position at the time, Hank Aaron, who had been director of minor league personnel for the Atlanta Braves since 1976. After praising Robinson and the Dodgers, Kahn added that Robinson, were he still alive, would share his wife's concerns. Koppel then turned to Campanis, whom 22 years earlier Lacy had praised for tutoring "colored" players Robinson and Maury Wills,[2] to ask why there were no black executives today. "I can't answer the question directly," Campanis replied from the Houston Astrodome over a satellite feed. As possible reasons, Campanis offered that one had to pay his dues, manage in the minors "where the pay isn't that good," and that many black stars had found lucrative employment outside of baseball after retiring. "You know in your heart of hearts that's a lot of baloney.... Is there still that much prejudice in baseball today?" Koppel asked. "No, I don't believe it's prejudice. I truly believe they may not have some of the necessities to be a field manager or perhaps a general manager," Campanis replied.[3] "Translated into racial language," wrote A. S. "Doc" Young, then a sportswriter for the African American weekly the *Los Angeles Sentinel*, "that means: They're too dumb!"[4]

"You really believe that?" Koppel asked incredulously, eliciting a nervous grin from Campanis. "I'm not saying that about all," Campanis said, "but how many quarterbacks do you have, how many pitchers are black?" "That sounds like the same kind of garbage we were hearing forty years ago about players," replied Koppel. "No, it's not garbage, Mr. Koppel," Campanis shot back. Then, in a curious non-sequitur, Campanis introduced another sport, swimming. "Why is it blacks are not good swimmers?" he suddenly asked Koppel. Answering his own question, the Dodgers' VP said, "Because they don't have the buoyancy." Koppel disagreed, saying, "they don't have access to all the country clubs and the pools."[5]

Koppel called Campanis during a commercial break, something he rarely did with any guest. "Do you understand what you're saying?" Koppel asked him. In a later interview, the *Nightline* host explained, "We knew he wasn't a blind, racist fool but he was coming across like he should have worn a robe that night." Back on the air, Koppel gave Campanis a chance "to dig yourself out of a hole because I think you need it." Following a nervous laugh, Campanis challenged Koppel with a question about how many blacks "are in your business?" Koppel replied there were some black anchors but no black executives, because whites running the broadcast business "were reluctant to give up power."[6]

Reactions rained down on Campanis. Dodgers owner Walter O'Malley fired him two days later. Benjamin Hooks, executive director of the NAACP, threatened to shut down major league baseball.[7] "Your words ... didn't hurt much at all.... We never believed what you people said anyway.... We hurt because you never *did* anything," African American tennis star Arthur Ashe wrote in an open letter to Campanis.[8] Three months after the interview, Billy Williams, an outfielder with the Chicago Cubs and the Oakland Athletics, used his July Hall of Fame acceptance speech to add his voice to those urging clubs to hire black executives. After noting that minorities had demonstrated their abilities as players for 40 years, Williams said, "Now we deserve the chance and consideration to demonstrate our talents as third base coaches, as managers, as general managers and as executives in the front office, and, yes, as owners of major league ball clubs themselves."[9]

Reggie Jackson, who had retired the year before and was one of the few African American players, active or retired, willing to speak out, said on a subsequent *Nightline* program, "We don't need affirmative action. We need definitive action. We've written about the Kennedys and the Martin Luther Kings for a long time; now we need to do something."[10] Hank Aaron said from Atlanta, "Campanis needs to apologize to every single black person in America. All that shows," Aaron added, "is how ignorant the man is."[11]

The ex-Dodgers VP did apologize. In doing so he expressed hurt and astonishment at the widespread and overwhelmingly negative reactions to his comments. "That one of baseball's best known executives could disgrace his sport as Campanis did, and have no clue that he'd done it, shows the depth of baseball's ugliest and most secret scandal," wrote *Washington Post* sportswriter Tom Boswell.[12] John B. Holway, noted Negro leagues historian, while not weighing in on Campanis' comments, took the occasion to accuse the media of hypocrisy for "clucking their tongues over Al Campanis," when of the 50 city daily papers covering baseball, only two, the *Boston Globe* and *Chicago Tribune*, had a full-time black sportswriter.[13]

Campanis' supporters chimed in. Dick Young jumped on Koppel, insinuating that the interviewer had waylaid an unsuspecting guest. "Campanis is no bigot," Young wrote. "Koppel led him down a sociological alley for which Campanis was not prepared."[14] Mike Downey, sportswriter for *The Sporting News*, said Campanis meant no harm. "He was misguided," Downey wrote, "not a misanthrope."[15]

* * *

The topic of no blacks in executive positions had come up before, but just as a topic of conversation among baseball executives. Baseball Commissioner Bowie Kuhn, 13 years earlier in 1974, had told Joe Durso of *The New York Times* that the time had come for clubs to hire black managers and executives. While he could not tell an owner whom to hire, the commissioner promised to "jawbone" owners to consider African Americans. Kuhn added, "It has been suggested there's a conspiracy or policy against black managers." Kuhn dismissed that suggestion. "That's humburg [*sic*]. If there was a conspiracy, I wouldn't stand for it. You can't just say bias is the reason we haven't had one. Competition is more like it. When a club thinks it can win with a black manager, it will name one," Kuhn said.[16] *Washington Post* reporter David DuPree raised the issue with Kuhn again in July 1979. Kuhn said then, "We think we have a good number of blacks in management roles but we are always looking for the opportunity to bring on more." He did not elaborate. Kuhn's assistant, Bob Wirz, added, "The opportunities are there. People just need to come forward and show interest."[17] DuPree said Kuhn's and Wirz's comments demonstrate that "Baseball continues to close its eyes to the situation and says it is doing all it can and needs to do."[18]

Now, however, the issue had spread beyond the commissioner's office to the media and the television screens of millions of Americans. Things began to happen. The racist remarks of a white man who had made hiring and firing decisions for a major league team for two decades got attention from the commissioner in a way that repeated pleas from African Americans Sam Lacy, Frank Robinson, "Doc" Young, Rachel Robinson and others never could. A week after the Campanis interview, Commissioner Peter Ueberroth promised immediate guidelines for minority hiring. He hired Harry Edwards, a black sociologist teaching at the University of California, Berkeley, as a special assistant. The two had first met in the mid–1960s at San Jose State University, where Ueberroth was a graduate student assistant track coach and Edwards the school's premier discus thrower. Edwards had since developed a national reputation as a sports sociologist and for trying, unsuccessfully, to persuade black athletes to boycott the 1968 Summer Olympics in Mexico City.[19] Edwards sported a bushy beard and a shaved head. He had characterized baseball as "a plantation-style system" on one of his several appearances on *Nightline*.[20]

Ueberroth's efforts met with mixed reviews. Dick Young, believing reform starts best at home, suggested Ueberroth first look around his own office while he was asking team executives to look around theirs. "Let me ask you something, Ubie," Young wrote. "How many black employees do you have in your office? Don't strain your brain. Zero. That's how many."[21] (Monte Irvin had retired from the commissioner's office in October 1984.) The Reverend Joseph Lowery, president of the Southern Christian Leadership Conference, a civil rights activist group founded by Dr. Martin Luther King, Jr., in 1957, met with Ueberroth several weeks after the interview. He pronounced their meeting "very profitable. The commissioner," Lowrey said, "is sensitive to the situation. I'm very encouraged."[22] Civil

rights activist and presidential aspirant Jesse Jackson struck a more chal-
lenging stance. He gave baseball executives two months to develop an
affirmative action program or face boycotts. After meeting with Ueberroth
and owners from each league, Jackson softened his tone. He told the press,
"Some adjustments have been made … since Mr. Al Campanis, the fall
guy, pulled the scab off the cancer."[23] Hank Peters recalled little urgency
coming from the commissioner's office. "He," Peters said, "didn't say there
was a quota but wanted clubs to be aware if they didn't have blacks and
had the means to correct it, please do so."[24]

* * *

Racial barriers had for years blocked African Americans in Baltimore
from ascending to top-level jobs in pursuits other than baseball. In
response to a 1972 finding that the Armco Steel Corporation discriminated
against blacks in promoting workers to supervisors, the Maryland Human
Relations Commission ordered the company to promote three black workers a year until blacks held 20 percent of the supervisor positions. If Armco
ignored the order, as it had a year earlier, by terming a similar order "out-
rageous," the commission would seek a court order. Armco ignored the
order for three more years. The commission got its court order. Armco
signed a consent order in Circuit Court. The order bound the company
to the terms of the original order but without admitting any wrongdoing.[25]

Armco had company. The U.S. Department of Labor had kept an eye
on Sparrows Point since its 1967 action against the Bethlehem Steel sub-
sidiary. In 1971, the Department detected that an employee who shifted
from one unit to another went to the back of the seniority line in the new
unit and often took a pay cut. The policy particularly discouraged blacks,
who generally held lower paying jobs due to 40 years of discrimination,
from seeking a better job in another unit. Using the threat of loss of federal
contracts, the Office of Federal Contract Compliance called for a
company-wide seniority system and a promise that no pay cut would
accompany a job change. A subsequent Department of Labor panel in
1973 found that proposal too extreme and instead settled on merging several units into larger units, giving blacks a larger pool of jobs to aspire to.
If the new job paid less, however, the employee had to accept the lower
pay but would not lose seniority.[26]

"The Old Boy Network," thought by many blacks to keep African
Americans out of executive positions in baseball, also worked against
blacks in the Maryland State House during the 1970s and 1980s. African

American delegate John Douglass (D–Baltimore) showed that from the mid–1970s to 1988, no black legislator had landed a state job upon leaving the Assembly, but that 49 white former legislators had. Douglass, an 18-year veteran of the Assembly and looking for a job himself, knew of five other black legislators who had received no help from the "old boy network." House Majority Leader John Arnick (D–Baltimore County) told *Washington Post* reporter Susan Schmidt that Douglass had been promised assistance in his quest for the deputy state treasurer's job in 1988 but had not been promised the job. Douglass did not mind the existence of the network but objected, he said, to "the systematic exclusion of black legislators from it."[27]

Other African American Baltimoreans besides steelworkers and legislators encountered racial discrimination in the work place. By 1986 30,000 people had no employment at all in Baltimore, 73 percent of them black. *Destiny 2000*, a report on black unemployment released by the Baltimore Urban League in 1986, suggested racial discrimination as the cause of the vast majority of the unemployed being black. The report noted, for instance, that the number of racial discrimination cases processed each year by the Maryland Commission on Human Relations rose 800 percent (163 to 1,317) from 1967 to 1986. Of those, 75 percent came from Baltimore city. The report did not indicate the outcomes of the cases but said the increased filings indicated more blacks felt they had been discriminated against and were increasingly willing to take action. Even though blacks outnumbered whites in the workplace (183,000 to 137,000), twice as many whites as blacks held managerial and professional jobs, many of them in Baltimore's expanding service sectors—banking, restaurants, hotels, and tourism. Blue collar, manufacturing jobs, which traditionally employed many blacks, continued to decline.

In another 1986 report, *Baltimore 2000: A Choice of Futures*, sponsored by the Morris Goldseker Foundation, Peter L. Szanton, the first President of the New York City-Rand Institute, noted that thousands of people commuted to Baltimore from the surrounding counties to jobs in the city. The number of commuters, Szanton said, demonstrated that "the skills and attitudes" of many unemployed Baltimore residents (mostly black) "are not as attractive to employers as those of residents of the surrounding counties (mostly white)," suggesting, Szanton said, a need for job training. *Destiny 2000*'s author, Baltimore journalist DeWayne Wickham, on the other hand, noted that "in the absence of documentation to the contrary, it is unreasonable to accept" that service jobs "are largely beyond the ability of a substantial number of black job seekers." Wickham did not use the word "necessities" in connection with those who thought service jobs to be beyond the ability of blacks, but he could have. Wickham agreed with Szanton on the importance of training but added, "a parallel effort to end racially-based employment practices" was also needed if the employment gap between whites and blacks in Baltimore were to narrow.[28]

In an effort to boost the economy and create jobs at all levels for both blacks and whites, William Donald Schaefer, Baltimore's mayor from 1971 to 1987 and a Baltimore native, led a building boom during the middle 1980s that transformed downtown Baltimore. No longer would the city be "an avoidable stop on the road from Washington, D.C., to New York City."[29] With hotels, restaurants, an aquarium, a convention center, long-vacant factories converted to condominiums, and high-rise office buildings dotting the skyline around "Harbor Place," Baltimore's downtown had become an urban showcase. Harbor Place attracted tourists as well as high-income, white collar residents who paid more in taxes than they received in services. *Esquire* magazine named Schaefer the nation's best mayor in 1984.[30]

Critics charged that Schaefer's initiatives had been accomplished at the expense of improvements needed in the inner city. Baltimore's poor blacks now had, Schaefer's detractors alleged, fewer services and jobs than they had earlier. Many blacks had been intimidated into leaving their neighborhoods to make room for the new development, according to Bobby Cheeks, president of the Baltimore Welfare Rights Organization. The city's population continued its four-decade decline as affluent whites continued to vote with their feet. Teenage pregnancies skyrocketed. New office buildings encroached on downtown stores. "I'm not sure if the money used for revitalization of the Inner Harbor has any impact on the city's poor black residents," said African American Rep. Parren J. Mitchell.[31]

Schaefer's response to critics concerned about "the rot beneath the glitter" often contained profanity coupled with promises to help the poor.[32] Schaefer insisted that the wealth produced in the Inner Harbor would "trickle down" to other parts of the city. Many inner-city residents disagreed. Sharon Garner, 42, a single mother of three who lived in a three-bedroom apartment in Baltimore's west side, said, "Nothing trickles down here but the water through the roof."[33]

Kurt Schmoke, Baltimore's first elected black mayor (1987–1999), a Baltimore native and Harvard Law School graduate, defended Schaefer. "It was easy to point to the Harbor," Schmoke said in a 2013 interview. "It was harder to see a new housing initiative. Schaefer invested much more money in the neighborhoods than he did in downtown."[34]

Schmoke, at age 38, heralded a new breed of young, well-educated, pragmatic post-civil-rights-era African American politicians.[35] As mayor he led efforts to improve low-income housing projects, sponsored a needle exchange program for drug addicts, maintained a stable tax rate, and helped attract the Ravens professional football team (the former Cleveland Browns) to Baltimore. In a city with a population of 720,000 and up to 200,000 functionally illiterate adults, Schmoke started a literacy campaign. His slogan read, "Baltimore, the City That Reads." "Not glitzy," the mayor acknowledged, "but a matter of survival."[36] "At the receiving dock, it used to be the guy would just unload the truck. Now he has to enter the information into a computer," noted Charles Zimmerman, a Westinghouse executive.[37]

Schmoke turned to the Orioles for help with his reading initiative. He enlisted Calvin Hill, quarterback at Yale before playing in the National Football League, while Schmoke threw touchdown passes for the Elis' junior varsity. Hill gave free Orioles tickets to any public school fifth grader who read six extracurricular books between February 18 and April 18, 1988. When asked by a student at Barclay Elementary School for recommendations, the mayor suggested Dr. Seuss' *Green Eggs and Ham*. Students who qualified picked up their tickets at the O's "Read Like a Pro Day" in May.[38] They could bring a parent, a teacher, or their school's principal.[39] Cal Ripken, Jr., the Orioles' Hall of Fame shortstop, was, Schmoke said, a "tremendous leader" in a quasi-public corporation, Baltimore Reads, established by the mayor. Cal's wife Kelly and her father served on the Board. The corporation donated money to the city's reading program every time Cal scored or batted in a run, both of which he did often.[40] President George H. W. Bush awarded Schmoke the National Literacy Award in 1992 for his work to improve literacy in the city.

Even with the reading program and investments in the city's neighborhoods, Schmoke recalled that major challenges still faced the city during his time as mayor. "How could a city with the Harbor and Camden Yards also be the site for the TV show 'Homicide'?" he asked in a 2013 interview. The show portrayed the city's police homicide unit investigating violent crimes in Baltimore during its 1993–1999 run. "We had outstanding examples of urban progress, yet we also had the highest concentration of urban poverty in the state. We had both," the former mayor said.[41]

* * *

Challenges also lay ahead for the Orioles. Edward Bennett Williams responded to Campanis. Realizing a week after the interview that the Orioles' front office employed but one African American, Williams called a press conference on April 17, 1987, to express his concern and a plan of attack. "I will take second place to no one," Williams emphatically told reporters, "in the United States on sensitivity to racial justice. And if you want documentation on that over the last 40 years, I will give it to you."[42]

Williams was perhaps referring to his role in integrating the Washington Redskins' front office during the time he owned the team. "I think," he said in July 1979, "it behooves management to push hard to get outstanding black athletes into management positions." He cited his Redskins, with one top executive (Bobby Mitchell) and two scouts (Charlie Taylor and Dickie Daniels), as a good example of his racial justice record.[43]

After the Campanis interview he said, "I am really embarrassed that our front office has such a horrible ratio of minority workers.... It did not come about because of any bigotry.... We have just gone along with a color-blind hiring policy. We are switching instantly to a very positive affirmative-action program."[44] Hank Peters, who agreed with Williams on very little at that time, did agree with Williams' explanation saying the lack of blacks in the front office, "was not a deliberate thing. We just didn't look far enough ahead."[45]

The NAACP offered to help Williams and Peters look ahead. George N. Bunting, Jr., executive secretary of the Baltimore chapter, wrote Williams requesting a meeting with the Orioles in late April. "They [the Orioles] don't necessarily have the expertise to do it [establish an affirmative action program] and we do," Buntin explained. Buntin let Peters know that "Our patience is short but we will give them a reasonable amount of time to respond to the letter." He signaled the NAACP's activist intentions, saying, "There is a fine line between getting positive action and telling a business how to conduct its affairs. But we're going to make sure we get as close to that line as possible."[46] A month later, Orioles Vice President for Business Affairs Bob Aylward acknowledged to *Sun* reporter Kent Baker, "The fact of the matter is that we have not done a good job seeking minority representation.... We are correcting it."[47] So far, however, the response from the O's had been all talk.

The NAACP's national office, on the other hand, was ready to join its Baltimore affiliate in action. Benjamin Hooks convened the NAACP Sports Advisory Group. Members included Richard Powell, former GM of the Negro leagues Baltimore Elite Giants, Arthur Ashe, golfer Lee Elder, Hall of Fame basketball players Oscar Robertson and Sam Jones, and black football players from the Philadelphia Eagles and Detroit Lions. The group, Hooks said, had started negotiations with professional baseball, basketball, and football teams. Should the negotiations not bear fruit, "We will have to rely on our time-honored direct action activity which includes boycott," Hooks promised.[48]

As Williams considered his options, two mind-sets, one white and one black, about hiring minorities emerged. "Blacks," Peters noted, "rarely expressed an interest. I can't remember," he told *Sun* sportswriter Mark Hyman on Opening Day 1987, "that I have ever had a minority player come to me and say 'I am really interested in getting into front office work.'" Frank Robinson gave Hyman two reasons why not. Blacks saw the all-white composition of the front office and never heard of a black even being interviewed for a front office position, so they said to themselves, "I have no chance, so why apply?" Secondly, Robinson observed, those who did get hired did not apply. They gained their positions by the "good ole boy network."[49]

Robinson suggested the O's scrap the "good ole boy" approach, advertise openings and invite applications. That approach, Peters acknowledged, would have required a change of attitude because "our minds don't function that way. We have found that there have been so many people interested that we did not have to seek out people." Peters also acknowledged, however, that there could have been merit in taking "a more aggressive" approach to filling front office positions. "Maybe," Peters offered, "we have been remiss in not going up to a guy ... and saying, 'hey, you ought to think about getting into management.'"[50]

* * *

Prodded by pressure from the NAACP and his own embarrassment, Williams swung into action. He promised to "change greatly the club's hiring practices." In July 1987, he took the first step by appointing Calvin Hill to the 13-member Orioles Board of Directors.[51] Hill, a Baltimore native, former NFL running back, and grandson of a slave, replaced the deceased Jack Dunn III.[52] The O's expanded a summer internship program to include three minorities and hired two African American ball girls.[53] Joe Durham, who had complained in April that he could not "figure out why a man who has been around the Orioles forever is not qualified for a full-time baseball job,"[54] landed a position in November as a community director of baseball organizations. He visited schools to promote baseball and "helped out" during the season with the O's farm team, the Hagerstown Suns. Cuban-born Cristobal Rigoberto Carreras "Minnie" Mendoza, a former minor league second baseman, held down the first base coaching job for the 1988 season. Club executives, led by Orioles Vice President Larry Lucchino, a graduate of Princeton University and Yale Law School, whom Edwards had hired as his deputy when he bought the team, and still an attorney in Williams' law firm, Williams & Connolly, met with NAACP representatives throughout the year.[55]

In another response to the Campanis interview fallout, the O's hired Quay Rich, 39, in the fall of 1987 as the assistant director of season tickets and groups. He grew up in the West Baltimore neighborhood of Edmondson, where blockbusting and the drug trade flourished. The 1968 riots had hit the area particularly hard. His father worked at the post office. His mother managed the home. "Baseball," Rich said, "kept me from drinking and off the streets. We'd play all day. I didn't have a girl friend 'til I was 21." He made the All-Maryland Scholastic Association Team in 1967 for his play with the Redskins (now Red Storm) of Edmonson High (now Edmonson-Westside High) and won a baseball scholarship to Florida A and M University, a black university in Tallahassee. Homesickness brought him back home, where he finished his studies at Morgan College.[56]

Rich's previous sales position had been with Bell Atlantic (now Verizon Communications), where he was the only African American in the marketing department. "I had a big bush haircut and a statue of a fist on my desk in those days," he said. "The white guys, they were very conservative. They all looked a little nervous as they walked by my desk. I think I frightened them," he said with a smile. He left Bell Atlantic shortly after the Campanis interview and applied for a position with the O's. "I met," he said, "Mr. Lou Michelson, Director of Marketing, who rushed from around from his desk and hired me on the spot. Timing is everything. They were looking for talent after the Campanis interview."[57]

Rich participated in weekly staff meetings chaired by Lucchino. At every meeting "the demographic question came up. The panic was on," Rich recalled. The O's were losing, the press carried articles critical of the lack of African Americans on the office payroll, and few blacks could be seen in the stands. To put more blacks in the stands, Rich initiated the Jackie Robinson Program. He called on corporations such as Coca-Cola and prominent African Americans like boxer Sugar Ray Leonard for donations that he used to buy tickets for black youngsters to attend games, which they did by the hundreds.[58]

In addition to the demographic panic, the team's 1987 record, 67–95, frustrated Williams further. Not since their first two years in Baltimore had the O's lost as many games in a single season. "I am lower than a snake's belly over the state of the Orioles,"[59] Williams wrote to New York City sportscaster Warner Wolf before instigating a front office shake-up. He fired Peters, who said he "was relieved at being relieved," and farm system director Tom Giordano. Both had been with the club for 12 years. Williams replaced Peters with Roland Hemond, former general manager of the Chicago White Sox for 16 years, and, most recently, an assistant to Ueberroth charged with heading up the commissioner's minority hiring efforts. Williams announced he would now hire all department heads himself. There was to be no application process, as suggested by Frank Robinson.[60] He promoted Robinson into a new position, vice president and advisor to the owner, but retained Ripken, Sr., as manager. In November 1987, Williams gave Hill the additional responsibility, as vice president for administrative personnel, to monitor the team's hiring of African American and Latino workers.[61]

Lacy lauded Williams for appointing Robinson. "It took the 'lip service' stigma," Lacy said, out of Williams' promise six months earlier in April to set up an affirmative action program. Robby's presence "at the elbow of Williams can go a long way" toward improving race relations in the "Orioles and in baseball generally," Lacy added.[62]

Williams announced the changes at a November press conference. There he made the startling comment that race may have influenced the judgments of Peters and Giordano in their evaluations of players.[63] Williams gave as examples that, of 100 Orioles players currently under minor league contract, only seven were black, and that the O's had selected only one African American out of 30 drafted in 1987.[64] "I always resented that Williams made that statement," Peters said, "because it was a bunch of crap. I've hired and signed many blacks."[65] Looking back over his career, Peters, however, acknowledged that "Black people were not given the opportunities they should have.... I fought in World War II for three years and didn't have a black soldier next to me. Did that mean I should have done something about it? No. That's the way life was at the time. So we made do with the way things were. As times changed we all tried to change with them. I certainly feel no guilt at all about the decisions I made in my career."[66]

Giordiano, a special assistant to Peters after Peters became general manager of the Cleveland Indians in late 1987, told reporters he did not know what Williams meant. "I'll stand on my name and my reputation," he told *Sun* reporter John Eisenberg. "You'll have to ask him [Williams] what he meant."[67]

Peters and Giordiano had in fact signed many African American players. If few minorities appeared on the O's 1987 minor league rosters, the 1987 40-man roster for the "big club" listed nine African Americans and two Latinos. Though speculation appeared in the press about possible reasons for the low percentage of minorities in the O's minor league farm system in 1987, no definitive answer emerged.[68]

Asked how a team with a history of black players of the caliber of Robinson, Murray, Don Baylor, and Ken Singleton could lack sensitivity to blacks, Williams shrugged his shoulders and said, "I don't know.... I really assumed we were doing the right thing in this area with minorities.... I didn't have the time to go to each ballpark. I looked at the statistics and all, and they don't say if a player is black or white."[69]

* * *

While Williams explained his front office shake-up, two national initiatives to bring blacks into front office jobs had emerged. Commissioner Ueberroth had hired not only Harry Edwards but also Clifford Alexander, the nation's first African American Secretary of the Army and former chairman of the Equal Employment Opportunity Commission. Ueberroth asked Alexander, president of his Washington, D.C., consulting firm, Alexander and Associates, and Edwards to create a minority hiring process.

The two men mailed a questionnaire to former minority major league players to complete, with the intention of inviting those interested to meet with major league executives at regional job fairs. At the same time, Robinson and Willie Stargell, the retired Hall of Fame slugger for the Pittsburgh Pirates and currently a coach with the Milwaukee Brewers, formed the Baseball Network, an association of former black players. The Network's agenda was similar to Alexander's and Edwards': spread information about job openings, send lists of minority job applicants to all teams, and provide career, financial, and marriage counseling to interested black players, past and present.[70]

Robinson had changed his earlier reluctance to take an active role in civil rights. "Thanks, but politics and sports don't mix," Robinson had told Gabe Paul when Paul offered to buy a NAACP membership for his star in the early 1960s. Robinson later declined a plea from Jackie Robinson to get involved in civil rights activities. By this time, however, though he had discussed discrimination in baseball for years, sometimes with the press, this was his first public action.[71]

Robinson felt so strongly about the Network that he gave up the opportunity to possibly become the O's general manager. He decided not to apply for the position in order to devote full time to the Network. "I thought of such a committee years ago. So had others, but we never pulled it together, maybe because I never said it," he told Claire Smith of the *Hartford Courant*.[72]

The two groups clashed immediately. Prior to the first meeting between representatives from Ueberroth's office and the Network in Dallas on November 9, 1987, Robinson let it be known that "Edwards hasn't exactly reached out to us.... We truly do not know what they are doing which is why we're meeting." Asked if Edwards represented blacks seeking baseball jobs, Stargell replied, "I don't even know the man." Robinson promised that the Network would remain independent of the commissioner's office.[73]

Tensions resurfaced at the meeting. Edwards, Alexander, and Major League Baseball vice president Ed Durso represented Commissioner Ueberroth. Robinson, Stargell, Curt Flood, and Don Baylor, the Minnesota Twins' designated hitter and former Orioles outfielder from 1970 to 1975, represented the Network. "To unilaterally select a group of people to represent me, I have a problem with that," Flood complained after the meeting. When asked if he would work closely with the players, Edwards replied, "We have been working closely together all along." Robinson said little about Edwards' work other than "If an individual wants to fill it [the questionnaire] out and send it to Harry Edwards, that's fine with me."[74]

Edwards' and Alexander's backgrounds, however, were not fine with Robinson. The fact that neither man had any baseball experience meant, Robinson said, "they were not familiar with the problems faced by minority players." Impatient with Edwards' plans for a three- to five-year program, Robinson noted that Edwards' salary of $250,000 per year, a budget of $250,000, and speeches that paid the sociologist $5,000 each allowed him to take a long view. "I know," an exasperated Robinson said, "black ex-ball players who are willing to work in baseball right now for three of Edwards' speeches yet can't find a job."[75]

Ueberroth finally met with the Network for three hours in early December, again in Dallas, but this time without the tensions of the November meeting. Robinson felt "very pleased." Ueberroth reported "we're making progress.... We are destroying, properly so, and with everybody's help ... some of the old-boy network that held opportunities away from minorities in the past."[76]

By June 1988 the Network, whose executive director Ben Moore had been an aide to Robinson in San Francisco, had 80 dues-paying members, a 387-member mailing list, and, according to Moore, "some kind of involvement in 47 jobs."[77]

The Network, however, did not play a major role in increasing the number of front office minorities. "You had the sense it was going to be an important organization," recalled Mark Hyman, who covered the meetings for the *Sun*. "Here you had Frank Robinson, Willie Stargell, Curt Flood, who came with moral authority of very few players, Don Baylor, and there were many others. It did help raise awareness, but it never became part of the formal process."[78]

As efforts to place minorities in front-office jobs began to unfold, Sam Lacy, in November 1987, hailed them "as testimony to the claim that the antebellum days in baseballs front offices are now under concerted attack."[79]

* * *

The question of how successful the attack had been came up a year to the day after the Campanis interview. Ueberroth issued a report on April 6, 1988, the first of its kind in baseball history. The report showed that minorities, including women, made up 180 of the 542 people hired by the 26 major league clubs during the previous 12 months. Robinson saw a ray of hope in the results. "Hirings that would not have taken place have come about and hirings in the future will happen that otherwise wouldn't," he said. Minorities, however, still filled none of the highest level positions—manager, general manager, president—save Cuban-born Cookie Rojas, who assumed Gene's Mauch's job as manager of the California Angels when Mauch retired. Pointing this out, Baylor slammed the results. "There are no black managers, still no third base coaches. There are a few hitting coaches, a few office jobs and some scouts, but everything else remains the same." Ueberroth, in turn, replied: "Anyone who says that is incorrect.... The rest of the progress will come naturally, and that's the right way."[80] Seven months after the report and seeing no significant changes, Robinson turned critical. Owners and baseball's top executives "are," he told *The Sporting News*, "thumbing their nose at people, saying 'Hey, we're gonna do it the way we've always done it.'"[81] Edwards, who promised to redouble efforts to "fill the full spectrum of positions," acknowledged, "We'll come into a great deal of criticism" if no team hired a black manager in the coming year, but he promised "we're prepared for that."[82]

Edwards did not have to wait a year. A week after Ueberroth issued his report, a week during which the O's went 0–6 to start the 1988 season,

Williams fired Cal Ripken, Sr. This time Robinson got the job, bringing the total of minority major league managers to two. The novelty of a black manager attracted attention in the press. The lead sentence in the *Los Angeles Times*' account of Robinson's hiring read, "The number of minority managers in baseball doubled Tuesday." Ueberroth pronounced himself "very pleased.... This is not tokenism. Frank Robinson is a quality guy."[83]

As a caution against premature self-congratulations, Dave Anderson, *New York Times* sportswriter, warned, "One black manager and one Hispanic manager are not enough to let other clubs off the hook that Al Campanis hung them on."[84]

Anderson's caution rang unfortunately true at the two-year mark of the interview. Noticeable numerical progress had been made by blacks and other minorities, who obtained 33 percent of the major league front-office jobs that had become available since the fateful day two Aprils ago. Minorities, however, still had made little progress in cracking the high-profile positions. Of the 27 such positions available since April 1987, only one, Frank Robinson's, had gone to a minority.[85]

* * *

Williams hoped Robinson would pull the O's out of their tailspin. Following the Washington Redskins' Super Bowl victory over the Denver Broncos in January 1988, Williams lavished praise on the 'Skins general manager, Bobby Beathard. "You have done a brilliant job," Williams wrote to Beathard. "I wish to God I could find your counterpart in baseball. All my problems would be over."[86] Williams' problems, however, continued. Even with Robinson as their manager, the Birds struggled through the rest of the 1988 season. They lost their first 15 games under the new pilot and finished the season with their worst record ever, 54–107.

* * *

Two months after the O's most depressing season ever ended, two events occurred that further dampened African Americans' enthusiasm for the O's. On December 3, 1988, Eddie Murray finally got his wish to be traded (to the Los Angeles Dodgers). Fans, radio show hosts, and sportswriters, primarily white, had kept the criticism of Murray alive for the past two seasons as Murray's output continued to fall from what it had been from 1980 to 1985. He, nevertheless, had the team's second highest batting average (.277) in 1987 and led the team in hits, home runs, and runs batted in during the 1988 season.

Murray's trade bewildered African Americans. "No black baseball fans wanted him to leave," exclaimed William H. "Billy" Murphy. "No black fan expressed outrage at his demeanor or at his unwillingness to run out meaningless groundballs. How," Murphy wondered, "can a ballplayer who consistently produced as a superstar get run out of town by predominantly white fans?"[87] *Sun* reporter Mike Preston called Murray's departure "one of the lowest moments in this city's sports history." Preston compared Murray's exit to the Colts slinking off to Indianapolis under the cover of darkness and allowing its legendary quarterback, Johnny Unitas, to wear a San Diego Chargers' uniform.[88] "The way the Murray situation ended was a setback [to black fans' opinion of the Orioles]. I don't think there's any doubt about it," said John Eisenberg, long-time sportswriter for the *Sun*, in 2013.[89] The Orioles, in a move that was too little, too late, retired his uniform number 33.[90]

The second disappointment came three days after Murray's trade. Lawyers for the estate of Edward Bennett Williams, who had lost a heroic 11-year battle with cancer on August 13, 1988, put an abrupt end to former Orioles owner Jerold Hoffberger's aspiration to re-purchase the team.

In an unparalleled move in American professional sports, Hoffberger joined forces with ten black businessmen led by Raymond V. Haysbert, Sr., president of Baltimore's Park Sausage Company, whose haunting slogan "More Park's sausages, Mom... Please!" Baltimoreans recall to this day. Other Baltimore-based members of Haysbert's group included Allen Quille, parking lots and garages owner, James H. McLean, travel agency owner, Kenneth O. Wilson, owner of a downtown marina, Otis Warren, Jr., real estate executive, Osborne Payne, owner of several McDonald's restaurants, and William "Little Willie" Lloyd Adams, real estate developer. Owner of the Coca-Cola Bottling Company of Philadelphia, J. Bruce Llewellyn, Philadelphia 76ers basketball star Julius "Dr. J" Irving, and entertainer Bill Cosby rounded out the group. The group intended to make an offer to buy the team from Williams' widow, Agnes.[91]

Hoffberger, however, failed to deliver his group's bid to the estate's attorneys by the 2:30 p.m., Monday, December 6 deadline. "My pen was in the air" (that is, ready to sign the proposal) Hoffberger said when he received a call from the estate's lawyers at 3:00 p.m. telling him he need not bother to come to their office. Instead, Williams' representatives accepted an offer from New York financier and attorney Eli Jacobs, Larry Lucchino, and R. Sargent Shriver, a former high-ranking official in the Kennedy and Johnson administrations. Shriver's eldest son, Bobby, completed the group.[92]

A disappointed Hoffberger said, "Baseball needs black ownership just as it needs black management."[93] "Baseball," Haysbert lamented upon hearing the news, "has missed a great opportunity. Fact is one of the reasons blacks never have been [in] great attendance is because they haven't felt involved. An opportunity to show the nation that baseball did not exclude blacks in ownership was simply missed," he added.[94] Haysbert, long active in Baltimore business and civic affairs and one of the vice-chairmen of the committee that sponsored the Bob Boyd Night in 1957,[95] appealed the decision to the Commissioner's office to no avail.[96] Mayor William Donald Schaefer backed the Jacobs' bid and ducked questions about the Hoffberger-Haysbert attempted bid at a December 8, 1988, news conference.[97] Maryland State Delegate Howard P. "Pete" Rawlings, 51, first elected in 1979 and a member of the Black Caucus, also expressed disappointment. "I'm concerned," he told *Sun* reporter Brian Sullam, "that the Lucchino deal did not make any effort to bring minorities into this deal."[98]

Rawlings, a Baltimore native who grew up in public housing and had earned a reputation as an activist and statesman in the African American community, did more than express concern. With fellow delegate Curt

An aerial view of Oriole Park at Camden Yards taken in May 2006. The Inner Harbor, a source of controversy, can be seen in the background. Some thought it revitalized Baltimore. Others saw it as the "gilt" that siphoned attention away from the needs of the inner city (Library of Congress, Prints and Photographs Division, LC-DIG-highsm-04854; photograph by Carol Highsmith).

Anderson, first elected in 1983 and chairman of the Maryland State House's Black Caucus, the two had approached Governor Schaefer in 1987 as he sought support from the General Assembly to build a new ball park. Many legislators favored increasing spending on education and housing, not a ball park. Rawlings and Anderson saw job opportunities for African Americans. "We," Anderson said, "went to Schaefer and said, 'Look, we'd be willing to throw all our [Black Caucus] votes behind this if we can be sure some of the new jobs include minority businesses and hiring minorities.'"[99] Schaefer agreed. To insure that Schaefer's promise would be honored, the Black Caucus included in the legislation a proviso that minority firms and individuals would participate. "We always did that with any significant capital project," Clarence Davis, another member of the Black Caucus, recalled in 2013. "You couldn't rely on goodwill and builders and contractors, so we had to lock it in the legislation."[100]

As the new stadium rose from the aged rail facility, Camden Yards, 20 percent of the jobs had gone to minorities. Anderson monitored the participation of minority firms and employees—"reviewing contracts and requests for proposals, going over manifests, talking with supervisors and foreman. In the process," Anderson recalled," I got to know Larry Lucchino who, like me, was at the site most every day."[101]

CHAPTER 11

"I'm Just So Damn Mad"

As Anderson and Lucchino supervised the construction of Camden Yards, Murray's departure and the team's lackluster performance the year before confronted manager Frank Robinson with a tall order. He told the team in spring training 1989 to forget last year. Starting anew, he hired four African American coaches; Al Jackson, a ten-year major league veteran with the New York Mets and a pitching coach in their system; Tom McCraw, a first baseman and outfielder for 13 major league seasons who had coached under Robinson in Cleveland and San Francisco; Curt Motton, an Orioles outfielder from 1967 to 1974; and Orioles bullpen coach Elrod Hendricks. Robinson retained Cal Ripken, Sr., as third base coach and hired Johnny Oates, a former major league catcher, to coach at first. "They were hired on ability, and it just so happens four are black," Robinson said about his coaches. "Maybe this will quiet rumors that minorities can't handle pennant winning ball clubs."[1]

Handle a pennant-winning club they did, almost. Robinson led the 1989 Orioles to an 87–75 record to achieve the third-best year-to-year turnaround in major league history, a remarkable achievement by any standard. The O's led the American League for 116 days in spite of distractions posed by umpires Robinson believed were prejudiced. Telling reporters, "I can't go out and defend my team. I can't say anything if I believe they missed a call," Robinson considered stepping down. "They [the umpires] resent him. What else would they resent him for? Frank's a bright guy, and I think some of them are having trouble dealing with that," Tommy McCraw explained to the press.[2] Hemond asked Robby not to resign, promising to take his complaint to the commissioner's office. Fortunately for the Orioles, Hemond prevailed. Unfortunately, the Toronto Blue Jays, under African American manager Cito Gaston, nosed out the O's for the pennant on the next to the last day of the season. Gaston's appointment early in the 1989 season made him baseball's third minority manager that season. Gaston went on to lead the Blue Jays to the 1992 World Series title, becoming the first African American manager to do so. Robinson won the "Manager of the Year" Award for the American League in 1989. After a five-year fall from prominence, the O's had staged a comeback under the leadership of African Americans.[3]

Robinson would not see that level of managerial success again. The O's landed in fifth place in the American League East in 1990. After a disappointing 13–24 start to the 1991 season, trainer Richie Banells tapped Robinson on the shoulder during batting practice in Memorial Stadium on the afternoon of May 23. "Could you stop by Hemond's office after the game?" Banells asked Robinson. Turning toward Banells and drawing a finger across his throat, Robinson said simply, "I'm gone." He was right. Johnny Oates replaced him.[4] Hemond appointed Robinson to an assistant general manager's position to keep the Orioles' two front office African Americans as the team moved from Memorial Stadium to Oriole Park at Camden Yards to start the 1992 season.

* * *

Five years had now passed since the Campanis interview. Progress had been painfully slow and everyone knew it. "We have only three minority managers in the major leagues, only three black assistant general managers … and not one black manager in the minor leagues. That is unacceptable," Fay Vincent, Bart Giamatti's successor as baseball commissioner, told the National Urban League's Conference in San Diego in August 1992.[5]

Vincent omitted one historic event from his speech. In the midst of the controversy over the lack of black executives in front offices, National League owners unanimously offered Bill White the league presidency in February 1989. White accepted to became the first African American league president and the highest-ranking black executive in baseball. Outspoken during his 13-year playing career (1956–1969) and as a broadcaster for the New York Yankees alongside Phil Rizzuto, White had been one of only a few black players who went on record against segregation in Florida spring training camps and in minor league cities throughout the South. Peter O'Malley, Dodgers owner and chairman of the search committee, said that White was the best man for the job, and "that race was not a factor." White's appointment pleased Alexander. He termed White's appointment "highly significant" and congratulated baseball on "setting a standard that others can emulate." But, he cautioned, "If we think one appointment is the beginning and the end, it isn't."[6]

White was not unaware of the significance of his appointment. He told *Ebony* in 1992 that he hoped his tenure as president would serve to show people that blacks could handle significant responsibilities as well as anyone. White's five-year tenure proved him right. Following White's resignation in 1993, the owners selected African American Leonard S. Coleman to succeed him. Coleman stayed in the job until 1999, when baseball abolished the offices of American and National League presidents while leaving the office of commissioner, in the person of Bud Selig at the time, to preside over the game.[7]

Slow progress did not deter Rawlings from organizing the African American Task Force on Professional Sports (AATFPS). The group consisted of elected officials, church officers, educators, and members of Baltimore's community organizations. The task force set two objectives for itself, to increase black attendance at games and to insure that blacks gained a fair share of the economic benefits derived by the O's from the city. The votes of black caucus legislators and the city residents' purchase of lottery tickets (whose proceeds went toward funding Camden Yards) represented, Rawlings argued, substantial African American support for the team.

Discussions between the task force and the O's went smoothly for a year. Then in March 1992, Rawlings charged the O's with dragging their feet on an AATFPS proposal to involve blacks in the celebrations to inaugurate the new ballpark in April 1992. "I'm just so damn mad that it's been before them for three months, and they've done nothing," Rawlings fumed to a *Philadelphia Tribune* reporter. The O's inaction showed, Rawlings charged, lack of awareness "that the city is 60 percent African American." More outreach to the black community, Rawlings reasoned, would solve the problem "of very few African Americans coming to ball games."[8]

Rawlings got no satisfaction. Lucchino, now the face of the O's to the city as new owner Jacobs, in decided contrast to Williams, stayed out of day-to-day management, wanted to study Rawlings' complaint before responding. O's public relations manager Bob Miller, wanting to publicize the O's level of outreach, proudly ticked off a list of community programs initiated by the Birds "to serve the community regardless of race, creed, color, and handicaps." Rawlings, unimpressed, wanted the O's to advertise in the *AFRO*, give away 5,000 tickets to an exhibition game to students with good attendance at school, and invite the choir from Morgan State to sing the national anthem on Opening Day. Community relations director Julie Wagner responded by saying that 1,000 Opening Day tickets would be given to a local radio station to disperse.[9]

Despite Rawlings' frustration, the two groups met again in October

1992. The meeting involved Rawlings, Anderson, 12 other task-force members, Lucchino and three other Orioles officials. The meeting only served to increase the tension between the O's and the AATFPS. Lucchino deemed unrealistic the task force's proposal for a $2 million marketing campaign over three years designed to bring black attendance at games up to 10–15 percent. He did agree to increase the team's marketing efforts in the black community. An unfortunate misunderstanding occurred during the discussion, which had it been ironed out, would have avoided hard feelings. Based on the results of a marketing study conducted by Brenda Hulbert, wife of Maurice (Hot Rod) Hulbert, African American and general manager of radio stations WEBB and WBGR, Lucchino proposed to rely more on radio stations than on newspapers, as Rawlings had proposed. The study convinced Lucchino that radio would reach more people than would newspapers. Ray Gilbert, a reporter for *Afro-American Red Star*, did not see it that way. He characterized Lucchino's proposal as "negative and insulting," because it implied "that African Americans don't or can't read." The task force also proposed that minority business firms supply 25 percent of the concessions sold at the stadium. Of the 25 percent, 15 percent should be African Americans and the other 10 percent should consist of "minorities that are identified both in the city and state procurement regulations." The meeting ended on an inconclusive note.[10]

While the task force waited for a response from Lucchino, the Rev. Jesse Jackson took the occasion of Opening Day 1993 to mount a protest at Camden Yards. He called for a 1,000-person picket line at the ballpark as the O's faced the Texas Rangers. Jackson directed his protest at all of major league baseball, not just Baltimore. He chose Camden Yards only because President Bill Clinton would throw out the first ball.[11] In a letter to the White House Chief of Staff, Thomas F. "Mack" McLarty, Jackson spelled out what he saw as "baseball's institutional racism and sexism." The letter did not specifically ask the President to cancel his appearance, but such was Jackson's intent.[12] Denying any racism or sexism, institutional or otherwise, Lucchino issued a statement saying the O's "are proud of their record of the past five years ... and we must and we shall improve our record in achieving objectives that are fundamental in our country's promises to all Americans."[13] Clinton threw out the first pitch. Only 200 people answered Jackson's call for picketers.

* * *

Jackson's call for a protest revealed differences of opinion in Baltimore's African American community over the best way to increase the

Orioles' minority hiring. Jackson urged the General Assembly's Black Caucus to support his campaign to have more blacks and minorities hired in baseball's front offices. Rawlings and Anderson pledged the caucus's support and applauded the Reverend's message. "The first steps have been encouraging," Anderson said.[14] Jackson telephoned Joseph Haskins, Jr., president of Harbor Bank, in which the O's had earlier deposited $100,000. Jackson told Haskins, who also presided over the Presidents Round Table, "We'd like you to have your suite dark to support the picketing."[15] The Presidents Round Table, an association of African American business leaders, had bought the suite in response to Governor Schaefer's call to African Americans to support the Greater Baltimore Committee. "Professional basketball and football players, actors and actresses, businessmen, attorneys, and every political person you could think of, frequented the suite. We helped to raise the visibility of the African American business community and show we play our part as do others," Haskins said in 2013. He took Jackson's request to the other Round Table members. "They told me," Haskins said, summarizing his colleagues' replies, "'You know Joe, we busted our chops and it cost us a fortune to have this suite and we're all for the cause but why now? Sometimes progress costs a little more than people feel they should be paying.'"[16] The lights stayed on.

The game began at 1:30 p.m. Jackson's pickets, including Delegate Clarence Davis, carried protest signs and leaflets. Marchers shouted, "Hey, hey, ho, ho, racism has got to go" and "No women allowed in the game, the front office is just the same."[17] Haskins and his guests watched the game from the Presidents Round Table Suite. Baltimore Mayor Kurt Schmoke and Kweisi Mfume, a U.S. Congressman from Baltimore and chairman of the U.S. House of Representatives Black Caucus, watched the game from box seats with President Clinton. The different choices confused and upset Courtland Milloy, columnist for the *Washington Post*. "I couldn't figure out the 'protest' against racism at Camden Yards," Milloy admitted. Mfume disagreed with Milloy that the situation looked confusing. "We have developed a political sophistication," Mfume told Milloy, "that recognizes waging battles on all fronts simultaneously." Mfume defended his choice by saying he talked about his concerns directly with Clinton, which he could not have done had he been on the picket line. Milloy did not buy it. People, Milloy asserted, had one of three choices: "take a swing at racism" as Jackson did, "see where" participating in both the picketing and the dialogue with Clinton "would get them," as Ronald Walters, a political science professor at Howard University, suggested

Schmoke and Mfume should have done, "or just stand there, as Schmoke has, and take the pitch."[18]

* * *

Talks between the O's and the task force began again on July 8, 1993. They met at the Orchard Street Church, Baltimore's oldest standing structure, built by African Americans and headquarters at the time for Baltimore's Urban League. The Orioles sent their top executives, including Lucchino, Hill, Robinson, Aylward, and public relations director Julie Wagner. Quay Rich, who also attended, described the tone of the meeting as friendly. Members of the task force believed the Orioles had agreed to create a plan to boost African American attendance at games and increase the club's business with black-owned firms.[19] Rawlings came away feeling pleased. "It is," he said immediately afterward, "clearly unparalleled for a professional sports team." Rawlings, nevertheless, felt more had to be done. The team's failure to set specific goals for hiring more minority workers and purchase more from minority firms was, Rawlings said, "a disappointment."[20]

Later in July Lucchino, more connected with the black community than any Orioles executive before him, issued a "mid-season report." Thirty-three percent of the O's advertising budget now went to outlets, print, radio, and television, serving primarily African Americans. Minority-owned Harbor Bank held a $100,000 deposit from the team, thanks to, according to bank president Joseph Haskins, Jr., Lucchino reaching out to the black community.[21] A local, African American-owned firm would now print the team's stationery.

Cooperation between the task force and the Orioles continued during preparations for the 1993 All-Star Game at Camden Yards. As the only African American member of the 12-person All-Star Host Committee, Anderson arranged for the African American actor, James Earl Jones, to speak the national anthem while the Morgan State Choir sang it in the background. Anderson had convinced the committee that the planned appearance of country singer Garth Brooks might not appeal to African Americans. Anderson also arranged for local black fraternities to perform step shows in a parking lot outside the stadium.[22]

* * *

While promising, these events failed to address major league baseball's front office hiring practices. On the eve of the All-Star Game, the

Rev. Jackson's Rainbow Commission on Fairness in Athletics announced that no minority held an executive position in a major league front office: owner, president, general manager, chief scout, or director of player personnel. Clifford Alexander took issue with Jackson's assessment. Alexander claimed that "top executive employment has gone from about 2 percent to 8 percent and that the percentage of managers and coaches has risen from 12 percent to 20 percent since 1987." Some of the teams, Alexander allowed, "are not doing the job at all, but the overall picture is improv-

MARYLAND
HOUSE OF DELEGATES

HOWARD P. RAWLINGS
CHAIRMAN
COMMITTEE ON APPROPRIATIONS

MEMORANDUM

TO: MEMBERS OF THE AFRICAN-AMERICAN TASK FORCE ON PROFESSIONAL SPORTS

FROM: DELEGATE PETE RAWLINGS

DATE: JULY 1, 1993

RE: MEETING TO RESPOND TO DOCUMENTS PRESENTED BY THE BALTIMORE ORIOLES

There will be a meeting of the African-American Task Force on Professional Sports on **THURSDAY, JULY 8, 1993 AT 8:00 A. M.** in the office of the BALTIMORE URBAN LEAGUE, 520 ORCHARD STREET, BALTIMORE, MARYLAND 21201.

This meeting is called for the purpose of obtaining a task force response to the documents presented to us by the Baltimore Orioles. The documents will be presented to you at the meeting.

If you have any questions regarding the above, please call me at my District Office (466-4224). I look forward to seeing you on **THURSDAY, JULY 8, 1993 AT 8:00 A.M.**

A copy of the memo that delegate Peter Rawlings sent to task force members informing them of the meeting with Orioles representatives at the Orchard Street Church on July 8, 1993 (author's collection).

ing. It needs to improve more."[23] Hank Aaron, unswayed by Alexander's percentages, said the increases could be explained by women hired as secretaries and a few blacks in low-level positions. The only significant hire, in Aaron's opinion, occurred when the Houston Astros hired African American Bob Watson as assistant general manager. "When all was said and done," Aaron wrote in his autobiography, "I don't believe Alexander and Edwards made one damn bit of difference."[24]

Regardless of the figures, there were precious few blacks in the front office positions for which African Americans, Campanis had stated, lacked the necessities. When asked why, Alexander suggested "unknowing discrimination" as a likely explanation. As different from flat-out bigotry, Alexander pointed out that one's reactions to "what we read and how we are educated influence our actions and decisions in ways we may not be fully aware of. If certain groups have been portrayed negatively and such portrayal influences one's opinion about the group however slightly, and one does not take those reactions into account when making personnel decisions then," Alexander told author John Eisenberg, "you are acting in a discriminatory fashion." He gave as an example the frequent negative portrayals of Hispanics in the late 1980s. "That can seep into the thinking of some people," he said. "You may not think it, but it does."[25]

Perhaps "unknowing discrimination" explained Campanis' remarks as well as those by veteran Orioles scout Fred Uhlman during spring training in 1993. Mexican players run poorly, but are good infielders and dancers because they have good rhythm, Uhlman told *Washington Post* reporter Mark Maske. "It's a genetic thing," Uhlman explained.[26] The National Council of La Raza, a Hispanic lobbying group, demanded Uhlman's firing. Lucchino, following a meeting with the Council, said the O's would stand by Uhlman but not what he said. "Any type of racial or ethnic stereotyping," Lucchino told Maske, "is offensive and wrong, and we regret the comments that were made along those lines."[27] Uhlman, like Campanis, did not realize the impact of his statement at the time, apologized, and said he "didn't mean in any way for it to come across like that. If I offended anyone in any way, I certainly want to apologize."[28] In an effort to stem further such incidents, Lucchino sponsored a cultural diversity sensitivity training program for Orioles employees.[29]

* * *

In August 1993, a month after the Orchard Street Church meeting, the O's changed ownership. Peter G. Angelos led a group of investors who bought the Orioles for a then-record sum of $173 million. Other investors included film director Barry Levinson, novelist Tom Clancy, tennis player Pam Shriver, and ABC sports commentator Jim McKay. The new owner had created a lucrative law practice following a political career. He served on the city council from 1959 to 1963, the first Greek-American to do so, where he advocated for fair housing. He ran unsuccessfully for mayor in 1964 with an African American as his running mate, the first bi-racial ticket in Baltimore history, and he mounted three unsuccessful campaigns for a seat in the Maryland General Assembly during the 1960s.[30]

Angelos met with the task force in October 1993, the only meeting he would have with the group. There he proposed several community initiatives, including a pavilion for kids from all parts of the city who would receive free tickets. He noted afterwards, "That didn't seem to interest Rawlings that much." He also said he did not think the Orioles had a binding agreement with the task force.[31]

Angelos was right about Rawlings's attitude toward free tickets.

Hawkins did think, however, that the task force did have a binding agreement with the O's. He pursued it. After failing to re-establish contact with Angelos, Rawlings, in a May 1994 letter to task force members which he published in the *AFRO*, compared Angelos to the U.S. Supreme Court's *Dred Scott v. Sanford* decision. That ruling concluded that African Americans were property, not citizens. "It appears that 137 years later," Rawlings wrote, "Peter Angelos has revisited the Dred Scott case."[32] The comparison angered Angelos. "The Orioles will not be coerced, threatened, or insulted as I was by Rawlings.... Let me tell him publically he owes me an apology," Angelos fired back. Joe Foss, Orioles vice chairman of business and finance, added, "The Orioles do not discriminate. Our organization will report to Major League Baseball, not the Task Force."[33]

The task force met to consider its next steps. It ruled out a boycott, a tried and true civil rights protest activity, since "that would be a big joke. Peter Angelos would hardly notice," observed Rawlings, making reference to the sparse African American attendance at games.[34] Rawlings instead decided to reach out to the Baptist Ministers Conference of Maryland, with 100 African American churches statewide. The Conference voted unanimously to support the Task Force's work, thereby joining the NAACP, the Urban League, the Council for Business and Economic Opportunities, members of the City Council, and the House of Delegates, who had previously announced their support for the task force's objectives.[35]

Reports in late June 1994, that Angelos was selecting a group of blacks to work with him on minority issues, further alienated many African Americans. The *Afro-American Red Star* ran an editorial titled "Warning, Mr. Angelos." The writer called such a move evidence of "a shocking degree of contempt for the intelligence and good sense of African Americans. Long ago," the editorial continued, "we learned to be wary when people outside our community began telling us who our leaders were. We recognized the technique for what it is, 'divide and conquer,' and realize it is an effort to split the black community into competing factions."[36]

Soon afterward Angelos severed all ties with the task force. At the same time he promised to meet with any member of the community to discuss any issue. He assured the city, "There's nothing wrong with the Orioles. There is no discrimination practiced against anyone."[37]

In a final effort to engage Angelos, the task force addressed an open letter to him in July stating, in part, "We find it completely unacceptable that you have, in effect, rendered our good faith agreement with the Baltimore Orioles null and void." Thirty-two people signed the letter. Signers included Delegates Rawlings, Anderson, Davis, and Elijah Cummings, future U.S.

Open letter to Peter Angelos
Owner, Baltimore Orioles

Dear Mr. Angelos:

Last year at the Orchard Street Church, we entered into an historic agreement for fairness and justice between the African-American Task Force on Professional Sports (AATFPS) and the Baltimore Orioles.

That agreement addressed our grave concerns about both the limited participation of African Americans as fans at the ballgames and the meager economic benefits derived from one of the most profitable businesses located in Baltimore.

We wish to remind you that the Baltimore Orioles are now drawing huge profits because of the public support that built Oriole Park at Camden Yards.

The construction of the stadium would not have even occurred without the substantial support of the elected officials from the African-American community. Also, the debt service payments on the stadium construction bonds are derived from the lottery which our community plays in significant numbers.

We find it completely unacceptable that you have, in effect, rendered our good faith agreement with the Baltimore Orioles null and void. We're also appalled by your lack of responsiveness at our repeated attempts to discuss the agreement further.

We are calling for immediate action on the July 1993 agreement in its entirety. It's that simple. A process must be established to assure that the Baltimore Orioles will act with integrity and immediacy to honor the tenets of our agreement. The AATFPS will continue to pursue this matter until fairness and justice prevails.

Sincerely,

Delegate Howard P. Rawlings
Chairman, AATFPS

Delegate Curtis S. Anderson	*Joy Bramble*
Delegate Elijah E. Cummings	*Ovetta Moore*
Delegate Clarence Davis	*Dr. Charles W. Simmons*
Delegate Salima Siler Marriott	*Stanley Tucker*
Councilman Melvin Stukes	*Steve Walden*
Councilwoman Sheila Dixon	*Arnold Hawkins*
Councilwoman Iris Reeves	*Naomi C. Booker*
Dr. Anne O. Emery	*Roger Lyons*
Donna Stanley	*George Buntin*
Joseph Haskins, Jr.	*A. Bernice Hunley*
Rev. William Calhoun	*Frances M. Draper*
Rev. John Louis Wright	*Meldon Hollis*
James McLean	*Valerie Clifford-Howze*
Michael A. Gaines, Jr.	*Lonnie Carr*
Maurice Robinson	*Morning Sunday*
Lewis Long	*Delores West*

HIT A HOME RUN FOR JUSTICE! Support the African-American Task Force on Professional Sports by sending this open letter to:

Mr. Peter Angelos, Owner
THe Baltimore Orioles
333 W. Camden Street
Baltimore, MD 21201

I support the position of AATFPS.

NAME:

The open letter, with a few stain marks, that the African American Task Force on Professional Sports sent hundreds of signed copies of to Orioles owner Peter Angelos, taking him to task for not living up to "the good faith agreement" between the task force and himself (author's collection).

Congressman from Baltimore; three city council members including future Baltimore Mayor Shelia Dixon; ministers, educators, and others. The letter promised, "The AATFPS will continue to pursue this matter until fairness and justice prevail." Over 500 Baltimore citizens, "black, white, male, female," recalled Clarence Davis, signed copies of the letter.[38] Anderson, representing the task force, Baltimore Urban League representative Marvin McFadden, and Interdenominational Ministerial Alliance representative the Rev. Daki Napata delivered the copies to Angelos's office on July 27, 1994. Angelos was unavailable.[39] No more was heard from the task force.

* * *

Two years later, in a move applauded by white and black Baltimoreans and Orioles players alike, Angelos negotiated a trade with the Indians that brought Eddie Murray back to Baltimore eight years after his tumultuous 1988 departure. Cheers of "Ed-dee !!, Ed-dee !!" again rang in his ears. Parents no longer kept their children away from the first base box seats. Players eagerly sought his advice. Murray gave it willingly. On September 6, 1996, a year to the day after Cal Ripken, Jr., broke Lou Gehrig's consecutive game streak by appearing in his 2,131st consecutive game, Murray, with a sizzling line drive into the right-center field stands, joined baseball's immortals. With that home run he became only the third player in major league history to achieve 500 home runs and 3,000 hits. As an indication of how much progress had been made on the field since Jackie Robinson's 1946 debut in Baltimore, fans gave Murray a nine-minute standing ovation. Just two other players have achieved the feat: Cuban-born Rafael Palmeiro and New York Yankee Alex Rodriguez. After passing the 500-homer mark as a member of the Texas Rangers, Palmeiro got his 3,000th hit in an Orioles uniform against the Seattle Mariners on July 15, 2005. Rodriguez got his 3,000th hit, a home run (number 667), against the Detroit Tigers on June 19, 2015, at Yankee Stadium.

So sweet for Murray was his return that his Baltimore-based agent, Ron Shapiro, predicted after Murray's record blast that he would enter the Hall of Fame representing the team he began his career with, the Orioles.[40] On July 27, 2003, at a ceremony in the village of Cooperstown, New York, Murray, who had played for the Orioles for 12 of his 21 major league seasons and also for the Dodgers, Mets, Indians, and Angels, proved Shapiro right. On August 11, 2012, the Orioles unveiled a larger-than-life-sized bronze statue of Murray. Murray's statue joined those of the Orioles' other Hall of Famers: Frank Robinson, Jim Palmer, Brooks Robinson, Earl Weaver, and Cal Ripken, Jr.

Epilogue

In 1999, near the end of his last term as mayor, Kurt Schmoke characterized Baltimore's heart "as still working class even if the economic realities have changed." The city continues to eschew "anything elegant or stylish. We have," Schmoke continued, "this world famous institution, Johns Hopkins, in our midst, but it has never quite won the affection of ordinary Baltimoreans." Closer to the hearts of Baltimoreans at that time, in the eyes of *New York Times* reporter R. W. Apple, Jr., were its "unpompous politicians," two U.S. Senators, "a tough, wise-cracking Polish American Barbara Mikulski, a cerebral Greek-American Paul Sarbanes, and a wacky former mayor and governor [William Donald Schaefer] who settled a bar bet by diving into the seal pool at the National Aquarium." Apple also singled out "gritty" sports heroes Johnny Unitas, Frank Robinson, and Cal Ripken Jr., "who never blew their own horns," as other beloved Baltimoreans.[1]

Curt Anderson noted in 2013 that over the past 25 years whites voted for blacks in municipal elections for mayor and city council seats in ever increasing numbers as the number of African Americans holding elected office continued to rise. Schools, while constitutionally integrated, remained segregated in practice as most white parents sent their children to private or Catholic schools, expressing concern over possible violence or instruction "not to their liking." Blacks and whites tended to associate among themselves. "There are hardly any integrated churches," Anderson said. "If you go to the cafeteria in a state office building," he added, "you're likely to see whites sitting with whites and blacks sitting with blacks." Racial tension, however, was at an all-time low, Anderson added, save for that caused by the city's policemen, who have a "reputation for not respecting citizens."[3]

Matthew Death, inner-city resident and coordinator of community relations for the Orioles, had similar observations of life in Baltimore in

2013. "It's segregated," he said when asked about the ethnic make-up of his Upper Fells Point neighborhood. "Across the street from me," Death said, "is a section of 8A Housing mostly for African Americans, directly to the right of me the majority of people are Latino, and closer to the water it is predominately Caucasian. People pretty much keep to themselves creating an unofficial segregation, but there's no tension. I walk or ride my bike through these neighborhoods to and from the office. Of course it is the inner city and you have to be prepared, but I've never felt threatened."[4]

Looking into the future in 2013, Schmoke predicted that Baltimore will "remain a tale of two cities for awhile where one will find some wonderful urban living and, at the same time, real challenges in dealing with the problems of the poor." The city, Schmoke believed, "needs to become more creative" as state and federal monies fall off but thought the city "is moving in the right direction. More folks are moving back into the city. Home purchases move along at a steady clip. Community relations are at a good level. People want to work together."[5]

Two years after Schmoke's observations, racial tension went from an all-time low to front and center. Six Baltimore police officers, three black and three white, arrested Freddie C. Gray, Jr., a 25 year-old African American, on April 12, 2015, near Baltimore's Gilmor Housing Project, an area known for high rates of poverty, crime, and drug dealing. Charged with possession of an illegal switchblade knife, Gray lapsed into a coma in a police van. Officers took him to a trauma center where he died on April 19 of spinal injuries suffered in the van. A grand jury indicted the officers on charges ranging from reckless endangerment to second-degree murder. Hundreds of protesters took to the streets looting and burning neighborhood businesses including a CVS drug store. Maryland State Police sent eighty-two of its officers to patrol the streets. Maryland governor Larry Hogan declared a state of emergency. He brought in the National Guard. The Orioles postponed a game against the White Sox and, in an unprecedented move, barred fans from attending the next scheduled game against the Sox. By May 3, the Guard had started withdrawing from the city and the city-wide night curfew was lifted. On May 8 U.S. Attorney General Loretta Lynch initiated a Department of Justice review of the Baltimore police department for alleged use of excessive force, unlawful practices, and discriminatory policing. Outward calm had returned to the city, but racial tensions continued to fester.[2]

* * *

Sixty years after the Orioles arrived in Baltimore, the increase in African Americans in the stands noted by Lacy in 1985 has fallen off. A long-serving African American usher, when asked during a Sunday afternoon game in 2013 how many attend games replied, "A lot fewer than you'd think." The Orioles do not publicize attendance figures by race, gender, or ethnicity, but it is a safe bet that black attendance is less than ten percent. The percentage of African American residents in the city approaches 65 percent. Flagging interest on the part of the younger generation, cost, the effects of segregation, and the presence of few African American players on the team explain the low turnout.

"Baseball's not a major draw for black kids like basketball and football are," said Al Bumbry in 2012.[6] "It's easy to get a ball and go into a gym. It also has to do with the heroes young black kids grow up idolizing, like Michael Jordan."[7] Clarence Davis bought a house near Memorial Stadium "so my kids could enjoy the games with me. Now," he continued, "they catch me watching a game on TV and say 'Dad, there you go with the O's again.'" Davis, who "played baseball six days a week growing up," cited baseball's slow pace as the reason for his kids' disinterest.[8]

Cost is another impediment. "It's expensive," Curt Anderson said. Anderson, a 60-year resident of northeast Baltimore and a 24-year member of the Maryland House of Delegates, added, "Taking your kids to a game is reserved for the well-to-do. Not many families in northeast Baltimore can afford the $100 to $200 it can cost for a family of four."[9]

Joseph Haskins, Jr., agreed. "While people do not always like to talk about it," he said in 2013, "cost is the primary reason black attendance is so low. After tickets, a hot dog, and a drink, a family of three to four can be into a hundred dollars, and the per capita income of blacks in the city is fairly low."[10]

The effects of segregation remain an impediment. Negative feelings of blacks toward teams like the Red Sox and Yankees, two of the last teams to integrate and who visit Camden Yards every year, "have persisted," according to Judge William H. "Billy" Murphy, Jr.[11] The Rev. Quay Rich, now pastor emeritus at Baltimore's New Huntington Baptist Church, cited the city's history of segregation as "still a sting in the craw for guys my age [60 and over]," as a reason for the low turnout.[12] Quay also cited John Denver's "Thank God I'm a Country Boy," played during the seventh-inning stretch, as another deterrent to blacks attending games. "It's a hard song for inner-city blacks to relate to. It has a certain red-neck tone and reminds people of farms and plantations in the South," Quay said. "How you gonna draw us in if you have John Denver signing that song?"[13]

Not all African Americans share Quay's assessment of Denver's song. Schmoke recalled, "I've seen everybody singing along. I'm sure there are some people who don't like it, but I never viewed it having anything to do with race."[14] Curt Anderson concurred. "I've been to lots of games," he said, "and I see blacks singing along like they know the words."[15]

Having few black players is another contributor to a low African American turnout. "People that I know in my district root for the Orioles but very few go to the games. One reason being the product on the field is not representative of us," Anderson noted.[16] The percentage of African America players in the majors has fallen from a high of 20 percent during the 1970s through the early 1990s to eight percent in 2013.[17] The Orioles experienced a similar decline. The 2014 40-man roster carried but three, including center fielder Adam Jones, the team's highest-paid player at $13 million for the 2013 season. The other two were outfielder Delmon Young and second baseman Jemile Weeks. Of the team's ten coaches in 2014, one, Wayne Kirby at first base, was an African American. The Orioles, like many teams, now feature a strong international contingent. The 2014 roster carried players from Taiwan, Mexico, Dominican Republic, Curacao, Venezuela, Cuba, and South Korea.[18]

The low African American turnout has not, however, discouraged Orioles management from initiating extensive contacts with city residents, black and white alike. The Orioles, through an aptly-named initiative, OriolesREACH, gave away over 100,000 free tickets in 2012, which included 12,000 tickets for children from disadvantaged areas. A number of Orioles players contributed money to this effort. With the tickets came food, drink, Orioles t-shirts and caps, and transportation to and from the games. The other tickets went to non-profit, volunteer, and service organizations such as schools, churches, the NAACP, and the Urban League. The free tickets accounted for about five percent of the season's attendance.[19]

OriolesREACH also conducts a myriad of activities within the stadium and the community. Stadium events include Jackie Robinson Day, Military Appreciation Day, hosting a high school all-star game, and sponsoring special days for safety patrols and Little Leaguers. Community activities include partnering with the schools in the summer to help thousands of students master basic skills and supporting Reviving Baseball in the Inner City (RBI), which helps teenagers, both boys and girls, build self-esteem while learning the game. African American firms provide concessions at Camden Yards and print the club's stationery.[20]

Angelos takes an active role. "He is very thoughtful with resources in the African American community," Haskins said of Angelos's initiatives in the African American community.[21] Angelos twice contributed $5,000 to Curt Anderson to underwrite the cost of taking 300 youngsters from Baltimore to the Baseball Hall of Fame in Cooperstown, New York, for both Eddie Murray's and Cal Ripken, Jr.'s induction. "I couldn't have done it without him," Anderson said.[22] "We have a very positive working relationship with the Orioles," said J. Howard Henderson, President and C.E.O. of the Greater Baltimore Urban League, in a 2013 interview. Henderson also noted that the O's provide tickets to kids to attend games, provide players to speak at events, and support youth leagues with donations and equipment. Judge Murphy credited Angelos, "one of the most racially enlightened people from the white community that I've ever met," with reaching out to the black community. "He's done many things," Murphy said, "but hasn't been more successful [in attracting African Americans to games] than anyone else in the country has."[23]

Noticeably less progress has been made in integrating the front office. It remains practically an all-white group that calls the shots both on the field and within the city. As assistant general manager from 1992 to 1995, Frank Robinson was the O's last black executive. At the staff level women have made significant gains in the front office. Of the 115 front office personnel pictured in the Orioles' 2013 Media Guide, 47 were women. African Americans have not fared as well. Only three who appear from their photographs to be African American are shown in the 2013 Media Guide: manager of mail room operations, mail room assistant and main receptionist. "We are still pushing for more blacks in high level front office positions to complete that part of the pie," Henderson said in 2012.[24]

The lack of blacks in the Orioles' executive ranks does not put the club in the minority: only five blacks have held a general manager position in all of Major League baseball. Only one African American, Hall of Fame basketball player Earvin "Magic" Johnson, has been involved as an owner. He is a part of the ownership structure of the Los Angeles Dodgers. See the Appendix for a list by team of black major league baseball managers, general managers and owners.

Afterword

Peter Angelos

Angelos remains the primary owner of the Orioles as of this writing. Since purchasing the team he has been the subject of some criticism. *Sports Illustrated* rated him as the worst owner in the major leagues in 2009. Disillusionment among fans has grown as the Orioles have won only one division title during the Angelos era. That may be changing as the 2014 Orioles captured their division title for the first time since 1997. Well-known for his acts of charity and philanthropy, Angelos is the largest individual donor to the University of Baltimore and reportedly donated $300,000 to keep the city swimming pools open during the hot summer of 2010. He breeds and races thoroughbred horses.

Spiro Agnew

Agnew nominated Richard Nixon for president at the 1968 Republican National Convention. Nixon selected him as his running mate, and they beat Hubert Humphrey and Edmund Muskie in the fall election. The U.S. Attorney's Office investigated Agnew in 1973 on charges of extortion, tax fraud, bribery, and conspiracy. Agnew pleaded no contest to one charge of tax evasion and resigned the vice presidency. He became a trade executive, published a memoir implying that Nixon and others planned to assassinate him if didn't resign, and wrote a novel about a vice president done in by his own ambitions. He died on September 17, 1996, at age 77 in Berlin, Maryland, from leukemia.

Thomas D'Alesandro, Jr.

The winner of 22 elections to public office, D'Alesandro served as a delegate in the Maryland Assembly, a member of the Baltimore City Council, a member of Congress, and as Baltimore's mayor from 1947 to 1959. His son, Thomas D'Alesandro III, followed him as mayor from 1967 to 1971. His daughter, Nancy Pelosi, won election to the U.S. House of Representatives from San Francisco and has served as Speaker of the House. After retiring as mayor he worked in appointed public service positions as a member of the Federal Renegotiation Board from 1961 to 1969 and the Parole Commission from 1971 to 1981. He died of a heart attack on August 23, 1987, in Baltimore at age 84.

Curt Anderson

Elected Chairman of the Legislative Black Caucus of Maryland in 1987, the same year as the Campanis interview, Anderson sponsored Maryland's Minority Business Enterprise Act. The subsequent act increased minority participation in state projects, including the building of Camden Yards. Defeated in a race for a Maryland State Senate seat in 1994, he practiced law for eight years before winning election to a seat in the Assembly, where he serves as of this writing. Following his re-election, Anderson strongly opposed the introduction of slot machines, a position he held throughout the long debate on the issue. Pro-slots forces eventually prevailed.

Paul Blair

Traded to the New York Yankees in 1977, Blair played for the Yankees and, briefly, the Cincinnati Reds before retiring from major league baseball in 1980. He stayed active in baseball until 2002 as a coach for the Houston Astros and the Rochester Red Wings, and head baseball coach at Fordham University and Coppin State College. He managed the Yonkers Hoot Owls, in the newly formed Northeast League, for its one year of existence in 1995. After retiring from coaching he appeared often in celebrity golf and bowling tournaments. He collapsed during a practice round for a bowling tournament in Pikesville, Maryland, on December 26, 2013, and died of heart failure on the way to the hospital at age 69.

Sam Bowens

After leaving the Orioles in 1967, he played for the Washington Senators for two seasons, 1968–1969. He had his best season with the Orioles, 1964, but an alcohol addiction and being hit in the head by a pitched ball shortened his career. He returned home to Wilmington, North Carolina, where he died March 28, 2003, at age 64.

Joe Durham

After being released by the St. Louis Cardinals in 1959, Durham played in the International League with the Richmond Virginians and the Rochester Red Wings from 1961 to 1964. He worked as a salesman for the Churchill Liquor Distributors in Baltimore and pitched batting practice for the Orioles for many years. Now retired, he lives in Maryland and serves as an Orioles Baseball Club representative.

Harry Edwards

Edwards is a professor emeritus of sociology at Berkeley. He continues his advocacy for African Americans in sports and all walks of life. During his career, Edwards has served as a staff consultant to the San Francisco 49ers football team and to the Golden State Warriors basketball team. He is the author of several books, including *The Revolt of the Black Athlete* and *The Struggle that Must Be*; and numerous published articles for *Time Magazine*, *Sports Illustrated*, *Psychology Today* and *Atlantic Monthly*.

Jehosie Heard

Heard pitched in the minors through the 1957 season. He returned to Birmingham as a supervisor in a cotton mill until retiring in 1985. He died of cancer in a nursing home in 1999 at age 79, leaving behind his wife Mildred and a daughter, Doris Robinson, of Birmingham.

Jerold Hoffberger

After selling the Orioles to Edward Bennett Williams in 1979, Hoffberger continued as president of the National Brewery Company and stayed involved in many civic and philanthropic activities. Beneficiaries of his generosity included the Johns Hopkins University Hospital; Mercy, Sinai, and Harbor Hospitals; and the Baltimore Hebrew Congregation. He served as president of the Council of Jewish Federations and Welfare Funds and the worldwide Jewish Agency. He indulged his passion for horses by establishing a farm for thoroughbreds in Howard County, Maryland. The Rev. Melvin Tuggle, president of the Clergy United for East Baltimore, credited Hoffberger with helping to diffuse racial tensions in the city by acquiring Frank Robinson. The former Orioles owner died of a heart attack two days after his 80th birthday on April 9, 1999.

George Mahoney

Mahoney continued to run for public office and lose. In 1970 incumbent U.S. Senator Millard Tydings prevailed in the Democratic primary. In his last attempt at public office, he lost the 1974 race for Baltimore county executive to Theodore Venetoulis. He served one term as chairman of the Maryland Lottery, sold his construction company, Mahoney Brothers, in 1985, and in 1987 bought Christ's Episcopal Church in downtown Baltimore, because, he said, he liked the bells. He died of congestive heart failure in his suite at the Belvedere Hotel on March 18, 1989.

Theodore McKeldin

Prevented by law from running for a third consecutive term as governor, McKeldin threw his hat in the ring for the 1959 Baltimore mayor's race and was soundly beaten. Taking his defeat in stride, he returned to giving flamboyant speeches and handing out autographed pictures of himself. He built up his law practice and added to his collection of antiques and gold coins. He again ran for mayor in 1963. This time he won easily. While mayor he broke ranks with his party to support Lyndon Johnson's campaign for President due to remarks on immigration made by Barry Goldwater's running mate, William Miller. Infuriated Republicans turned away from him. Johnson rewarded him with appointments as special ambassador to the Philippines' presidential inauguration in 1965 and as a member of the United States observer group for the 1967 South Vietnamese elections. He kept his hand in the affairs of his beloved Baltimore and was appointed to the City Zoning Commission in 1971. He died of cancer at his home on August 10, 1974, at age 73.

Eddie Murray

Murray played nine more seasons for the Dodgers, Mets, Indians, Orioles and Angels before retiring in 1997 with 504 home runs. He served as a batting coach for the Indians from 2002 to 2005 and the Dodgers for the first half of the 2007 season. Before leaving Baltimore, his generous donation to the Baltimore City Parks and Recreation Department established the Carrie Murphy Nature Center, named after his mother. In 2012 the Securities and Exchange Commission charged Murray with insider trading based on a tip received from former teammate Doug DeCinces. Murray paid a fine to settle the charges without admitting or denying wrongdoing. He makes his home in California.

Hank Peters

Peters continued his career as a major league baseball executive in Cleveland, where he served as the Indians' president until 1992, closing out his baseball career. He had begun with the Browns in 1946 when he answered a newspaper ad for a job with their minor league teams. He was inducted into the Orioles Hall of Fame in 2001. He died from complications from a stroke on January 4, 2015, at age 90 in Highland Beach, Florida, where he lived during retirement.

Howard Peter "Pete" Rawlings

Rawlings served in the Maryland House of Delegates from 1979 to 2003. Appointed Chairman of the Appropriations Committee in 1992, he led the efforts to reform Baltimore inner-city schools, ban racial profiling, and secure funding for the Reginald F. Lewis Museum of Maryland African American History & Culture. He also served on many boards and task forces, including the Maryland Historical Society, the Maryland Low Income Housing Coalition, and the Task Force on Education Funding Equity. He died of cancer while in office on November 14, 2003.

Paul Richards

Richards continued his career as a baseball executive as general manager of the Houston Astros from 1962–1965 and the Atlanta Braves from 1966 to 1972. He returned to baseball at the invitation of Bill Veeck for one year to manage the Chicago White Sox in 1976. He was inducted into the Georgia Hall of Fame in 1996 for his role as manager of the minor league Atlanta Crackers in 1938 and 1941. The Paul Richards Park in Waxahachie is a Texas Historical Landmark. He died of a heart attack on May 4, 1986, while playing golf, a game some said he loved more than baseball, on the 13th fairway of the Waxahachie Country Club.

Earl Robinson

In 1966 Robinson coached the basketball team at Merritt College in Oakland, California, becoming the first African American basketball coach in the California junior college system. He later coached basketball at Berkeley and Laney College, where he also taught speech and communications classes. Subsequent civic activities included serving as vice president for the Oakland Zoo's board of trustees and as a board member with the South Berkeley YMCA, Oakland Police Athletic Association, and the Oakland Boys and Girls Club. He died of a cardiac arrest in Oakland on July 4, 2014, at age 77.

Frank Robinson

After leaving the Orioles' front office in 1995, Robinson served as Vice President of On-Field Operations for Major League Baseball in the commissioner's office until 2002. In 2002 he was hired as manager of the Montreal Expos and followed the team in that capacity to Washington, D.C., as manager of the Washington Nationals. In a poll of 450 major league players sponsored by *Sports Illustrated*, Robinson was voted the worst manager in the majors in 2005 and again in 2006. During Robinson's time as the Nationals' manager, President George W. Bush awarded him the Presidential Medal of Freedom on November 9, 2005. The Nationals did not renew his contract for 2007 but did offer to honor him before a game against the Orioles. Robinson declined. On April 28, 2012, the Orioles unveiled his bronze statue at Camden Yards. He returned to MLB in 2007 as a senior executive, where he remains as of this writing.

Jim Russo

The man who did as much as anyone to find African American players for the Orioles joined the Browns in 1951. Russo came with the team to Baltimore. Over the next 35 years he developed the well-earned nickname "Super Scout" for not only identifying players like Frank Robinson, Fred Valentine, and Sam Bowens for the Orioles, but also Jim Palmer, Boog Bowell, Dave McNally, and Davey Johnson. He died in Grover, Missouri, at age 81 on February 8, 2004.

Earl Weaver

After his second retirement from the Orioles, Weaver returned to Pembroke Pines, Florida, a suburb of Miami, to play golf and plant tomatoes. Fans saw him several times in 2012 at Camden Yards, where he participated in statue unveilings of Orioles Hall of Famers, including one dedicated to himself on June 30. He received a standing ovation each time. He was inducted into the Baseball Hall of Fame in 1996. A heart attack two years later convinced him to quit his two-pack-a-day cigarette habit. He died of a heart attack on January 19, 2013, at age 82 while aboard the cruise ship Celebrity Silhouette during a baseball-themed outing.

Fred Valentine

After one season, 1970, of playing baseball in Japan for the Hanshin Tigers, Valentine attended George Washington University and the Antioch Law School. He then began his career in the Clark Construction Group in Washington, D.C., working in employee relations and subcontractor administration. With other former ball players, he helped found the Major League Baseball Players Alumni Association, of which he was co-chair as of this writing. He lives in Washington, D.C.

Appendix:
African American
Major League Executives
as of 2014[1]

Managers

Frank Robinson—Cleveland Indians (1975–1977)
Larry Doby—Chicago White Sox (1978)
Maury Wills—Seattle Mariners (1980–1981)
Frank Robinson—San Francisco Giants (1981–1984)
Frank Robinson—Baltimore Orioles (1988–1991)
Cito Gaston—Toronto Blue Jays (1989–1997)
Hal McRae—Kansas City Royals (1991–1994)
Dusty Baker—San Francisco Giants (1993–2002)
Don Baylor—Colorado Rockies (1993–1998)
Davey Lopes—Milwaukee Brewers (2000–2002)
Don Baylor—Chicago Cubs (2000–2002)
Lloyd McClendon—Pittsburgh Pirates (2001–2005)
Hal McRae—Tampa Bay Devil Rays (2001–2002)
Jerry Royster—Milwaukee Brewers (2002)
Frank Robinson—Montreal Expos (2002–2004)
Dusty Baker—Chicago Cubs (2003–2006)
Willie Randolph—New York Mets (2005–2008)
Frank Robinson—Washington Nationals (2005–2006)
Ron Washington—Texas Rangers (2007–2014)
Cecil Cooper—Houston Astros (2007–2009)
Jerry Manuel—New York Mets (2008–2010)
Dusty Baker—Cincinnati Reds (2008–2013)
Cito Gaston—Toronto Blue Jays (2008–2010)
Dave Clark—Houston Astros (2009)
Marquis Donnell "Bo" Porter—Houston Astros (2013–2014)
Lloyd McClendon—Seattle Mariners (2014–current)

General Managers

Bill Lucas—Atlanta Braves—1977–1979 (VP of player personnel)
Bob Watson—Houston Astros—1994–1995
           —New York Yankees—1996–1997
Kenny Williams—Chicago White Sox—2001–2012
Tony Reagins—Los Angeles Angels of Anaheim—2007–2011
Michael Hill—Miami Marlins—2007–2013

African American MLB Owners

Earvin "Magic" Johnson (as a partner of Guggenheim Baseball Management)
   —Los Angeles Dodgers—2013–present

Chapter Notes

Preface

1. Howard Bryant, *Shut Out: A Story of Race and Baseball in Boston* (Boston: Beacon Press, 2002); Stephanie M. Liscio, *Integrating Cleveland Baseball: Media Activism, the Integration of the Indians, and the Demise of the Negro League Buckeyes* (Jefferson, NC: McFarland, 2010).

Introduction

1. Howard Bryant, *Shut Out: A Story of Race and Baseball in Boston* (Boston: Beacon Press, 2002).

Chapter 1

1. Bill Glauber, "Powell's Records, Memory Are Key to Historic Past," *Baltimore Sun*, April 29, 1990.
2. Buck Leonard, with James A. Riley, *Buck Leonard: The Black Lou Gehrig* (New York: Carroll & Graf, 1995), 19–20.
3. Jules Tygiel, *Past Time: Baseball as History* (New York: Oxford University, 2001), 130.
4. James A. Riley, *The Biographical Encyclopedia of the Negro Baseball Leagues* (New York: Carroll & Graf, 1994), 208.
5. Bob Luke, *The Baltimore Elite Giants: Sport and Society in the Age of the Negro Leagues* (Baltimore: Johns Hopkins University, 2009), 180–181.
6. http://www.slate.com/articles/sports/sports_nut/2014/02/william_edward_white_baseball's_first_black_player_lived_his_life_as_a_white.html, accessed April 12, 2015.
7. "M'Graw Signs Indian," *Baltimore Sun*, March 16, 1901; "Tribute to Charlie Grant," *Baltimore Afro-American*, July 15, 1916.
8. "McGraw Laughs at Hanlon," *Boston Daily Globe*, March 29, 1901.

9. "McGraw Signs Indian," *Baltimore Sun*, March 16, 1901.
10. A variety of accounts can be found on how the rumor proved true. Some say Grant's black fans gave him away by presenting him with a large floral wreath at the Giants' hotel after which Charles Comiskey, owner of the Chicago White Sox, pointed out that Grant's father, an African American, trained horses in Cincinnati. Another account has a black Elk brass band greeting the Giants at a train station. The former account squares with the fact that Grant grew up in Cincinnati. However it happened, Charlie Grant (sometimes spelled Charley), a.k.a. Tokahoma (sometimes spelled Tokohoma) never played in a major league regular season game even though two newspaper articles report McGraw ordered Grant to join the team in Boston in late May.
11. "Oriole Park Insults Patrons with Jim Crow," *Baltimore Afro-American*, April 22, 1933.
12. *Ibid.*
13. "West Measure Knocked Out," *Baltimore Sun*, August 6, 1913.
14. "Baltimore Tries Drastic Plan of Race Segregation," *New York Times*, December 25, 1910.
15. *Ibid.*
16. *Ibid.*
17. "Baltimore Race Riot," *Washington Post*, September 26, 1913.
18. "Thousands to See Howard-Lincoln Contest; All White Commission Picked by Lansing for Liberia; New Segregation Measure Cannot Stand Legal Test," *Baltimore Afro-American*, November 28, 1919.
19. "Elites to Use Oriole Park," *Baltimore Afro-American*, April 10, 1937.
20. "Play Ball! And Homers Fly," *Baltimore Afro-American*, May 22, 1937.
21. "Major Leaguers to Play Star Colored

Nine," *Baltimore Afro-American*, September 23, 1939.

22. "McDonald Hurls Shutout Ball, But All-Stars Lose," *Baltimore Afro-American*, October 14, 1939.

23. Amateur baseball was as segregated as pro ball in the city. Dick Hall, who played 19 years in the majors, 11 with the O's from 1961 to 1971, moved to Baltimore in 1947 during the middle of his sophomore year in high school and played for a Boys Club team. "The teams," Hall said, "were either all white or all black. We played mostly white teams." Hall recalled one game against a black team that arrived in an open-panel truck with the players standing up inside. "We played the game and had no problems at all," he said. (Dick Hall, author telephone interview, March 27, 2013.)

24. "10,000 Watch Elites Open NAL Season," *Baltimore Afro-American*, May 13, 1950.

25. Sharon Melvin, Office Assistant, Dr. Bernard Harris, Sr. Elementary School, telephone interview by author, January 22, 2015.

26. "Dunn Urges Better Pact With Stadium," *Baltimore Sun*, April 26, 1950.

27. E. B. Rea, "Orioles Won't Use Colored Players," *Baltimore Afro-American*, January 8, 1944.

28. Sam Lacy, "Baltimore White Fans Have High Praise for Colored Ball Players," *Baltimore Afro-American*, October 20, 1945.

29. Jackie Robinson, as told to Alfred Duckett, *I Never Had It Made* (New York: G. P. Putnam's Sons, 1972), 59.

30. "Biased Baltimore Fans Slur Jackie Robinson During Recent Series," *Baltimore Afro-American*, May 4, 1946.

31. Frank Lynch, interview by author, Baltimore, December 5, 2006.

32. Richard Armstrong, telephone interview by author, October 24, 2012.

33. Michael Olesker, *The Colt's Baltimore: A City and Its Love Affair in the 1950s* (Baltimore: Johns Hopkins University, 2008), 128.

34. Michael Olesker. *Journeys to the Heart of Baltimore* (Baltimore: Johns Hopkins University, 2001), 17.

35. *Ibid.*, 34–35.

36. James Edward Miller, *The Baseball Business: Pursuing Pennants and Profits in Baltimore* (Chapel Hill: University of North Carolina, 1990), 38.

37. Frank McDougald, interview by author, Baltimore, August 10, 2012. Morgan College became Morgan State College in 1975 and later Morgan State University with the addition of graduate programs.

38. Miller, *The Baseball Business*, 28.

39. "W. T. Dixon Dies; Former Councilman," *Baltimore Sun*, July 10, 1980, C1.

40. Ruth Jenkins, "I Only Heard," *Baltimore Afro-American*, January 5, 1952.

41. NAACP Papers, Section II, Box A329, Folder 1, Manuscript Division, Library of Congress, Washington, D.C.

42. Sam Lacy, "2 Former K.C. Stars in St. Louis Lineup," *Baltimore Afro-American*, July 26, 1947.

43. "St. Louis Browns Drop Negroes," *Chicago Defender*, August 30, 1947.

44. Larry Moffi and Jonathan Kronstadt, *Crossing the Line: Black Major Leaguers, 1947–1959* (Jefferson, NC: McFarland, 1994), 14.

45. Hank Peters, interview by author, June 14, 2012.

46. James A. Riley, 599–600.

47. Peters interview.

48. *Ibid.*

49. Moffi and Kronstadt, vii–viii.

Chapter 2

1. "Stadium Move by Mayor Seen Today," *Baltimore Sun*, September 30, 1949.

2. "Heroes' Reception Given Men Who Landed Browns," *The Sporting News*, October 7, 1953.

3. "Baltimore Ready to Celebrate Return to Big League Status," *Washington Evening Star*, September 30, 1983

4. James M. Cannon, "Welcome," *Baltimore Sun*, October 1, 1953; James H. Bready, *Baseball in Baltimore* (Baltimore: Johns Hopkins University, 1998), 222.

5. "Dinner for Miles Nov. 24 Sellout," *Baltimore Sun*, November 14, 1953. Financial pressures had forced Bill Veeck, major league baseball's preeminent promoter from the 1940s through the 1980s, to sell his 79 percent controlling interest in the St. Louis Browns for $2,475,000 on September 29, 1953, to a group of Baltimore investors at a meeting of American League owners in New York City. ("Browns Move to Baltimore: Bill Veeck Out," *Chicago Daily Tribune*, September 30, 1953).

6. "Frontiers Hear Orioles Pledge Unprejudiced Team," *Baltimore Afro-American*. January 2, 1954; Bready, *Baseball in Baltimore*, 223.

7. Sam Lacy, "From A to Z," *Baltimore Afro-American*, October 31, 1953.

8. Al Wolf, "Angels to Bid for Services of Satch Paige," *Los Angeles Times*, January 27, 1954.

9. Sam Lacy, "From A to Z," *Baltimore Afro-American*, February 20, 1954.

10. Reid E. Jackson, "Baltimore Hotel Owners Pass the Buck," *Baltimore Afro-American*, April 17, 1954.

11. *Ibid.*; Edward C. Burks, "Orioles Give Satch Paige His Release," *Baltimore Sun*, Jan-

uary 27, 1954. Ehlers did not like the special treatment that Veeck accorded Paige. Veeck allowed Paige to show up at the park midway through a game, amble out to the bullpen, and take his repose in a padded rocking chair made especially for him. Browns manager Marty Marion shared Ehlers' dislike of Paige's special status. Marion refused to sign Paige in October following the 1953 season, after Satch skipped an exhibition game in Providence, RI. "Sign him if you want to win," Veeck implored Marion. "I wouldn't sign Paige if you gave him to me," Marion replied. "You can't have a player like Satchel on the team with that kind of name and let him do one way and the team do another way" (Larry Moffi, *This Side of Cooperstown* (Mineola, NY: Dover Publications, 2010), 7. Paige produced a 3–4 won-lost record in 1951, 12–10 in 1952, and 3–9 in 1953 for a team perennially on life support. His earned run average of 3.53 in 1953, third-best on the Browns' staff, bested those of Joe Coleman (4.00) and Frank Fanovich (5.55), both age 31, for the seventh-place Athletics, and Vern Bickford (5.28), 33, of the second-place Boston Braves in the National League. Fanovich failed to make the O's roster and finished his career in the minors. Bickford's sole appearance for the 1954 Birds amounted to four innings in which he gave up five hits and four runs. He never played in another major league game. Coleman staged a surprising improvement with a 13–17 record and an ERA of 3.50.

12. "Baltimore Ships Three Players to Richmond," *Chicago Daily Tribune*, March 28, 1954.

13. "Satch Paige Nixes Offers by Three Major League Clubs," *Baltimore Afro-American*, September 1, 1956; Paul Dickson, *Bill Veeck: Baseball's Greatest Maverick* (New York: Walker Publishing, 2012), 223.

14. Sandy Banisky and Bill Carter, "Of Bats and Birds—Or Opening Day Fever," *Baltimore Sun*, April 14, 1978.

15. *Pittsburgh Press*, November 10, 1953, as quoted in Dickson, *Bill Veeck*, 214.

16. Edward C. Burks, "Miles Seeks 'At Least Couple' of Negro Players for Orioles," *Baltimore Sun*, December 7, 1953.

17. "Race Is No Barrier," *Cleveland Call and Post*, October 24, 1953.

18. "Frontiers Hear Orioles Pledge Unprejudiced Team," *Baltimore Afro-American*, January 2, 1954.

19. "Greenberg Rejects Deals," *New York Times*, December 11, 1953.

20. "Frontiers Hear Orioles Pledge Unprejudiced Team."

21. Edward C. Burks, "Orioles," *Baltimore Sun*, December 9, 1953.

22. "Signing of Negro Star Surprise to Armstrong," *Baltimore Sun*, October 24, 1945.

23. Robert Elmer, "Eight Clubs Get Franchises in New Eastern Shore Loop," *Baltimore Sun*, October 22, 1945; "Ints Re-Elect Shaughnessy," *Baltimore Sun*, November 11, 1952.

24. "Frontiers Hear Orioles Pledge Unprejudiced Team."

25. Louis M. Hatter, "Yuma Rushes Remodeling on Bird Camp," *Baltimore Sun*, January 9, 1954; "Yuma First in State Growth," *Arizona Sun*, February 26, 1954.

26. "Ehlers Helps out Lonesome Rookie—Loans Him TV Set," *The Sporting News*, March 10, 1954.

27. Bill Rives, "Texans Lead in Paving Way for Lifting of the Color Line," *The Sporting News*, February 6, 1952.

28. James A. Linthicum, "Sunlight on Sports," *Baltimore Sun*, April 6, 1954.

29. High school transcript in Heard's player file, Baseball Hall of Fame and Museum, Cooperstown, New York.

30. Rick Swaine, *The Black Stars Who Made Baseball Whole: The Jackie Robinson Generation in the Major Leagues, 1947–1959* (Jefferson, NC: McFarland, 2006), 261.

31. Larry Lester, *Black Baseball's National Showcase: The East-West All Star Games, 1933–1953* (Lincoln, NE: University of Nebraska, 2001), 360.

32. John Eisenberg, "The Quiet Pioneer," *Baltimore Sun*, April 23, 2004.

33. Gil Coan, telephone interview by author, May 25, 2012.

34. Peter Richmond, *Ballpark: Camden Yards and the Building of an American Dream* (New York: Simon & Schuster, 1993), 85; *1955 Baltimore Orioles Sketch Book*, 4; Eisenberg, "The Quite Pioneer."

35. Curt Anderson, telephone interview by author, June 29, 2013.

36. Lee W. Weinrich, "A Maryland Man with Pagentry," *Baltimore Sun*, November 1, 1959.

37. Sam Lacy, "46,354 Fans in Stadium for Orioles' Opening Game," *Baltimore Afro-American*, April 24, 1954; Robert J. Brugger, *Maryland: A Middle Temperament* (Baltimore: Johns Hopkins University, 1988), 553.

38. Joseph M. Sheehan, "Baltimore Hails Return to Majors," *New York Times*, April 16, 1954.

39. John Van Camp, "46,354 See Orioles Defeat White Sox, 3 To 1," *Baltimore Sun*, April 16, 1954.

40. Ned Burks, "Orioles Use Four Hurlers as White Sox Win 14–4," *Baltimore Sun*, April 25, 1954; Al Sweeney, "Heard Stays with Birds," *Baltimore Afro-American*, May 22, 1954.

41. "White Sox Defeat Orioles 11–6, 14–8," *New York Times*, May 28, 1954.

42. "Orioles Option Heard Back to Portland Club," *Chicago Daily Tribune*, June 7, 1954.

43. Hugh Trader, Jr., "Orioles Making Feathers Fly in Feud with Yankees," *The Sporting News*, June 16, 1954.

44. "E-X-C-L-U-S-I-V-E: Why the Orioles Released Heard," *Baltimore Afro-American*, June 19, 1954.

45. "Orioles' Rookies Nip Senators, 4–3," *New York Times*, September 11, 1954.

46. Ned Burks, "Orioles." *Baltimore Afro-American*, September 13, 1954.

47. James Bready, *Baseball in Baltimore: The First Hundred Years* (Baltimore: Johns Hopkins University, 1998), 214, as quoted in Paul Dickson, *Bill Veeck: Baseball's Greatest Maverick* (New York: Walker, 2012), 214.

48. Chris Bready, telephone interview by author, January 20, 2013.

49. Herb Mangrum, "Orioles," *Baltimore Afro-American*, September 25, 1954; "Orioles Add Three to Squad," *Baltimore Sun*, September 7, 1954.

50. Billy O'Dell, telephone interview by author, May 31, 2012.

51. Ron Hansen, telephone interview by author, September 24, 2012.

52. Jerry Sachs, interview by author, August 27, 2012.

53. *Ibid.*

54. Joe Durham, interview by author, June 14, 2013.

55. *Ibid.*

56. http://www. Baseball-reference.com/bullpen/Joe_Durham, accessed January 28, 2015.

57. John Eisenberg, *From 33rd Street to Camden Yards: An Oral History of the Baltimore Orioles* (New York: McGraw-Hill, 2001), 63.

58. Olesker, *Journeys*, 124.

59. "Baltimore Mixed Schools Under Fire," *Chicago Defender*, October 9, 1954.

60. *Ibid.*

61. "N.A.A.W.P. Sets Up Office Here, Plans State-Wide Drive," *Baltimore Sun*, November 21, 1954.

62. "Williams in Senate Race as Strong Segregationist," *Baltimore Sun*, January 19, 1956, 10.

63. Jesse Glasgow, "Hearings End of 'Baby FEPC,'" *Baltimore Sun*, February 9, 1956.

64. "Williams Hits Integration," *Baltimore Sun*, March 30, 1957.

65. Antero Pietila, *Not in My Neighborhood: How Bigotry Shaped a Great American City* (Chicago: Ivan R. Dee, 2010), 92–93.

66. "Baltimore Hotels Bar Ball Players," *Chicago Defender*," April 17, 1954.

67. Marshall Skelton, "The Human Side of Sports," *The Crusader*, April 16, 1954.

68. "Baltimore Hotels Bar Ball Players."

69. "Two More Groups Dodge City's Hotel Jim Crow," *Baltimore Afro-American*, December 8, 1956.

70. *Ibid.* As an example of McKeldin's comfort in working with people on opposite sides of the fence from him, the governor appointed Harris to the Maryland Employment Security Board a year later. Said McKeldin of Harris, "Few, if any, in the state are as well versed in the requirements ... of State services as is Mr. Harris." At the time Harris served as counsel to the Public Service Commission and the Maryland Classified Employees Association. ("Lawyer Here Is Appointed to Job Board," *Baltimore Sun*, May 3, 1955).

71. "Hotels Stand by Ban upon Negroes," *Baltimore Sun*, April 8, 1954.

72. Al Sweeney, "Cleveland Players Hope Hotels Will Change Policy," *Baltimore Afro-American*, May 1, 1954, 17.

73. "The Hotel Incident," *Baltimore Sun*, May 1, 1954.

74. Al Sweeney, *Cleveland Players*.

75. Sam Lacy with Moses J. Newson, *Fighting For Fairness: The Life Story of Hall of Fame Sportswriter Sam Lacy* (Centreville, MD: Tidewater, 1998), 91.

76. Harold Lotham, "Major Clubs Should Be Denied Jim Crow Cities," Special to *The Labor's Daily*, no date, in NAACP Papers, Group III, Box A 111, Folder 1, Manuscript Division, Library of Congress, Washington, D.C.

77. Edgar Williams, "The Low Down on Baltimore: It's Hot, It's Cold," *Baseball Digest* (May 1954), 57.

78. "Board Backs Miles' Plans for Orioles," *Washington Post and Times Herald*, September 8, 1954.

79. "Oriole Directors to Get Miles Out, Predicts Writer," *Boston Daily Globe*, September 6, 1954.

80. "Board Backs Miles' Plans For Orioles."

Chapter 3

1. Bob Maisel, "Morning After," *Baltimore Sun*, April 7, 1974.

2. "Plans Machine Gun Use in Fishing War," *Baltimore Sun*, July 27, 1926.

3. Ned Burks, "Richards," *Baltimore Sun*, September 15, 1954; Tim Kurkjian, "Richards, Ex-manager of Orioles, Dies at 77," *Baltimore Sun*, May 5, 1986.

4. Warren Corbett, *The Wizard of Waxahachie: Paul Richards and the End of Baseball As We Knew It* (Dallas, TX: Southern Methodist University, 2009), iv.

5. Sachs Interview.
6. Tim Kurkjian, "Richards, Ex-manager of Orioles."
7. Sachs Interview.
8. Ned Burks, "Richards."
9. Ned Burks, "More Oriole Scouts Due," *Baltimore Sun*, September 25, 1954.
10. *Ibid.*
11. Joseph L. Reichler, ed., *The Baseball Encyclopedia* (New York: Macmillan, 1988), 2,478, 2,673.
12. "Willie Miranda, 70, Shortstop in Majors," *New York Times*, September 9, 1996.
13. *Ibid.*; Howard Sigmand, "Yanks Begin Flag Rebuilding Drive," *Atlanta Daily World*, November 20, 1954.
14. "Indians Get Cox, Woodling; Tigers Buy Phils' Torgenson," *Chicago Daily Tribune*, June 16, 1955.
15. Bob Kuzava, telephone interview by author, May 31, 2012.
16. Jim Russo with Bob Hammel, *Super Scout: Thirty-Five Years of Major League Scouting* (Chicago: Bonus Books, 1992), 38.
17. "Bonus Rule Violation Brings About Levies of $2,000 and $2,500," *Baltimore Sun*, September 24, 1955.
18. Jim Hennenman, author interview, February 19, 2015.
19. Lee MacPhail, *My Nine Innings: An Autobiography of 50 years in Baseball* (Westport, CT: Meckler Books, 1989), 68–69.
20. Jesse A. Linthicum, "Sunlight on Sports," *Baltimore Sun*, March 22, 1955.
21. C. M. Gibbs, "Orioles Sign 2 Ex-Members of Army All-Star Team," *Baltimore Sun*, October 28, 1954.
22. Fred Rasmussen, "Sensations," *Baltimore Sun*, May 17, 1987.
23. Jesse A. Linthicum, "Sunlight on Sports," *Baltimore Sun*, January 20, 1955.
24. Lou Hatter, "First Orioles Arrive at Miami Beach," *Baltimore Sun*, February 28, 1955.
25. C. M. Gibbs, "Birds Sign 2 Players for Farm Teams," *Baltimore Sun*, November 11, 1954.
26. Bob Maisel, "Orioles Open Spring Training Drills Today," *Baltimore Sun*, March 1, 1955.
27. "Harlan Vote Mar. 9," *Baltimore Afro-American*, March 12, 1955.
28. "34 Players Are Retained by 12 of the Major Leagues' 16 Teams," *The New Journal and Guide*, May 28, 1955.
29. "Sonny Glover Signs with Orioles' Farm," *Baltimore Afro-American*, April 2, 1955.
30. Sam Lacy, "A to Z," *Baltimore Afro-American*, April 30, 1955.
31. Corbett, *The Wizard of Waxahachie*, 184.

32. "Pope Warmly Received in Oriole Debut," *Baltimore Afro-American*, June 25, 1955.
33. Lacy with Newson, *Fighting For Fairness*, 116.
34. Sam Lacy, "From A to Z," *Baltimore Afro-American*, May 21, 1955.
35. Bob Maisel, "Birds-Indians Deal Settled," *Baltimore Sun*, June 21, 1955.
36. Sam Lacy, "From A to Z," *Baltimore Afro-American*, June 25, 1955.
37. "Pope Warmly Received in Oriole Debut."
38. James H. Bready, *Home Team: A Full Century of Baseball in Baltimore, 1859–1959; a Patriotic Study* (no publisher or date cited), 49.
39. Jesse A. Linthicum, "Sunlight on Sports," *Baltimore Sun*, June 18, 1955.
40. Jesse A. Linthicum, "Sunlight on Sports," *Baltimore Sun*, November 8, 1955.
41. "Clarence Miles Resigns Berth," *Christian Science Monitor*, November 7, 1955. "Oriole Directors to Get Miles Out, Predicts Writer," *Boston Daily Globe*, September 6, 1954.
42. Bob Maisel, "1955 Profits Nearly 'Zero' for Orioles," *Baltimore Sun*, November 22, 1955; Lou Hatter, "Keelty Elected Oriole President," *Baltimore Sun*, November 19, 1955.
43. Ward Allan Howe, "Arizona's Scottsdale Resorts Put Accent on Western Theme," *Christian Science Monitor*, December 4, 1956.
44. Linda C. Boone, "The Days of Haze: A Personal Journey Down the Back Road to Brown v. Board of Education" *Arizona Attorney* (March 2000), 38–40.
45. Ira Morton, "A Judge for Equal Rights," *Jewish News of Greater Phoenix On-Line*, September 16, 2005 (accessed January 2, 2013).
46. "Nurse Refused Service at Upton's," *Arizona Sun*, April 19, 1956.
47. "No Colored Trade Solicited," *Arizona Sun*, January 27, 1956.
48. Howard Bryant, *Shut Out: A Story of Race and Baseball in Boston* (Boston: Beacon Press, 2002), 10.
49. Jim Ellis, "Orioles Okay Scottsdale as '57 Camp Site," *The Sporting News*, March 28, 1956; Sam Lacy, "I Lost My Sleep But It Was Worth It," *Baltimore Afro-American*, October 20, 1973; Ward Allen Howe, "Arizona's Scottsdale Resorts Put Accent on Western Theme."
50. "5 in camp as Orioles Open Drills," *Baltimore Afro-American*, February 25, 1956.
51. Moffi & Kronstadt, *Crossing the Line*, 54.
52. "Birds Sign Former Tenn. State Star," *Baltimore Afro-American*, July 28, 1956.
53. 1959 Baltimore Story booklet. Pre-

sented by Phillies. Published by *Sports Illustrated*, 25.

54. "Two Handsome Gifts for Thanksgiving," *Baltimore Afro-American*, December 3, 1955.

55. B. M. Phillips, "If You Ask Me," *Baltimore Afro-American*, March 5, 1955.

56. "Gains Noted as Hotels Hold Out," *Baltimore Afro-American*, May 2, 1956.

57. "Bar Vote Welcomed," *Baltimore Sun*, June 18, 1957.

58. "Park Officer is Fined for 'boy' Insult," *Baltimore Afro-American*, June 22, 1957.

59. Lou Hatter, "Orioles Re-Acquire Evers from Indians for Pope," *Baltimore Sun*, May 14, 1956.

60. Lou Hatter, "Birds Assess Billy Pierce," *Baltimore Sun*, July 20, 1956.

61. Jim Russo and Bob Hammel, *Super-Scout*, 47.

62. Bob Addie, "Valentine Doesn't Rue Being Football 'Dropout,'" *Washington Post Times-Herald*, March 4, 1966.

63. Fred Valentine, author interview, April 25, 2012.

64. Bob Maisel, "Honors Due Johnson on His 'Night,'" *Baltimore Sun*, August 28, 1956; "Mayor's Proclamation," *Baltimore Afro-American*, September 8, 1956; "Photo Stand-alone," *Baltimore Afro-American*, September 8, 1956.

65. Elizabeth Murphy Oliver, "'Sinker Kid' Cost $40,000," *Baltimore Sun*, October 13, 1956.

66. Lou Hatter, "Beamon Gains First Shutout," *Baltimore Sun*, September 27, 1956.

67. Oliver, "Sinker Kid."

68. "Gains Noted as Hotels Hold Out," *Baltimore Afro-American*, May 12, 1956.

69. "Sheraton-Belvedere Relaxes its Policy, Houses Morticians," *Baltimore Afro-American*, March 30, 1957.

70. Sam Lacy, "Hotel Bar 'a Problem,'" *Baltimore Afro-American*, April 6, 1957.

71. Don Larsen, telephone interview by author, June 12, 2012.

72. "Asks Help of Clubs in Hotel Fight," *Baltimore Afro-American*, May 25, 1957.

73. NAACP Papers, Section II. Box A329. Folder 1, Manuscript Division, Library of Congress, Washington, D.C.

74. Sam Lacy, "Baltimore Hotels Lift Racial Bars," *Baltimore Afro-American*, July 20, 1957.

75. "City Hotels to Change Race Policy," *Baltimore Sun*, July 13, 1957.

76. "Will Stay Downtown Next Year," *Baltimore Afro-American*, August 10, 1957.

77. Lou Hatter, "Orioles Sign Johnson, Hale," *Baltimore Sun*, January 18, 1957.

78. C. M. Gibbs, "Gibberish," *Baltimore Sun*, March 16, 1958.

79. Ed Rumill, "Red Sox Invasion of Arizona for Spring Training Intriguing Journey," *Christian Science Monitor*, February 18, 1959.

80. Dewey Webb, "Safari Tales." *Phoenix New Times*, May 22, 1997, http://www.phoenixnewtimes.com/1997-05-22/news/safari-tales/, accessed October 31, 2012.

81. Joe Durham, telephone interview by author, October 30, 2012.

82. Lou Hatter, "Nieman and Triandos Flop in Clutch," *Baltimore Sun*, March 17, 1957.

83. Lou Hatter, "Chance Aided Green's Bid," *Baltimore Sun*, March 13, 1957.

84. Fred Valentine, telephone interview by author, October 23, 2012.

85. Fred Valentine, telephone interviews by author, April 25, 2012, and October 23, 2012.

86. "Outfielder Joe Durham Recalled by Baltimore," *Philadelphia Tribune*, June 22, 1957.

87. October 30 Durham interview.

88. June 14 Durham interview.

89. "Fans Honor Bob Boyd at Pre-game Ceremony," *Baltimore Afro-American*, September 28, 1957.

90. Sam Lacy, "Eager to Play for Birds, Says Doby," *Baltimore Afro-American*, December 14, 1957.

91. Doc Young, "Inside Sports," *Jet*, December 19, 1957, as quoted in Joseph Thomas Moore, *Pride Against Prejudice: The Biography of Larry Doby* (New York: Praeger, 1988), 115–116.

92. Sam Lacy, "Eager to Play for Birds."

93. Sam Lacy, "Happy with Doby Declares Richards," *Baltimore Afro-American*, January 11, 1958.

94. Lou Hatter, "Orioles' Doby Bats a Thousand in Physical Checkup," *Baltimore Sun*, February 8, 1958; Sam Lacy, "Million Dollar 'Exploitation,'" *Baltimore Afro-American*, March 15, 1958.

95. Rosemary Paddleford, "The Training Camp Life of an Oriole Wife," *Baltimore Sun*, April 6, 1958.

96. Sam Lacy, "A to Z," *Baltimore Afro-American*, April 12, 1958.

97. "Orioles Trade Doby for Gene Woodling," *Baltimore Sun*, April 1, 1958; "Indians Get Doby in 5 Man Deal," *Chicago Tribune*, April 1, 1958.

98. "Doby's 'Friends' Lose a Friend," *Arizona Republic*, April 2, 1958.

99. Bob Maisel, "Willie Tasby Called Best," *Baltimore Sun*, August 23, 1958.

100. Bob Maisel, "Billy 13th Infielder on Roster," *Baltimore Sun*, December 6, 1958; "Louisville Negro Rookie of Year," *Chicago Defender*, September 6, 1958.

101. Lou Hatter, "Birds Send 2 to Vancouver," *Baltimore Sun*, March 10, 1959.

102. John Eisenberg, *From 33rd Street to Camden Yards: An Oral History of the Baltimore Orioles* (New York: McGraw-Hill, 2002), 61.

103. Doug Wilson, *Brooks: The Biography of Brooks Robinson* (New York: St. Martin's, 2014), 47.

104. Valentine interview, April 25.

105. Chuck Diering, telephone interview by author, May 31, 2012.

106. Louis Berney, *Tales From the Orioles Dugout* (Champaign, IL: Sports Publishing, 2007), 8.

107. Bowden, *The Best Game Ever*, 117–118.

108. *Ibid.*

Chapter 4

1. "Richards Says He Would Prefer Office Job to Piloting Orioles," *New York Times*, November 11, 1958.

2. Larry MacPhail to A. B. Chandler, April 27, 1945, Chandler Papers, Filson Club Historical Society, Louisville, KY, as quoted in Jules Tygiel, *Baseball's Great Experiment* (New York: Oxford University, 2008), 42.

3. David Halberstam, *October 1964* (New York: Fawcett Columbine, 1995), 55.

4. Sachs interview.

5. Sam Lacy, "Sports: A to Z," *Baltimore Afro-American*, June 14, 1958.

6. Odell M. Smith, "Anti-Bias Measure Is Killed," *Baltimore Sun*, November 25, 1958.

7. Sandy Banisky, "Jacob Edelman, Longtime Member of Council Dies," *Baltimore Sun*, August 31, 1984.

8. "You Can't Slow Down, Thurgood," *Baltimore Afro-American*, January 25, 1958.

9. "D'Alesandro Wins Senate Race," *Baltimore Sun*, May 2, 1958.

10. Laurence Stern, "Suburbia Cut D'Alesandro Dead," *Washington Post*, November 9, 1958.

11. James Edward Miller, *The Baseball Business*, 68.

12. Willie Tasby, telephone interview by author, June 11, 2012.

13. Valentine interview, October 23, 2012.

14. Alan Goldstein, "Sports Promote Race Relations," *Baltimore Sun*, February 6, 1979.

15. Jack E. Davis, "Baseball's Reluctant Challenge: Desegregating Major League Spring Training Sites, 1961–1964," *Journal of Sport History*, Vol. 19, No. 2 (Summer 1992), 144.

16. *Ibid.*

17. Sam Lacy, "Sam Lacy's A to Z," *Baltimore Afro-American*, March 28, 1959.

18. Jim Marshall, telephone interview by author, June 29, 2012.

19. John Eisenberg, *From 33rd Street*, 59–60.

20. Corbett, *The Wizard of Waxahachie*, 183.

21. Bill Nunn, Jr., "Change of Pace," *Pittsburgh Courier*, March 28, 1959.

22. Sam Lacy, "Orioles Pin Hopes on Willie Tasby," *Baltimore Afro-American*, April 11, 1959.

23. Tasby interview.

24. "Tan Orioles Absent as Teammates Are Toasted," *Baltimore Afro-America*, April 25, 1959.

25. Tasby Interview.

26. *Ibid.*

27. Sam Lacy, "Great Relief Hurling May Save Connie," *Baltimore Afro-American*, July 11, 1959.

28. Lou Hatter, "C. Johnson Cut, Hale Retained by Orioles," *Baltimore Sun*, April 10, 1959.

29. "Pearson Goes to Orioles: Nats Lose," *Washington Post*, May 27, 1959.

30. Sam Lacy, "Orioles Want Tan Fans and Players, Vow MacPhail, Richards in Baltimore," *Baltimore Afro-American*, June 17, 1961.

31. Lou Hatter, "Taylor Sold to Vancouver; Orioles Seek Replacement," *Baltimore Sun*, July 27, 1959.

32. Valentine interview, April 25.

33. *Ibid.*

34. *Ibid.*

35. *Ibid.*

36. Sam Lacy, "Sox, Yanks Loom as Threats–Boyd," *Baltimore Afro-American*, February 6, 1960.

37. Lou Hatter, "Tasby Loses Center Field Job," *Baltimore Sun*, March 4, 1960.

38. Sam Lacy, "Bonuses for Baseballers: the $100,000 Question," *Baltimore Afro-American*, August 23, 1958.

Chapter 5

1. "Fans See Birds Ending Season in 1st Division," *Baltimore Afro-American*, August 20, 1960.

2. Bob Brown, telephone interview by author, March 2, 2014.

3. Sam Lacy, "Harry is Scary.... $28 per Foot.... I'll Take Paul," *Baltimore Afro-American*, August 2, 1960.

4. *Newark-Star Ledger*, March 4, 1998, as cited in Paul Dickson, *Bill Veeck*, 143.

5. Jesse Glasgow, "Hearings End of 'Baby FEPC,'" *Baltimore Sun*, February 9, 1956.

6. Bob Luke, *The Most Famous Woman in Baseball: Effa Manley and the Negro Leagues* (Washington, D.C.: Potomac, 2011), 137.

7. Bill Stanton, telephone interview by author, March 2, 2014.

8. Vince Bagli, telephone interview by author, February 10, 2014.

9. Bob Maisel, telephone interview by author, February 9, 2014.

10. Lou Hatter, "Keelty Elected Oriole President; 13 Directors Are Headed by Iglehart," *Baltimore Sun*, November 19, 1955.

11. "Classified Ads," *The Baltimore Sun*, October 12, 1956.

12. "'Hiring by Merit' Talks Planned," *Baltimore Sun*, April 8, 1959.

13. Edward C. Burks, "Council Gets Rid of Rights Bill Quickly," *Baltimore Sun*, March 31, 1959.

14. Edward C. Burks, "New Rights Law Sought by City," *Baltimore Sun*, June 9, 1959; Edward C. Burks. "Bill Offered to Repeal Fair Employment Law," *Baltimore Sun*, June 14, 1959; "Sit-ins Assistance Group Commends Grady," *Baltimore Afro-American*, June 9, 1960.

15. "Restaurants Study Policy," *Baltimore Afro-American*, April 30, 1960.

16. Monte Irvin, telephone interview by author, April 22, 2012.

17. "The Sports Pad," *Baltimore Afro-American*, April 6, 1946.

18. Roscoe McGowen, "Florida City Bars Montreal Negroes," *New York Times*, March 22, 1946.

19. Davis, "Baseball's Reluctant Challenge," 144–151.

20. "Common Sense Will Solve Race Problems," *The Sporting News*, April 5, 1961.

21. Davis, "Baseball's Reluctant Challenge," 153.

22. *Ibid.*, 159.

23. Henry Aaron with Lonnie Wheeler, *I Had A Hammer: The Hank Aaron Story* (New York: HarperCollins, 1991), 154.

24. Jim Ellis, "Orioles' Chico Only 5 Days Late at Camp," *The Sporting News*, March 11, 1959.

25. Lou Hatter, "1961 Oriole Pact Signed by Robinson," *Baltimore Sun*, February 3, 1961.

26. John Drebinger, "Ditmar and Coates of Yankees Blank Phils; Mantle Belts Homer and Double," *Baltimore Sun*, March 16, 1961; Jack E. Davis, "Baseball's Reluctant Challenge," 160.

27. "Wendell Smith's Sports Beat," *Pittsburgh Courier*, March 4, 1961.

28. "Orioles' Camp Third in Florida to Integrate," *Jet*, March 30, 1961, 51.

29. "Oriole Site Integrated," *New York Times*, March 19, 1962.

30. http://alumni.berkeley.edu/california-magazine/just-in/2014–07–28/going-bat-earl-robinson-we-ve-got-do-something-help-robbie. Accessed February 6, 2015.

31. Sam Lacy, "Why Earl Robinson Chose Jim Crow," *Baltimore Afro-American*, March 25, 1961.

32. Sam Lacy, "Lacy Says Orioles Would Lower Bar," *Baltimore Afro-American*, March 18, 1961.

33. Bruce Porter and Marvin Dunn, "The Miami Riots," *Chicago Tribune*, May 22, 1981; "Sir John Hotel Tops in Luxury," *Chicago Defender*, April 20, 1957; Tommy Picou, "Tommy's Corner," *Chicago Defender*, February 17, 1962.

34. Bill Nunn, Jr., "Bonus Baby Earl Desires Tan Hotel at Miami Beach," *Pittsburgh Courier*, March 1, 1961.

35. "Majors Ease Florida Issue," *Baltimore Sun*, November 16, 1961.

36. Sam Lacy, "Orioles Want Tan Fans and Players Vow MacPhail, Richards in Baltimore," *Baltimore Afro-American*, June 17, 1961.

37. *Ibid.*

38. Sachs interview.

39. "Paul Richards Quit Orioles for Houston," *Washington-Post Times Herald*, August 30, 1961.

Chapter 6

1. Douglas Brown, "Educated, Astute, Diplomatic, Thorough, Patient...," *Baltimore Sun*, April 8, 1962.

2. Lou Hatter, "Billy Hitchcock, 43, to Manage Orioles Next Year," *Baltimore Sun*, October 8, 1961.

3. Sam Lacy, "Archie Moore: 'Everyone Picks on Me,'" *Baltimore Afro-American*, October 21, 1961.

4. Lou Hatter, "Versatility Makes Virgil Valuable Bird," *Baltimore Sun*, March 8, 1962.

5. Russo, *Super Scout*, 48.

6. "Orioles Call up McGuire," *Baltimore Sun*, August 25, 1962.

7. "Opening Games Set Record for Tan Participation," *Baltimore Afro-American*, April 21, 1962.

8. "Boycott of Oriole Games Threatened," *Baltimore Afro-American*, July 21, 1962.

9. "MacPhail Insists He'd Hire Qualified Negro Players," *Baltimore Afro-American*, July 16, 1962.

10. *Ibid.*

11. Sam Lacy, "The Orioles and Earl Robinson," *Baltimore Afro-American*, July 7, 1962.

12. Bob Maisel, "The Morning After," *Baltimore Sun*, September 30, 1962.

13. Orioles Buy Joe Gaines, *New Journal and Guide*, January 5, 1963; Bob Maisel,

"Morning After," *Baltimore Sun*, April 15, 1963.

14. Paul Blair, interview by author, October 2, 2012.

15. Eisenberg, *From 33rd Street to Camden Yards*, 64.

16. Sam Lacy, "Everybody Belongs in D.C. 'March,'" *Baltimore Afro-American*, August 24, 1963.

17. Joe Gaines, telephone interview by author, July 27, 2012. For an excellent discussion of Flood's challenge, see Brad Snyder, *A Well Paid Slave: Curt Flood's Fight for Free Agency in Professional Sports* (New York: Viking, 2006).

18. Lou Hatter, "Miller, Bowens Join Birds, May Face Boston Tonight," *Baltimore Sun*, September 6, 1963.

19. Russo, *Super Scout*, 48.

20. "Orioles Hunting Manager," *Baltimore Sun*, October 6, 1963.

21. William Akin, "Billy Hitchcock," http://sabr.org/bioproj/person/95b45e6e, accessed July 23, 2012).

22. Barney Kremenko, "Lee MacPhail: Subdued Success," *New York Journal American*, November 16, 1966.

23. "Hank Bauer, 84, World Series Star, Dies," *New York Times*, February 10, 2007.

24. Lou Hatter, "Blefary Goes to Rochester and Blair Too," *Baltimore Sun*, March 31, 1964.

25. "2 More Orioles Sign Contracts," *Baltimore Sun*, February 13, 1964.

26. "Orioles Obtain Willie Kirkland," *Washington Post Times-Herald*, December 5, 1963; "Birds Sign Davis, Jackson, Brunet," *Baltimore Sun*, February 1, 1964; "Pulled Muscle Shelves Aparicio for 5-Game Set with White Sox," *Baltimore Sun*, June 16, 1964.

27. Gaines interview.

28. *Ibid.*

29. *Ibid.*

30. Bob Luke, *The Baltimore Elite Giants*, 21–22.

31. Frederick Lonesome, interview by author, Baltimore, October 10, 2006.

32. *Ibid.*

33. Gaines interview.

34. "Orioles Win 4–2, and Regain First," *New York Times*, August 22, 1964; "Nats Buy Kirkland from Orioles," *Washington Post Times-Herald*, August 13, 1964; Jim Elliot, "Orioles Buy Lenny Green, Fill Roster at 40 Players," *Baltimore Sun*, September 6, 1964.

35. Lou Hatter, "McNally Hurls 1-Hitter; Bunker Rebuked by Pilot," *Baltimore Sun*, October 2, 1964.

36. "Birds Drop Sam Jones," *Baltimore Sun*, October 18, 1964.

37. Jim Elliot, "Earl Robinson Angers Bauer," *Baltimore Sun*, March 25, 1965.

38. Jim Elliot, "Senators Get McCormick, Cubs' E. Robinson from Birds," *Baltimore Sun*, April 4, 1965.

39. "Orioles Send Blair to Rochester Farm," *The Baltimore Sun*, July 4, 1965; "Birds Recall Blair, Farm Sam Bowens," *Baltimore Afro-American*, August 14, 1965.

40. Bob Maisel, "Morning After," *Baltimore Sun*, September 12, 1965.

41. *Ibid.*

42. "Letters to the Editor," *Baltimore Sun*, August 3, 1965.

43. George W. Collins, "The High Cost of a Bad Image," *Baltimore Afro-American*, October 9, 1965.

44. http://www.thebaseballpage.com/history/jerry-hoffberger, accessed November 3, 2013.

45. Richard Goldstein, "Jerold Hoffberger, 80, Owner of Series-Winning Orioles, Dies," *New York Times*, April 12, 1999.

46. Collins, "The High Cost..."

47. Maisel, "Morning After," September 12, 1965.

Chapter 7

1. Lou Hatter, "Hoffberger Becomes Chairman of Orioles Board of Directors," *Baltimore Sun*, June 12, 1965; Lou Hatter, "Club Drops GM Title in Alignment," *Baltimore Sun*, December 8, 1965.

2. Jim Elliot, "Party Given for MacPhail," *Baltimore Sun*, December 15, 1965.

3. Bob Maisel, "Morning After," *Baltimore Sun*, December 10, 1965; Jim Elliot, "Orioles Get Frank Robinson from Cincinnati Reds for Milt Pappas, Dick Simpson, Jack Baldschun," *Baltimore Sun*, December 10, 1965; Jim Elliot, "Oriole Ticket Sales Are Up," *Baltimore Sun*, February 9, 1966.

4. William (Sheep) Jackson, "Reds Announce Putting Robinson on the Block," *Cleveland Call and Post*, December 11, 1965; Elliot, "Oriole Ticket Sales Are Up."

5. "Baseball 'Stunned' by Robinson Trade," *Pittsburgh Courier*, December 18, 1965.

6. A. S. "Doc" Young, "Good Morning Sports," *Chicago Daily Defender*, August 12, 1966.

7. http://en.wikiquote.org/wiki/Bull_Durham, accessed January 25, 2015.

8. Douglas Brown, "The Orioles Frank Robinson," *Baltimore Sun*, April 10, 1966.

9. http://espn.go.com/classic/biography/s/robinson_frank.html, accessed January 15, 2015.

10. Jim Elliot, "Orioles Get Frank Robinson from Cincinnati Reds..."

11. Dick Hall, telephone interview by author, March 27, 2013.

12. Sam Lacy, "Frank Robinson Gives His Side of 'Hard-to-handle' Tag," *Baltimore Afro-American*, February 5, 1966.

13. Sam Lacy, "From A to Z," *Baltimore Afro-American*, June 2, 1956.

14. Frank Robinson with Al Silverman, *My Life in Baseball* (Garden City, NY: Doubleday, 1975), 111–116.

15. "Grand Jury Holds Robinson," *Chicago Defender*, February 25, 1961.

16. "Reds' Robinson Fined $250 on Gun Charge," *Washington Post Times-Herald*, March 21, 1961.

17. Lee MacPhail, *My Nine Innings*, 80.

18. Russo, *Super Scout*, 66.

19. Doug Brown, "Ticket, Ad Buyers Come Alive with Robinson in Birds' Nest," *The Sporting News*, December 25, 1965.

20. Frank Cashen, telephone interview by author, September 24, 2012.

21. Doug Brown, "Ticket."

22. Kent Baker, "Frank Robinson, Bumbry Are Saluted at Banquet," *Baltimore Sun*, December 3, 1980.

23. Frank Robinson, 170.

24. Ken Nigro, "Cooperstown Welcomes a Favorite Oriole," *Baltimore Sun*, August 2, 1982.

25. McDougald interview.

26. Ken Nigro, "It's Frank Robby Day in Cooperstown," *Baltimore Sun*, August 1, 1982.

27. Goldstein, "Jerold Hoffberger, 80."

28. Frank Robinson with Berry Stainback, *Extra Innings* (New York: McGraw-Hill, 1988), 59–60.

29. Pietila, *Not In My Neighborhood*, 96.

30. *Ibid.*, 177.

31. "Lawrence Cardinal Shehan Dies; Retired Archbishop of Baltimore," *New York Times*, August 27, 1984.

32. Scott Sullivan, "Foes of Bill On Housing Boo Cardinal," *Baltimore Sun*, January 14, 1966.

33. Scott Sullivan, "Fair Housing Bill Killed in 13–8 Vote," *Baltimore Sun*, January 18, 1966.

34. "Letters to the Editor," *Baltimore Sun*, January 21, 1966.

35. "Mayor Deplores Boos, Catcalls," *Baltimore Sun*, January 17, 1966.

36. "Citizen Protests, Brutality Pleas Ignored by Schmidt, Report Says," *Baltimore Sun*, January 10, 1966; "Brutality Charges Lead to Baltimore Shakeup," *Chicago Defender*, January 15, 1966.

37. Richard H. Levine, "Pomerleau Named City Police Head," *Baltimore Sun*, September 16, 1966.

38. "CORE Plan Upsets Baltimore's Mayor," *New York Times*, April 17, 1966.

39. George W. Collins, "ROBED Order Incites Anger, New Tensions," *Baltimore Afro-American*, May 14, 1966.

40. John E. Woodruff, "Apartment Integration Gains Seen," *Baltimore Sun*, May 21, 1966; "Integration Pledged by Nine Apartments," *Baltimore Sun*, June 4, 1966. Among the apartments involved in addition to Horizon House were Belvedere Towers, Village of Cross Keys, University One Apartments, 611 Park Avenue Apartments, Park Wheeler Apartments, and Carlyle Apartments.

41. "Apartment Integration Bid Slowed," *Baltimore Sun*, August 10, 1966.

42. Joel N. Shurkin, "Baltimore Rally Sparks Violence," *Boston Globe*, July 29, 1966.

43. "'Buy Guns' Baltimoreans Told; Segregationists Indicted," *Baltimore Afro-American*, August 6, 1966.

44. *Ibid.*; David Simon and DeWitt Bliss, "Perennial Candidate Mahoney Dies," *Baltimore Sun*, March 20, 1989.

45. Ben A. Franklin, "Mahoney Victory in Maryland Is Laid to 'Backlash' Sentiment," *New York Times*, September 15, 1966.

46. Alan L. Dessoff and Peter A. Jay, "Democrats Map 'Golden Silence' Plan on Mahoney," *Baltimore Sun*, October 6, 1966.

47. Jim Hoagland, "Agnew Hits Mahoney, President," *Washington Post Times-Herald*, October 12, 1966.

48. Bart Barnes, "Agnew Calls Mahoney Menace to Maryland," *Washington Post Times-Herald*, November 1, 1966.

49. Charles V. Flowers, "Agnew Defines Negroes' Vigil," *Baltimore Sun*, October 12, 1966.

50. Alan L. Dessoff, "Baltimore Vote Is Key to Agnew Race," *Washington Post, Times-Herald*, October 27, 1966.

51. *Ibid.*

52. Oswald Johnston, "State Chided by Edwards on Rights Lag," *Baltimore Sun*, October 27, 1966.

53. David Leip, "1966 Gubernatorial General Election Data Graph, 2012," http://uselectionatlas.org/RESULTS/datagraph.php?year=1966&fips=24&f=0&off=5&elect=0, accessed August 29, 2012.

54. Alan Goldstein, "Another Day: Sports Promote Race Relations," *Baltimore Sun*, February 6, 1979.

55. Doug Wilson, *Brooks: The Biography of Brooks Robinson*, 24.

56. Goldstein, "Another Day."

57. Bob Maisel, "Morning After," *Baltimore Sun*, November 12, 1977.

58. Bob Maisel, "Morning After," *Baltimore Sun*, December 16, 1978.

59. Quay Rich, interview by author, February 25, 2013.

60. Robinson, *My Life,* 179.

61. Robinson, *Extra Innings,* 63.

62. *Ibid.*

63. Blair interview.

64. Robinson, *Extra Innings,* 60.

65. *Ibid.*

66. Tom Adelman, *Black and Blue: The Golden Arm, the Robinson Boys, and the 1966 World Series That Stunned America* (Boston: Little, Brown, 2006), 31–32.

67. Robinson, *My Life,* 183.

68. "Tavern Light Opera Troupe Sing to Birds' Final Score," *Baltimore Sun,* October 7, 1966.

69. "Baltimore's Mayor Bids Bars End Bias," *New York Times,* October 5, 1966.

70. "Taverns Drive Gains Support," *Baltimore Sun,* October 7, 1966.

71. "Bar Bias Called Usual," *Baltimore Sun,* October 8, 1966.

72. Mark Millikin, *The Glory of the 1966 Baltimore Orioles and Baltimore* (Haworth, NJ: St. Johann Press, 2006), 183.

73. Bijan C. Bayne, interview by author, October 5, 2012.

74. Lou Hatter, "Powell Vows No Guessing," *Baltimore Sun,* September 10, 1964.

75. Blair interview.

76. "McKeldin, Robinson Team Up," *Baltimore Sun,* September 27, 1966.

77. "Board Knocks Robinson Out of the Park After Delay," *Baltimore Sun,* November 16, 1966.

78. Joseph Durso, "Frank Robinson Is Honored Here," *New York Times,* October 13, 1966.

79. "F. Robinson AL Most Valuable," *Chicago Daily Defender,* November 9, 1966.

80. Sam Lacy, "'Year Complete' says Frank's Wife," *Baltimore Afro-American,* November 5, 1966.

81. http://hickokbelt.com/about/history/, accessed January 31, 2015.

82. "Brooke, Bill Cosby Among Russwurm Winners," *Norfolk Journal and Guide,* March 18, 1967.

83. Doug Brown, "Puzzles of a $100,000-a-Year Ball Star," *Baltimore Sun,* April 9, 1967.

Chapter 8

1. Lou Hatter, "Orioles Make 3 Roster Changes," *Baltimore Sun,* July 2, 1967.

2. "Group Wants Negroes and Baseball Executives," *Washington Post Times-Herald,* November 30, 1967; "Report Jim Brown Seeks Negro Major Executives," *Chicago Daily Defender,* November 30, 1967.

3. "Irvin Gets Post with Bill Eckert," *Hartford Courant,* August 22, 1968.

4. http://digital.archives.alabama.gov/cdm/singleitem/collection/voices/id/2952/rec/5, accessed January 19, 2015.

5. "B'ham's Police Dogs Shock World," *Baltimore Afro-American,* May 18, 1963.

6. "Garbage Trucks Haul Kids," *Baltimore Afro-American,* June 8, 1963.

7. "Year-old Birmingham Church Blast Unsolved," *Baltimore Afro-American,* September 26, 1964.

8. Leon Daniel, "Tear Gas, Clubs Halt 600 in Selma March," *Washington Post Times-Herald,* March 8, 1965.

9. "McKeldin Dies at 73 of Cancer," *Baltimore Sun,* August 20, 1974.

10. "City Curfew Imposed; Agnew Sends Troops as Unrest Spreads," *Baltimore Sun,* April 7, 1968.

11. "Backbone of Riot Reported Broken; Return to Normal Could be Near," *Baltimore Sun,* April 10, 1968.

12. "Orioles' Richert Called to Duty for Riot Here," *Washington Post Times-Herald,* April 8, 1968; Lou Hatter, "Mark Belanger Rejoins Birds, to Play Tonight," *Baltimore Sun,* April 15, 1968.

13. "'Battle-Scarred' Richert Rejoins Birds in Oakland," *Baltimore Sun,* April 18, 1968.

14. Hennenman interview, February 20, 2015.

15. Lou Hatter, "Birds' Game with Braves Canceled," *Baltimore Sun,* April 6, 1968.

16. http://retrosimba.com/2013/03/29/bob-gibson-put-aside-grief-to-pitch-while-mourning-mlk/, accessed February 20, 2015.

17. Sachs interview.

18. "Agnew Angers Negroes," *New York Times,* April 12, 1968.

19. Don Buford, telephone interview by author, July 16, 2013.

20. James Macnees, "Congressmen Split on Plea by Agnew for Housing Bill," *Baltimore Sun,* April 9, 1968; James Macnees, "Two Vote No on Housing," *Baltimore Sun,* April 11, 1968.

21. Matthew J. Seiden, "Open Housing Bids Lag," *Baltimore Sun,* July 4, 1972.

22. *Ibid.*

23. Pietila, *Not in My Neighborhood,* xi.

24. Gene Oishi, "City School Segregation Found Rising," *Baltimore Sun,* August, 12, 1967; "N.E.A. Hits Inner City Schools," *Baltimore Sun,* April 9, 1967; John E. Woodruff, "School Board Criticized on Racial Stand," *Baltimore Sun,* September 15, 1967.

25. Andrew Barnes, "Baltimore Schools Shaken by Move to New Direction," *Washington Post Times-Herald,* July 5, 1973.

26. David E. Sloan, "Schools Can't Be Integrated without Leadership," *Baltimore Sun,* May 5, 1974.

27. Mike Dowler, "Schaefer Bids Baltimore Obey U.S. School Plan," *Baltimore Sun*, September 1, 1974.

28. Edward Berkowitz, 1997, "Baltimore Public School in a Time of Transition," *Maryland Historical Magazine*, no. 4 (Winter), 412–432.

29. Lawrence Feinberg, "Stormy Conflict in Baltimore," *Washington Post*, May 10, 1975.

30. "Dr. Roland Patterson; Led Baltimore Schools," *New York Times*, August 12, 1982; Edward Coltman, "Appeals Court Upholds Patterson Dismissal," *Baltimore Sun*, April 7, 1977.

31. M. William Salganik, "Racial Split Here Almost Unchanged," *Baltimore Sun*, May 17, 1979.

32. Robert A. Elandson, "Mayor Sees Orioles Briefly, Resumes Recovery Planning," *Baltimore Sun*, April 11, 1968.

33. Buford interview.

34. Fred Valentine, E-mail to author, September 28, 2012.

35. Hennenman interview.

36. "Weaver Named Orioles' Manager as Bauer Cites 2d 'Knife in the Back,'" *Washington Post Times-Herald*, July 12, 1968, 24.

37. Bill Madden, "Earl Weaver Dead at 82," *New York Daily News*, January 20, 2013.

38. http://espn.go.com/mlb/story/_/id/8859584/hall-famer-earl-weaver-former-manager-baltimore-orioles-dies-82, accessed January 29, 2015.

39. Madden, "Earl Weaver Dead."

40. Bruce Weber, "Earl Weaver, a Volatile, Visionary Manager, Dies at 82," *New York Times*, January 20, 2013.

41. Dick Hall, telephone interview, March 27, 2013; Eric Siegel, "Orioles Basketball," *The Baltimore Sun*, January 13, 1980.

42. Bill Rhoden, "O's Newcomers Brighten Place with Optimism," *Baltimore Afro-American*, April 21, 1973.

43. Al Bumbry, author telephone interview, October 22, 2012.

44. Mike Klingaman, "Hank Peters, Former Orioles GM, Dies at 90," *Baltimore Sun*, January 4, 2015.

45. Thomas Boswell, "Jackson Reports, Sees Why Needed," *Washington Post*, May 1, 1976.

46. Michael Janofsky, "The Other World of Reggie Jackson," *The Sun Magazine*, September 19, 1976, 20.

47. Sam Lacy, "New Bird Catcher Displays High Class and Confidence," *Baltimore Afro-American*, January 20, 1973.

48. Bill Rhoden, "O's Newcomers Brighten Place with Optimism," *Baltimore Afro-American*, April 21, 1973.

49. Ken Nigro, "Watch out, Orioles Outfielders! Bumbry's Stinging Ball at Rochester," *Baltimore Sun*, August 22, 1972.

50. Thomas Boswell, "Jackson Reports."

51. Seymour Smith, "Orioles Will Take a Good Look at Farmhands Murray, Parrill," *The Baltimore Sun*, February 2, 1977.

52. Seymour Smith, "Orioles Will Take a Good Look at Farmhands Murray, Parrill," *Baltimore Sun*, February 2, 1977.

53. Henneman interview.

54. Bob Brown, telephone interview by author, September 27, 2012.

55. *Ibid.*

56. Dave Ford, telephone interview by author, March 20, 2013.

57. Sam Lacy, "Slo-luv," *Baltimore Afro-American*, August 31, 1985.

Chapter 9

1. A. S. "Doc" Young, "Good Morning," *Chicago Daily Defender*, August 5, 1971.

2. "Denies F. Robinson Next Indians Boss," *Chicago Tribune*, August 8, 1971; "Frank Robinson Keeps Door Ajar for Pilot Job," *New York Times*, August 8, 1971.

3. Sam Lacy, "Frank Echoes Complaints of Others about Majors," *Baltimore Afro-American*, March 16, 1968.

4. "Clubs Must Open Office to Negroes," *Washington Post Times-Herald*, March 16, 1968.

5. Shirley Povich, "This Morning," *Washington Post Times-Herald*, March 18, 1969.

6. Leonard Shecter, "Frank Robinson's Cool Assault on the Black-Manager Barrier," *Time Magazine*, May 5, 1970, 83.

7. Shirley Povich, "This Morning."

8. "Frank Robinson Named Manager of the Year," *Baltimore Sun*, January 19, 1969.

9. "F. Robby Denies Tribe Pact has Managing Clause," *Baltimore Sun*, September 15, 1974.

10. "Cleveland Makes Robinson 'First' Big League Manager," *Baltimore Afro-American*, October 12, 1974.

11. "Judge Me on Field: Robby," *Chicago Tribune*, October 4, 1974; Dave Anderson, "Frank Robinson is First Black Manager," *New York Times*, October 4, 1974.

12. "Frank echoes complaints."

13. Valentine interview, April 25, 2012.

14. Sam Lacy, "And a Merry Christmas to You, Too," *Baltimore Afro-American*, December 27, 1975.

15. Sam Lacy, "Orioles Retain Image and Lily-white Staff," *Baltimore Afro-American*, August 16, 1977.

16. "Finally: Orioles Sign Black Coach," *Baltimore Afro-American*, December 8, 1977, 10.

17. Peters interview.

18. *Ibid.*

19. "Frank Robby Fired, Seeks Brewer Post," *Baltimore Afro-American*, December 3, 1977.

20. "O's Again Call on Old No. 20," *Baltimore Afro-American*, February 18, 1978.

21. Ken Nigro, "Frank Robinson to Pilot Rochester," *Baltimore Sun*, May 4, 1978.

22. Peters interview.

23. Dave Ford interview.

24. Bryan Burwell, "After Tough Rochester Year, Robinson Ponders Chances of Return to Majors," *Baltimore Sun*, September 12, 1978.

25. Ken Nigro, "Frank Robinson to Pilot Rochester."

26. Bob Maisel, "Frank Robinson Happy, Thriving on Work," *Baltimore Sun*, March 13, 1980.

27. Sam Lacy, "A Manager in Baseball? Think White," *Baltimore Afro-American*, October 27, 1979.

28. Bob Maisel, "Whatever the Reason, Baseball Isn't Getting as Many Blacks," *Baltimore Sun*, October 30, 1980.

29. Joseph Durso, "Giants Pick Robinson to Manage," *New York Times*, January 15, 1981.

30. *Ibid.*

31. "Hard Times in a Proud Town," *Time Magazine*, May 2, 1988, 73.

32. Joe Sargis, "How Frank Sees Giants," *Baltimore Afro-American*, April 11, 1981.

33. "Bits o' Briefs," *Baltimore Afro-American*, July 18, 1981.

34. "Giants Fire Robinson," *Chicago Tribune*, August 5, 1984.

35. Bill Free, "Weary Weaver Ready to Become Affluent Retiree at the 7th Hole," *Baltimore Sun*, August 6, 1982.

36. Bill Free, "Weaver Exits with Tears," *Baltimore Sun*, October 4, 1982.

37. Sam Lacy, "Why Not F. Robby for Birds?" *Baltimore Afro-American*, October 23, 1982.

38. "It's Official: Orioles Hire Robinson," *Washington Post*, December 16, 1984.

39. Sam Lacy, "Did the O's 'Shaft' Frank?" *Baltimore Afro-American*, June 22, 1985.

40. Kent Baker, "This Farewell Lacked the Passion of 1982," *Baltimore Sun*, October 6, 1986.

41. Tim Kurkjian, "Orioles Will Name Ripken Today," *Baltimore Sun*, October 6, 1986.

42. Tim Kurkjian, "Robinson, Peters Talk, but Ripken Still Favored," *Baltimore Sun*, October 1, 1986.

43. Judge Murphy, Jr., interview.

44. Mike Littwin, "Like Rest of Us, Murray Just Has to Face Imperfect World," *Baltimore Sun*, August 26, 1986.

45. "What the Fans Said," *Baltimore Sun*, September 3, 1986.

46. "Stung Murray Stuns O's with Request for Trade," *The Sporting News*, September 8, 1986; Sam Lacy, "Ed-dee!!" *Baltimore Afro-American*, September 6, 1986.

47. Peter Richmond, *Ball Park*, 76.

48. Tim Kurkjian, "Murray's Teammates on His Side," *Baltimore Sun*, August 26, 1986.

49. Thomas Boswell, "Past Success Magnifies Present Woes," *Washington Post*, August 25, 1986; Evan Thomas, *Edward Bennett Williams Ultimate Insider: Legendary Trial Lawyer* (New York: Simon & Schuster, 1991), 479–480.

50. Bob Brown, telephone interview by author, September 27, 2012.

51. Peters interview.

52. Thomas, *Edward Bennett Williams*, 480.

53. Peters interview.

54. Lacy, "Ed-dee!!"

55. Mark Hyman, "Pro Sports now Are Confronted by the Last Color Line," *Baltimore Sun*, April 12, 1987.

56. Richard Justice, "Speaking of 'Necessities'..." *Washington Post*, April 12, 1987.

Chapter 10

1. Al Campanis racist remarks on "Nightline" (April 6, 1987), http://www.youtube.com/watch?v=O4XUbENGaiY, uploaded January 18, 2011, accessed February 2, 2013.

2. Sam Lacy, "Wills Pays Tribute to Al Campanis," *Baltimore Afro-American*, October 16, 1965.

3. *Ibid.*

4. A.S. Doc Young, "Campanis' Remarks Should Bring some Change," *Los Angeles Sentinel*, April 16, 1987.

5. *Ibid.*

6. William Weinbaum, "The Legacy of Al Campanis," uploaded April 1, 2012, http://www.youtube.com/watch?v=O4XUbENGaiY, accessed February 2, 2013; Sam Lacy, "Wills Pays Tribute to Al Campanis."

7. "NAACP Threatens to Shut Down Baseball," *Los Angeles Sentinel*, April 16, 1987.

8. Arthur Ashe, "An Open Letter to Al Campanis," *Washington Post*, April 12, 1987.

9. Ira Berkow, "History and Hope Given Their Due at Cooperstown," *New York Times*, July 27, 1987.

10. Young, "Campanis' Remarks."

11. Mike Downey, "Aaron among Legions Campanis 'Shocked,'" *The Sporting News*, April 20, 1987.

12. Tom Boswell, "Baseball's Scandal Isn't Secret Anymore," *Washington Post*, April 10, 1987.

13. "Voice of the Fan," *The Sporting News*, April 27, 1987.

14. Dick Young, "Commissioner Ubie Leaves Blacks out of Cleanup Spots," *New York Post*, April 10, 1987.
15. *Ibid.*
16. Joseph Durso, "Kuhn Presses Owners, Says 'Now Is Time' for Black Pilot," *New York Times*, August 18, 1974.
17. David DuPree, "Blacks Remain Rare in Pro Front Office," *Washington Post*, July 1, 1979.
18. *Ibid.*
19. Mark Hyman, "A Season to Remember," *Baltimore Sun*, October 18, 1987.
20. "Campanis' Remarks to Stem Racism—Hopefully," *Los Angeles Sentinel*, April 16, 1987.
21. Dick Young, "Commissioner Ubie Leaves Blacks out of Cleanup Spots."
22. "Ueberroth 'Sensitive' to Minorities," *USA Today*, April 28, 1987.
23. "Jesse Jackson Cites Baseball Plan for Affirmative Action as 'Fresh Air,'" *Baltimore Sun*, June 11, 1987.
24. Peters interview.
25. "Md. Panel Orders Armco Steel Corp. to Name Blacks to Supervisory Jobs," *Washington Post Times-Herald*, April 22, 1972; George J. Hiltner, "Armco Agrees to Promote 10 Blacks to Supervisor," *Baltimore Sun*, January 18, 1974.
26. "Steel Plant Guilty of Bias, Study Says," *Washington Post Times-Herald*, January 6, 1971; Maia Licker, "Uphill Fight," *Wall Street Journal*, August 8, 1973.
27. Susan Schmidt, "Md. 'Old Boy Network' Excludes Blacks, Delegate Says," *Washington Post*, January 13, 1988.
28. "Destiny 2000: the State of Black Baltimore," *Baltimore Sun*, January 9, 1987.
29. Donald P. Baker, "Is Baltimore Truly Back?" *Washington Post*, November 24, 1984.
30. *Ibid.*
31. *Ibid.*
32. Philip Moeller, "The Rot Beneath the Glitter in the New Baltimore," *Baltimore Sun*, January 28, 1987; Baker, "Is Baltimore Truly Back?" "The Schaefer Era," *Baltimore Sun*, January 20, 1987.
33. *Ibid.*
34. Kurt Schmoke, interview by author, May 15, 2013.
35. Stuart Rothenberg, "A Crop of Politicians Who are Young, Black and Buttoned Down," *Baltimore Sun*, September 20, 1987.
36. Paul W. Valentine, "Baltimore Targets its High Rate of Illiteracy," *Washington Post*, August 27, 1990.
37. *Ibid.*
38. "Orioles Team with Schools in 'Read Like a Pro' Program to Encourage Pupils, Illit-

erate Adults," *Washington Post*, February 18, 1988.
39. Chuck Conconi, "Personalities," *Washington Post*, February 27, 1989.
40. Schmoke interview.
41. *Ibid.*
42. "Vow from Orioles Owner," *New York Times*, April 18, 1987; Hyman, "Pro Sports."
43. DuPree, "Blacks Remain Rare," 1979.
44. "Vow from Orioles Owner."
45. Peters interview.
46. Kent Baker, "NAACP Asks to Talk with Orioles about Setting up Affirmative Action Program," *Baltimore Sun*, April 23, 1987.
47. Kent Baker, "NAACP's Sports Campaign Drawing some Heavy Hitters," *Baltimore Sun*, May 28, 1987.
48. "NAACP Presses for Black Managers," *Los Angeles Sentinel*, June 4, 1987.
49. Mark Hyman, "Pro Sports now Are Confronted by the Last Color Line," *Baltimore Sun*, April 12, 1987.
50. Peters interview.
51. Mark Hyman, "Hill to Monitor Orioles Minority Policy," *Baltimore Sun*, November 11, 1987.
52. Johnette Howard, "Still Climbing Hills," *Washington Post*, May 31, 1993.
53. Rich interview.
54. Mark Hyman, "Pro Sports."
55. Kent Baker, "NAACP's Sports Campaign Drawing some Heavy Hitters"; Hyman, "A Season to Remember"; Tim Kurkjian, "Orioles Name Durham Area Goodwill Ambassador," *Baltimore Sun*, November 19, 1987; Mark Hyman, interview by author, February 26, 2013.
56. Rich interview.
57. *Ibid.*
58. *Ibid.*
59. Edward Bennett Williams papers, Container 9, Folder 7, Manuscript Division, Library of Congress, Washington, D.C.
60. "Orioles Start Housecleaning after a Dismal Season, Fire Peters," *Los Angeles Times*, October 6, 1987; Richard Justice, "Hemond Takes over Orioles' Operation," *Washington Post*, November 11, 1987.
61. "Birds' Owner Williams Names Calvin Hill Member of Board," *Baltimore Afro-American*, August 1, 1987.
62. Sam Lacy, "Robbie and the O's: a Job that Fits Him," *Baltimore Afro-American*, November 27, 1987.
63. Sam Lacy, "Hail the New Oriole Hierarchy," *Baltimore Afro-American*, November 21, 1987.
64. Justice, "Hemond Takes over Orioles' Operations."
65. Peters interview.
66. *Ibid.*

67. John Eisenberg, "Orioles' Hiring Practices Produce Saddest Stat of All," *Baltimore Sun*, November 22, 1987.

68. *Ibid.*

69. Justice, "Hemond Takes over Orioles."

70. Mark Hyman, "Minority-hiring Officials, Baseball Network Meet," *Baltimore Sun*, November 10, 1987.

71. Jane Leavy, "The Network that Robinson Built," *Washington Post*, June 21, 1988.

72. Claire Smith, "Blood, Sweat, Tears on the Field," *Hartford Courant*, November 15, 1987.

73. Hyman, "Minority-hiring Officials, Baseball Network Meet."

74. Mark Hyman, "Baseball Network Less than Ecstatic about Commissioner's Group," *Baltimore Sun*, November 9, 1987.

75. Frank Robinson, *Extra Innings*, 10–12.

76. Tim Kurkjian, "Ueberroth Push for Black Hires 'Very Productive,'" *Baltimore Sun*, December 8, 1987.

77. Leavy, "The Network that Robinson Built."

78. Hyman interview.

79. Sam Lacy, "Eureka!" *Baltimore Afro-American*, November 14, 1987.

80. Michael Martinez, "Judging the Hiring Upswing," *New York Times*, April 6, 1988.

81. Stan Isle, "Robinson Sees No Progress in Minority Hirings," *The Sporting News*, November 28, 1988.

82. Michael Martinez, "Judging the Hiring Upswing."

83. Ross Newhan, "Robinson, 1st Black Manager in 4 Years, Gets Orioles Job," *Los Angeles Times*, April 13, 1988.

84. Dave Anderson, "Frank Robinson Isn't Enough," *New York Times*, April 15, 1988.

85. Richard Justice, "Bill White Named Baseball's 1st Black League President," *Washington Post*, February 4, 1989.

86. Edward Bennett Williams to Bobby Beathard, February 3, 1988, Edward Bennett Williams Papers, Container 9, Folder 7, Manuscript Division, Library of Congress, Washington, D.C.

87. William H. "Billy" Murphy, Jr., telephone interview by author, July 1, 2013.

88. Mike Preston, "Star Deserved Far Better Treatment than He Got," *Baltimore Sun*, July 27, 2003.

89. John Eisenberg, telephone interview by author, March 20, 2013.

90. http://baltimore.orioles.mlb.com/bal/history/retired_numbers.jsp, accessed October 28, 2013.

91. Mark Hyman, "Black Investors May Seek other Teams for Baltimore," *Baltimore Sun*, December 8, 1988.

92. Brian Sullam, "Hoffberger 'Disappointed,'" *Baltimore Sun*, December 7, 1988.

93. *Ibid.*

94. Barnett Wright, "Black Investors Strike Out," *Philadelphia Tribune*, December 13, 1988.

95. "Fans Honor Bob Boyd at Pre-game Ceremony," *Baltimore Afro-American*, September 28, 1957.

96. Barnett Wright, "Black Investors Strike Out."

97. Steve Berkowitz, "Schaefer Backs Jacobs as Buyer of Orioles," *Baltimore Sun*, December 9, 1988.

98. Sullam, "Hoffberger 'Disappointed.'"

99. Anderson interview.

100. Davis interview.

101. Anderson interview.

Chapter 11

1. A. S. Doc Young, "1989, an All-Star Year for Blacks," *Los Angeles Sentinel*, July 13, 1989.

2. Earl Caldwell, "Frank Robinson and the Bitter Truth," *New York Daily News*, July 12, 1989.

3. Richard Justice, "Robinson Named Manager of the Year," *Washington Post*, November 2, 1989.

4. Richard Justice, "Robinson Fired as Manager of Orioles," *Washington Post*, May 24, 1991.

5. "Too Few Changes Since Campanis," *New York Times*, August 16, 1992.

6. Michael Martinez, "Bill White a Unanimous Choice to Head National League," *New York Times*, February 4, 1989.

7. Mark Kram and Tom Pendergast, "Bill White Biography," http://www.answers.com/topic/bill-white, accessed June 15, 2013; "Leonard S. Coleman: NL President 1994–1999," http://www.sportsecyclopedia.com/mlb/nl/coleman.html, May 12, 2002, accessed June 15, 2013.

8. "Black Legislator Says Orioles Have Neglected His Community," *Philadelphia Tribune*, March 6, 1992.

9. *Ibid.*

10. Ray Gilbert, "Oriole Concessionaire Uses more American Indians than Blacks to Meet 10% Minority Goal," *Afro-American Red Star*, October 31, 1992.

11. Tom Stuckey, "Black Lawmakers Welcome Help from Jesse Jackson on Minorities in Baseball," *Pittsburgh Courier*, April 17, 1993.

12. "Fanfare: Jackson Asks Clinton to Rethink Pitch," *Washington Post*, March 25, 1993.

13. Mark Asher, "Camden Pickets Planned," *Baltimore Sun*, April 1, 1993.

14. Stucky, "Black Lawmakers."

15. Joseph Haskins, Jr., telephone interview by author, July 23, 2013.

16. *Ibid.*

17. Paul Valentine, "Jackson, Protesters Call for More Women, Minorities," *Washington Post*, April 6, 1993.

18. Courtland Milloy, "Choosing a Game Plan for Protest," *Washington Post*, April 7, 1993.

19. Mark Hyman, "Angelos, Black Task Force at Odds over Input," *Baltimore Sun*, May 21, 1994; Quay Rich, telephone interview by author, October 10, 2013.

20. Mark Hyman, "Orioles 'Unparalleled,' Black Task Force Says Minority Marketing Support Praised," *Baltimore Sun*, July 9, 1993.

21. Joseph Haskins, Jr., telephone interview by author, July 24, 2013.

22. Anderson interview.

23. Leonard Shapiro, "Baseball Swings for Improvement," *Washington Post*, July 12, 1993.

24. Hank Aaron with Lonnie Wheeler, *I Had a Hammer: The Hank Aaron Story* (New York: HarperCollins, 1991), 325.

25. John Eisenberg, "Orioles Hiring Practices."

26. Mark Maske, "Hispanic Group Firmly Against Scout," *Washington Post*, March 10, 1993.

27. Mark Maske, "O's Scout Apologizes," *Washington Post*, February 26, 1993.

28. *Ibid.*

29. Mark Maske, "Employees Take Training in Cultural Diversity," *Washington Post*, June 16, 1993.

30. Mark Hyman, "Report Shows Minority Hiring on Upswing," *Baltimore Sun*, June 10, 1994.

31. Hyman, "Angelos, Black Task Force at Odds," *Baltimore Sun*, May 21, 1994.

32. M. R. Cheshire, "Task Force Charges Orioles Broke Pact," *Afro-American Red Star*, May 21, 1994.

33. M. R. Cheshire, "Ministers Join Critics of Orioles Front Office," *Afro-American Red Star*, June 18, 1994.

34. Hyman, "Angelos, Black Task Force at Odds."

35. "Warning Mr. Angelos," *Afro-American Red Star*, July 2, 1994.

36. *Ibid.*

37. M. R. Cheshire, "Task Force Writes Orioles; Demonstration or Boycott May Follow," *Afro-American Red Star*, July 30, 1994.

38. Davis interview.

39. M. R. Cheshire, "Task Force Writes Orioles."

40. Mark Maske, "Where He Belongs," *Baltimore Sun*, August 23, 1996; Murray Chass, "Murray Hits 500th Homer to Join Elite Group," *New York Times*, September 7, 1996.

Epilogue

1. R. W. Apple, Jr., "In Bawlmer, Hon, Crab Is King," *New York Times*, February 19, 2003.

2. Compiled from *Baltimore Sun* articles.

3. Anderson interview.

4. Matthew Death, interview by author, August 22, 2013.

5. Schmoke interview.

6. Al Bumbry, telephone interview by author, October 22, 2012.

7. *Ibid.*

8. Clarence Davis, telephone interview by author, September 17, 2013.

9. Anderson interview.

10. Joseph Haskins, Jr., telephone interview by author, July 24, 2013.

11. Judge William H. "Billy" Murphy, Jr., telephone interview by author, July 1, 2013.

12. *Ibid.*

13. Quay Rich, telephone interview by author, February 19, 2013.

14. Schmoke interview.

15. Anderson interview.

16. *Ibid.*

17. http://www.ajc.com/news/ap/education/mlb-forms-diversity-committee-black-players-focus/nXJWD/, accessed April 30, 2013.

18. http://baltimore.orioles.mlb.com/team/roster_40man.jsp?c_id=bal. http://espn.go.com/mlb/team/roster/_/name/bal/baltimore-orioles, accessed April 23, 2014.

19. Monica Barlow, Matthew Death, Kristen Schultz, Bill Stetka, interview by author, August 22, 2013; 2012 Orioles Media Guide, 26–32.

20. *Ibid.*

21. Haskins interview.

22. Anderson interview.

23. Judge William H. "Billy" Murphy, Jr., telephone interview by author, July 1, 2013.

24. J. Howard Henderson, telephone interview by author, July 11, 2013.

Appendix

1. Compiled by: Cassidy Lent, Reference Librarian, National Baseball Hall of Fame and Museum, April 8, 2014.

Bibliography

Aaron, Henry, with Lonnie Wheeler. *I Had a Hammer: The Hank Aaron Story.* New York: HarperCollins, 1991.

Adelman, Tom. *Black and Blue: The Golden Arm, the Robinson Boys, and the 1966 World Series That Stunned America.* Boston: Little, Brown, 2006.

Berney, Louis. *Tales from the Orioles Dugout.* Champaign, IL: Sports Publishing, 2007.

Bready, James H. *Baseball in Baltimore.* Baltimore: Johns Hopkins University, 1998.

Brugger, Robert J. *Maryland: A Middle Temperament.* Baltimore: Johns Hopkins University, 1988.

Bryant, Howard. *Shut Out: A Story of Race and Baseball in Boston.* Boston: Beacon Press, 2002.

Corbett, Warren. *The Wizard of Waxahachie: Paul Richards and the End of Baseball As We Knew It.* Dallas: Southern Methodist University, 2009.

Dickson, Paul. *Bill Veeck: Baseball's Greatest Maverick.* New York: Walker, 2012.

Eisenberg, John. *From 33rd Street to Camden Yards: An Oral History of the Baltimore Orioles.* New York: McGraw-Hill, 2001.

Halberstam, David. *October 1964.* New York: Fawcett Columbine, 1995.

Lacy, Sam, with Moses J. Newson. *Fighting for Fairness: The Life Story of Hall of Fame Sportswriter Sam Lacy.* Centreville, MD: Tidewater Publishers, 1998.

Leonard, Buck, with James A. Riley. *Buck Leonard: The Black Lou Gehrig.* New York: Carroll & Graf, 1995.

Lester, Larry. *Black Baseball's National Showcase: The East-West All Star Games, 1933–1953.* Lincoln: University of Nebraska, 2001.

Luke, Bob. *The Baltimore Elite Giants: Sport and Society in the Age of the Negro Leagues.* Baltimore: Johns Hopkins University, 2009.

_____. *The Most Famous Woman in Baseball: Effa Manley and the Negro Leagues.* Washington, D.C.: Potomac, 2011.

MacPhail, Lee. *My Nine Innings: An Autobiography of 50 Years in Baseball.* Westport, CT: Meckler, 1989.

Miller, James Edward. *The Baseball Business: Pursuing Pennants and Profits in Baltimore.* Chapel Hill: University of North Carolina, 1990.

Millikin, Mark. *The Glory of the 1966 Baltimore Orioles and Baltimore.* Haworth, NJ: St. Johann, 2006.

Moffi, Larry, and Jonathon Kronstadt. *Crossing the Line: Black Major Leaguers, 1947–1959.* Jefferson, NC: McFarland, 1994.

Moore, Joseph Thomas. *Pride Against Prejudice: The Biography of Larry Doby.* New York: Praeger, 1988.

Olesker, Michael. *The Colts' Baltimore: A City and Its Love Affair in the 1950s.* Baltimore: Johns Hopkins University, 2008.

_____. *Journeys to the Heart of Baltimore.* Baltimore: Johns Hopkins University, 2001.

Pietila, Antero. *Not in My Neighborhood: How Bigotry Shaped a Great American City.* Chicago: Ivan R. Dee, 2010.

Reichler, Joseph L. ed., *The Baseball Encyclopedia.* New York: Macmillan, 1988.

Richmond, Peter. *Ballpark: Camden Yards and the Building of an American Dream.* New York: Simon & Schuster, 1993.

Riley, James A. *The Biographical Encyclopedia of the Negro Baseball Leagues.* New York: Carroll & Graf, 1994.

Robinson, Frank, with Al Silverman. *My Life in Baseball.* Garden City, NY: Doubleday, 1975.

_____, with Berry Stainback, *Extra Innings.* New York: McGraw-Hill, 1988.

Robinson, Jackie, as told to Alfred Duckett. *I Never Had It Made.* New York: G.P. Putnam's Sons, 1972.

Russo, Jim, with Bob Hammel. *Super Scout: Thirty-Five Years of Major League Scouting.* Chicago: Bonus Books, 1992.

Snyder, Brad. *A Well Paid Slave: Curt Flood's Fight for Free Agency in Professional Sports.* New York: Viking, 2006.

Swaine, Rick. *The Black Stars Who Made Baseball Whole: The Jackie Robinson Generation in the Major Leagues, 1947–1959.* Jefferson, NC: McFarland, 2006.

Thomas, Evan. *The Man to See: Edward Bennett Williams, Ultimate Insider, Legendary Trial Lawyer.* New York: Simon & Schuster, 1991.

Tygiel, Jules. *Past Time: Baseball as History,* New York: Oxford University, 2001.

Wilson, Doug. *Brooks: The Biography of Brooks Robinson.* New York: St. Martin's, 2014.

Index

Numbers in **_bold italics_** indicate pages with photographs.